ACTS
OF ARGUING

SUNY series in Logic and Language
John T. Kearns, Editor

ACTS OF ARGUING

A RHETORICAL MODEL OF ARGUMENT

Christopher W. Tindale

State University of New York Press

Published by
State University of New York Press, Albany

For information, address State University of New York Press, State University Plaza, Albany, N.Y., 12246

Production by Diane Ganeles
Marketing by Nancy Farrell

Library of Congress Cataloging-in-Publication Data

Tindale, Christopher W. (Christopher William)
    Acts of arguing : a rhetorical model of argument / Christopher W. Tindale
        p.   cm. — (SUNY series in logic and language)
    Includes bibliographical references and index.
    ISBN 0–7914–4387–6 (hardcover: alk. paper).—ISBN 0–7914–4388–4
(pbk. : alk. paper)
    1. Reasoning. I. Title. II. Series.
BC177.T533 1999
168—dc21   99–15028
                                                        CIP

10 9 8 7 6 5 4 3 2 1

for Kathy

Contents

Acknowledgments

This project is the product of research and writing conducted over many years, but it came together as a manuscript during a sabbatical year of 1995–96. I am grateful to Trent University, Peterborough, Ontario for granting me the leave and for funds to support the research. I would also like to thank the staff of the InterLibrary Loans Office at Trent for the splendid service they provided in tracking down many items for me.

During the summer of 1995 Neil Mercer and Lyn Dawes handed over their Stony Stratford house to an unknown academic and to his family. I am sure this was not done without more than a little trepidation. But it proved to be a wonderful location for organizing the project and for working on the first draft. That short stay has led to several return visits and to a growing friendship based on mutual interests in language and reasoning.

Thanks for comments and criticisms is also due to the audiences of a number of conferences. In particular, I should mention the members of the DASA program in Amsterdam, where I read an early version of chapter 6 in May of 1996. Frans van Eemeren proved to be a gracious and thoughtful host on that occasion.

I am grateful to Springer-Verlag for permission to reprint parts of my paper "From Syllogisms to Audiences: The Prospects for Logic in a Rhetorical Model of Argumentation"; to the editors of *Argumentation,* for permission to reprint sections from "Audiences, Relevance and Cognitive Environments"; and to the editors of *Informal Logic,* for permission to reprint "Fallacies in Transition" and sections of "Contextual Relevance in Argumentation," which appeared in *New Essays in Informal Logic.*

Many people have contributed to my thinking, often in ways they might not have expected. There are several whose encouragement, conversation, or criticism have been especially valuable. These include Michael Billig, Tony Blair, John Burbidge, Frans van Eemeren, Michael Gilbert, Trudy Govier, David Hitchcock, Ralph Johnson, Erik C.W. Krabbe, Doug Walton, and John Woods. To those whose names deserve mention but who have been overlooked in this list, I apologize. None of those I have cited will agree with all that is written here, but I hope they will find my contributions as welcome as I have found their own. I regret that James Crosswhite's excellent *The Rhetoric of Reason* became known to me too late to be included in discussions of his work.

The interest and encouragement shown by Leo Groarke and Hans V. Hansen deserves separate mention. I have worked with both of them on different projects, always benefiting from their knowledge of the field and insightful observations. But I particularly value their support of this project.

The usual qualifiers and provisions apply. Any errors that remain are mine alone.

Introduction:
The Case for Rhetorical Argumentation

1. Models of Argumentation

"[R]hetoric," writes Michael Billig, "as the traditional study and practice of argumentation, provides an entry to an understanding of thinking" (1993:121). Billig's comment recaptures an ancient understanding: that there is an essential connection between rhetoric and argumentation (and thinking). It harkens back to the linking of these ideas in Aristotle's *Rhetoric*.[1] Commenting on that text, Myles F. Burnyeat notes that "the thought content of a speech . . . is fundamentally argument. More often than not, it is argument in a context where certainty and conclusive proof are not to be had . . . yet a judgment must be made" (1994:12–13). These contexts are public contexts. The argumentation at stake here is not, exclusively, the argumentation of academics but the broader domain of persuasive and investigative discourse that arises in the marketplace, in the media, on the internet, and in the everyday conversations of citizens, and that thence may find its way into the academy. "Argumentation" is the site of an activity, where reasons are given and appraised, where beliefs are recognized and justified, and where personal development is encouraged.

It is this sense of argumentation which, once recovered, incites us to ask anew what it is we do when we argue. What activities come into play? What goals do we aspire to reach? Such questions, as simple as they are to formulate, have provoked diverse and complex responses. While the study of argument, its nature and uses, has given rise to the discipline of Argumentation, those engaged in the discipline have not pursued it with like-minded interests or expectations. In fact, the contemporary cadre of argumentation theorists draws members from areas as closely associated as formal and informal

1

logic and as far apart as fallacy theory and cognitive psychology. From speech communication, pragmatics, discourse analysis, and rhetoric scholars with a practical or theoretical bent are drawn to the rich field of argumentation studies to contribute to, or share in, a wealth of interdisciplinary insights and developments.[2]

One of the attractions drawing so many is the possibility offered for new slants on very traditional issues: on the relations between speech and actions; on the heightened prospects for dispute resolution; and on the development of communities of people reasonable in their evaluations and discourse.

Yet outside of such common ventures the discipline itself, as a consequence of the diversity of attitudes contributing to its growth, often appears to lack any coherent theoretical core. Within the literature, three notable perspectives have emerged, none of which necessarily excludes the others. Ironically, given the discipline's claim to newness, these perspectives can be traced to divisions in Aristotle's *Organon*. In Aristotle's writings, Logic, Dialectic, and Rhetoric each has a claim to some key involvement in the activity of arguing.

It has been a consequence of the bias of the tradition that comes down to us that we tend to equate "argument" with Aristotle's logic, particularly the syllogism,[3] and neglect its other occurrences in his work. Aristotle, however, exhibits a broader conception of argumentation, with logical, dialectical, and rhetorical variants, and there is a different sense of "argument" that can be connected to each of these components.

The logical theory concentrates on the categorical syllogism and the demonstrations that are drawn from true and immediate premises. Here the sense of "arguments" at work, that which we associate with a traditional premise/premise/conclusion set (PPC), tends to be the most familiar.

Under the rubric of dialectic, however, the focus shifts to the reasoning employed in dialogues and debates. Instead of true and immediate premises, we find in the *Topics* and *Sophistical Refutations*[4] that dialectic employs probable premises "whereby we shall be able to reason from reputable opinions about any subject presented to us, and also shall ourselves, when putting forward an argument, avoid saying anything contrary to it" (*Topics* 100a20–22). The dialectical proposition concerns itself with what is "reputable to all men or to most men or to the wise" (104b10–11).

Much of the *Topics* involves advice for overthrowing a view or for establishing a view, although there are other aims of argument, such as for the sake of training or examination. In fact, Book VIII introduces rules for pedagogy rather than for competition. The *Sophistical Refutations* (165b9–12) notes this dual interest in the *Topics* between what are there called dialectical and examinational arguments, but addresses its attention to the use of arguments in competitions and contests. It is in this latter regard that the sense of dialectical argument as a dialogue game is evident. Here, "argument" is presented as a type of structured debate with rules to govern the steps and countersteps. Someone will put forward a thesis and, under regulated conditions, an opponent will attack it. Defender and attacker will each employ questions that contribute to the argumentation or counterargumentation. A dialogue game is won when the defender is led to allow theses that are contradictory. A variety of steps are appropriate in developing these dialogues, depending upon the subject matter involved.[5]

Given such details on argument to be found elsewhere in Aristotle's work, we might not expect to discover a further perspective on argument in the *Rhetoric*. After all, as its title would suggest, it is not a work in either logic or dialectic. But the *Rhetoric,* dealing as it does with public persuasion, contains its own distinctive sense of rhetorical argument. Writers from C. L. Hamblin (1970) to Paul Ricoeur (1977) have reminded us that the *Rhetoric* is concerned primarily with the presentation of arguments. But the sense of argumentation at stake is distinctive in the way in which it is grounded in the relation between speaker (to become arguer, for our purposes) and audience, and with its integrated concerns with character (ethos) and emotion (pathos). These features, along with the special meaning of the rhetorical enthymeme, gives rhetorical argumentation a broad sphere of influence, including not just logical argument but also an interest in the whole person.

2. Product, Procedure, and Process

In several discussions of argumentation, the Aristotelian triad has been identified with the three "p's" of product, procedure, and process (Brockriede, 1978; Wenzel, 1979; Habermas, 1984). Logic is concerned with the PPC products of argumentation, the texts and discourses proffering claims with supporting evidence, which can be judged valid or invalid, strong or weak. Dialectic sets its sights on the rules or procedures required for argumentation, if it is to be performed correctly and achieve goals of resolving disputes and promoting critical discussions. Rhetoric concentrates on the communication processes inherent in argumentation, on the means by which arguers make their cases for the adherence of audiences to the claims advanced.

As might be expected, these three approaches can give very different answers to the central question of what an argument entails. Consider the following proposals:

> 1. Argument: a unit of reasoning in which one or more propositions (the premises) purport to provide evidence for the truth of another proposition (the conclusion) (Kelley, 1994:A62).

> 2. Argument is then defined as a use of reasoning to contribute to a talk exchange or conversation called a dialogue. So conceived, reasoning is a narrower notion that is compatible with the point of view of traditional logic, whereas argument is a frankly pragmatic notion that has to do with the uses of reasoning in a context of dialogue (Walton, 1995a:254–55).

> 3. . . . we are dealing with theses presented in an argumentative discourse. . . . People who argue do not address what we call "faculties," such as intellect, emotion, or will; they address the whole person, but, depending on the circumstances, their arguments will seek different results and will use methods appropriate to the purpose of the discourse as well as to the audience to be influenced (Perelman, 1982:13).

These statements of what an argument, or arguing, entails reflect, respectively, the logical, dialectical, and rhetorical perspectives. (The last of these does not provide a succinct definition, but it is the very nature of the rhetorical perspective that this should be so.[6]) The conceptions do not exclude each other, but each sets its sights on a different goal—the production of valid arguments, the resolution of disputes, the adherence of an audience—and, accordingly, each adopts different criteria for determining success.

3. Habermas's Challenge

In spite of their productiveness in different spheres, the possibility of a synthesis of the three perspectives is an attractive prospect. Joseph W. Wenzel (1980, 1989) argues for the three to be brought together in a full theory of argument, and Jurgen Habermas is emphatic that "At no single one of these analytical levels can the very idea intrinsic to argumentative speech be adequately developed" (1984:26). This is because the basic concept corresponding to each perspective cannot survive critical scrutiny.[7]

Habermas illustrates his point with critiques of Wolfgang Klein and Stephen Toulmin. In each case Habermas's principal concern is with the need for objective standards of argumentation.

Klein is concerned with de facto argumentation, with how people actually argue. This, however, leaves Klein struggling to find an external perspective from which to judge arguments. He believes that it is from a "collectively shared, unproblematic knowledge" that reasons derive their power to convince (cited in Habermas 1984:28), but he can only account for the latter in a relativistic way. Habermas states his problem with this: "[Klein] screens out all internal relations between what is *de facto* accepted as valid . . . and what should have validity . . . in the sense of a claim transcending local, temporal, and social limitations" (ibid.). As a consequence, the concept of validity has been replaced by the concept of acceptability, the latter relative to persons and times. Klein does try to make sense of his notion of "collective validity," and looks for lawlike empirical regularities. But to try to depict the laws to which participants in argumentation are subject, without recourse to any objective validity, fails. The problem lies, Habermas believes, in the reliance on argumentation as process, in the attempt to sketch the logic of argumentation (fixed regularities) *exclusively* from the flow of communication *processes* (how people argue). Such a proposal lacks a concept of rationality as a measure between "valid for them" and "valid for us."

Toulmin's (1958) approach seems to be on a better course because he looks at a range of validity claims depending on the context, be it law, science, or medicine. And these different enterprises *appear* to owe their rationality to a common core that acts as a framework for possible argumentation. But sometimes, notes Habermas, "Toulmin is decidedly opposed to such a universalist view; he doubts that direct access to a fundamental and unchangeable framework of rationality is possible" (1984:33). This ambivalence seems to haunt Toulmin's text. He adopts an historical approach to the concept of rationality, which amounts to looking at the rationality of the various enterprises at any given time. But elsewhere being rational according to the standards of a particular time is not enough: Toulmin invokes the "impartial standpoint of rational judgment" that the historian should adopt. But, and this is Habermas's complaint,

Toulmin does not analyze this generally conceived standpoint of impartiality. Thus he delivers up the logic of argumentation to *preexisting* notions of rationality. "Toulmin does not push the logic of argument far enough into the domains of dialectic and rhetoric" (35).

These summaries of Habermas's critiques indicate only some of the problems that may arise when the different perspectives in argumentation theory choose separate paths. More will be explored in the chapters ahead. A more detailed consideration of Toulmin's approach is provided in chapter 1. My interest here is to acknowledge the desirability of a synthesis of the three perspectives and to recognize the concern behind Habermas's key complaint, namely, that in any ensuing theory of argumentation, primary attention must be given to objective standards of evaluation.

4. The Case for the Rhetorical

The question then arises how the three perspectives should align themselves within "a complete theory of argument." Or, to pose a more contentious question, whether one of the three perspectives should dominate the synthesis such that it forms the conditions for the presence of the other two. The pragma-dialectical account of argument, developed in the work of Frans H. van Eemeren and Rob Grootendorst (1984, 1992a), and to some extent in that of Douglas N. Walton (1989, 1992a, 1995a), is one such model. Adopting, as its name suggests, a fundamentally dialectical account, it looks to reconcile itself to the other two perspectives. This attempt is explicitly acknowledged: "In the dialectical approach, the product-oriented [logic] and the process-oriented [rhetoric] approaches to argumentation are combined" (van Eemeren and Grootendorst, 1988:281). And the point is demonstrated in attempts to show, for example, that a dominant rhetorical model like that proposed by Chaim Perelman with L. Olbrechts-Tyteca could enjoy "a fruitful integration" (van Eemeren and Grootendorst, 1995a:132) with the pragma-dialectical theory. The details of the pragma-dialectical account are examined in chapter 2. Chapter 1 subjects the product-oriented logical perspective to a similar review. The remainder of the book is devoted to developing, applying, and defending the perspective that is adopted here, the process-oriented perspective of the rhetorical. The thesis to be elaborated and defended is that the most appropriate synthesis of the main perspectives in argumentation theory is one grounded in the rhetorical.

Why the rhetorical? The answer to this question is threaded throughout the pages of this study. One of the claims to be defended is that the rhetorical approach avoids the shortcomings of the logical and the dialectical. But in its own right, with its focus upon the contexts in which argumentation occurs and the personalities of those who argue and consume arguments, a rhetorical model of argumentation offers the most complete and satisfying account of what arguing *is*, of what it is like to be engaged in argumentation, to be argued to, and to evaluate arguments. This claim too, of course, with its far-reaching ramifications, is to be defended in what follows.

5. Origins in the *Rhetoric*

Aristotle's *Rhetoric* is presented as an art of persuasion; ostensibly a manual to assist speakers in persuading an audience, although its lessons extend beyond the circumstances of the orator and the types of audience envisaged by Aristotle. It covers epideictic, forensic, and deliberative rhetoric, although it is the latter, with its concern for future courses of action, which receives particular attention. The text is controversial, and disjointed. It is judged on the one hand as an amalgamation of two works (bks. 1 and 2 on persuasive argument and bk. 3 on style and composition) revised over different periods (Kennedy, 1991; Burnyeat, 1994); and on the other hand, a coherent whole designed to respond to Plato's dismissal of rhetoric and Isocrates' all-inclusive embracing of the practice (McCabe, 1994).

It is the first two books, containing the theory of argument, which offers greatest rewards for contemporary argumentation theorists, although the ideas expressed there may not be those we tend to associate with "rhetoric." In fact, while I have suggested that the logical tradition has impressed upon us a particular sense of "argument" largely omitting the other senses, so Ricoeur detects a similar movement of exclusion in the history of rhetoric. What has survived, he insists, is a "restricted rhetoric," shorn from its roots in argumentation, and reduced to just one of its three parts—style. He concludes, rather harshly, that, as a result of this, rhetoric "became the erratic and futile discipline that died during the last century" (1977:28).[8] This may well account for the negative connotations that tend to attach to rhetoric in our own century, but such negativity is not justified toward the Aristotelian origins. Aristotle's rhetoric is grounded in method, linked to his dialectical and ethical works, and eschews the exploitation of audiences (Irwin, 1996).

Rhetoric is introduced as a counterpart to dialectic (1.1.1354a). While it shares some features with dialectic, it contains elements, such as the interests in ethos and pathos, which are not found there. Even its third major constituent, logical argument, suggests more than was conveyed by that concept in the dialectical works. Rhetorical arguments are concerned with *pisteis* (proofs or convictions [1.1.1355a]), which are a type of demonstration (*apodeixis*). And rhetorical *apodeixis* is the enthymeme, which is a type of reasoning (1.1.1355a). But the logic here is quite informal because, as Burnyeat notes, "not all the patterns of argument he illustrates can be fitted into the syllogistic mold" (1994:31). In fact, while the rhetoric is presented as an art, the *pisteis* involved comprise both artistic (entechnic) and nonartistic (atechnic) forms. The first, artistic, involves invention, the constructions of the arguer. The nonartistic are proofs that already exist in the form of witnesses, testimony, and the such (1.2.1355b). So, "proof" and "enthymeme" are central concepts in understanding rhetorical argument, but it is the second of these that is most disputed as to its meaning and that therefore requires a more extensive discussion.

6. Rhetorical Argument: Enthymeme

In Book 1 of the *Rhetoric,* the enthymeme is introduced as "a sort of syllogism [or reasoning]" which is different from "a logical syllogism" (1.1.1355a). Later Aristotle explains, "just as in dialectic there is on the one hand induction [*epagoge*] and on the other hand syllogism and the apparent syllogism, so the situation is similar in rhetoric; for the *paradeigma* ["example"] is an induction, the *enthymema* a syllogism. I call a rhetorical syllogism an enthymeme, a rhetorical induction a paradigm" (1.2.1356b). This appears to establish the enthymeme as the rhetorical equivalent of a deductive argument form. However, as Aristotle goes on to explain, it is "to show that if some premises are true, something else [the conclusion] beyond them results from these because they are true" (ibid.). The exact relation between premises and conclusion is not clarified and, as we will see from Burnyeat, there is a "relaxed" way of interpreting this. Finally here, we should note what is taken to be the key definition of the "enthymeme" in the *Rhetoric:*

> Thus, it is necessary for an enthymeme and a paradigm to be concerned with things that are for the most part capable of being other than they are—the paradigm inductively, the en-

thymeme syllogistically—and drawn from few premises and often less than those of the primary syllogism; for if one of these is known, it does not have to be stated, since the hearer supplies it. (1.2.1357a)

There are three important things to note about the enthymeme. The first is with respect to its content: it is concerned with things that are capable of being otherwise. That is, it deals with probability, not necessity. The second point has to do with its relation to the audience: it is not context free but anticipates, in its organization, the active involvement of the audience.

I will return to both of these points in the next section. It is the third point that concerns us here, and that has to do with the form of the enthymeme. The previous passage appears to endorse the traditional view of the (Aristotelian) enthymeme as an incomplete syllogism, comprising a premise and conclusion. Whether this is the Aristotelian view is the point in question, and answering this question will get us much closer to the meaning of "enthymeme" in the *Rhetoric*.

The tradition that understands *enthymeme* as an incomplete syllogism is so established that this is often seen as the definition of the term (see Hitchcock, 1985; Quine, 1972). As David Hitchcock notes, the tradition thus shifts away from Aristotle's principal concern in terms of the premises being "probabilities or signs" (1995a:116). George Kennedy agrees. In his commentary to the *Rhetoric* he observes that the enthymeme having an assumed premise, while often the case, "*is not a necessary feature* of the enthymeme" (1991:42) (italics mine). "The real determinant of an enthymeme in contrast to a syllogism is what a popular audience will understand . . . [rhetoric is] addressed to an audience that cannot be assumed to follow intricate logical argument." The understanding here is that an enthymeme should be a brief, noncomplex argument.

Burnyeat takes the analysis much further, including a challenge to the utility of the enthymeme as an incomplete syllogism, which has become "a useless relic of the textbook tradition" (1994:5). He attributes the understanding of enthymemes as abbreviated syllogisms to an integration of Stoic and Aristotelian logic in the commentaries of late antiquity (1996:91), with the principal idea being of Stoic origin (1994:42).

Burnyeat's challenge to the tradition is a double one. In the first instance, he traces the "confusion" to a line near the end of the *Prior Analytics:* "An enthymeme is an incomplete (*ateles*) *sullogismos* from likelihoods or signs" (70a10).

But the *ateles* here, omitted from most significant manuscripts, is wrong. The sentence without the term is repeated three times in the *Rhetoric:* "An enthymeme is a *sullogismos* from likelihoods or signs." But even here, and this is the second part of Burnyeat's challenge, he doubts whether Aristotle wrote the sentence.

> That is, the Aristotelian enthymeme is to be explained neither as an abbreviated syllogism in accordance with the traditional doctrine, nor as a syllogism from likelihoods and signs . . . nor even as a *sullogismos* in some other sense from likelihoods or signs. It may be true that the enthymeme is a *sullogismos* from likelihoods or signs, but that is not its definition. (1994:10)

The *enthymeme* is introduced by Aristotle with little or no explanation (1.1.1354a). This suggests that he expects his audience to be familiar with the term, which further suggests that he is drawing on a contemporary usage where it simply means the thoughts or ideas a speaker wishes to communicate to an audience. So the *enthymeme* here is not a technical term, not a syllogism in the accepted (by us) sense; it is a speech that conveys ideas to an audience in order to demonstrate something. Since this involves advancing arguments, the enthymeme is a kind of argument (*sullogismos*).

The passage from 1.2.357a still needs consideration since Aristotle specifically refers to the *enthymeme* being drawn from few premises, and often less than the primary syllogism. But of course, as we can now read this, "often" does not mean "always," and so that cannot be central to the definition of the term; nor does "few" mean "one" (as in the "traditional" enthymeme). In fact, one could insist that "few" entails more than one. All that really is required from this is that an enthymeme be brief so that it can be effective with its audience.

Although Aristotle illustrates the suppression of premises that an audience can supply with a two-premise argument in which one is commonly known, here (as at 2.21.1394a when he adds premises to maxims in a similar way) the resulting arguments are not syllogisms.

Finally, to show further that the repeated references to *sullogismos* need not mean "syllogism" in the accepted sense, Burnyeat (1994:28–29) recalls that Aristotle divides proofs into *sullogismos* and *epagoge* (normally translated as "deductive" and "inductive"). But, since some nondeductive inferences are not cases of *epagoge,* then *sullogismos* must include arguments in which premises do not purport to necessitate their conclusions.

Burnyeat's argument represents a compelling case for reading Aristotle's enthymeme as a more informal type of reasonable argument. It certainly lays to rest any vestiges of the incomplete syllogism of the tradition.

As forms of probable argument, enthymemes can take on a number of different strategies or lines of argument. In chapter 23 of Book 2, Aristotle details twenty-eight of such "topics," which include a number of strategies that should be familiar to contemporary argumentation theorists. Topic 6 involves "[turning] what has been said against oneself upon the one who said it" (2.23.1398a), for example, and others cover a range of topics from "definition" (Topic 7) and "division" (Topic 9), to induction (Topic 10) and precedent (Topic #11), to arguing from consequence (Topic 13) and "consequences by analogy" (Topic 15). A particularly effective aspect of enthymeme (since "people enjoy things said in general terms that they happen to assume ahead of time in a partial way" [2.21.1393b]) is the maxim (*gnome*), although Aristotle's successors tended to treat the gnomic utterance as a stylistic device rather than as the tool of logical argument that he considered it (Kennedy, 1991:182). The maxim serves to illustrate the popular nature or "publicness"[9] of rhetorical argument. In this regard, we shall recall, the enthymeme does not exhaust the category of common proofs (*pisteis*) but is joined by the paradigm or example. And the paradigm, in turn, can be "historical" or, in the form of fables, "fictional" (2.20.1393a-b). Thus, the sphere of rhetorical argumentation is widened even further to embrace the use of these types of "narrative."

The popularity alluded to here may be the most significant aspect of rhetorical argument, particularly in regard to its logical cousin. Mary Margaret McCabe (1994) reminds us of how "austere" Aristotle's model of argument is elsewhere—comprising collections of propositions that are related to a conclusion. Validity is then a *characteristic* of the argument, divorced from context. To its credit, the human mind has the capacity to *see* this validity. But on the downside, the mind is *passive* in doing so. Were this character to carry over to rhetorical argument, the arguer and audience would be insignificant. But this is exactly where rhetorical argument, in requiring the *active* involvement of arguer and audience, is distinctive. McCabe puts this well:

> Unlike pure syllogisms, they [enthymemes] cannot be purely formal, because they are embedded in the possibilities *that interest* us. . . . Enthymemes, that is, cannot be formalized away from their context in the easy way that syllogisms can. (1994:155)

Part of this context is the active involvement of the audience—supplying assumptions where required (thus completing the argument), assessing the reasoning, and judging the evidence for the action proposed. This role gives autonomy to the audience; audiences are not just pawns in a game "but active moral agents to be taken with due seriousness" (161).

In concluding these remarks on the nature of the enthymeme, I would emphasize the fact that as the primary model of rhetorical argument it should be seen as distinct from the formal model of "logical argument." And its relation to audience, particularly through its associations with ethos and pathos, illustrates how rhetorical argumentation is distinct from its strict dialectical counterpart. Relaxing the logical requirements of the enthymeme does not weaken or marginalize it; quite the opposite. Burnyeat himself acknowledges this:

> Aristotle's doctrine of the enthymeme embodies the claim that the clash of opposing arguments in deliberative and forensic gatherings is a positive expression of human reasonableness in a world where issues are complex and deciding them is difficult, because there really is something to be said on either side. As such, Aristotle's doctrine of the enthymeme is one of his greatest and most original achievements. (1996:91)

7. Rhetorical Argumentation

Rhetorical argumentation, as should be clear by this point, involves more than just the enthymeme. In fact, the tools of proof are not restricted to the enthymeme but also include the paradigm or example. We are now in a position to sketch the key features of rhetorical argumentation and to comment on their distinctiveness.

Next to the accessibility of the enthymeme, and connected with it, is the role of the audience. The sense of audiences for rhetorical argumentation is restricted by Aristotle to those interested in non-scientific, popular, less "rationally compelling arguments" (Irwin, 1996:143). In the current study the range of audiences appropriate to rhetorical argumentation will be considerably wider. McCabe (1994) has stressed the active, autonomous nature of the audiences in rhetorical argumentation. Other features follow from this characteristic. Since audiences are *affected* by the argument, they need to be appropriately disposed toward its ideas and strategies. This is the link to pathos. They also need to be so disposed toward the arguer. This is the link to ethos. In these terms, we can see that rhetorical argumentation is about context and that the context it is about includes, essentially, logos, ethos, and pathos.

Plato's *Phaedrus* had advocated the need for the "legitimate" rhetorical arguer to know the types of soul in an audience in order to address the appropriate discourses to the corresponding types. Aristotle handles this in two ways: he considers the nature of audiences in terms of their interests, speaking of those who are old, young, and in between; and, secondly, he discusses the emotions that can be brought about in an audience in order to move them in certain directions. In the *Rhetoric,* emotions, despite being nonrational, are subject to reason (Nehamas, 1994:263), they can be evoked and directed by rational considerations. (Aristotle also discusses the wrong way to appeal to emotions.) The conception of "pathotic argument" (Brinton, 1988b) which can be developed from this will be discussed in chapter 3. It involves not just the creation of emotions (moods) in an audience, but the more general appeal to such emotions like pity as a legitimate argumentative strategy.

Likewise, the discussion of ethos in chapter 3 of this study is a development of the Aristotelian position. Aristotle is concerned with the ethos (character) of the speaker, who needs to establish credibility and to demonstrate positive character traits (1.2.1356a; 2.1.1377b).[10] The reason why the speaker's character is important to the decisions of an audience is seen in the elements that are valued in that character: practical wisdom (*phronesis*), virtue (*arete*), and goodwill (*eunoia*) (2.1.1378a). Character comprises a person's capacities and habits that direct her or his actions and ends. Thus, as Amelie Oksenberg Rorty points out, "a person's character can be summarized by his ends: they form an organized system of ordered preferences, the structure of his practical reasoning" (1996:13). A person who is known to reason well, an audience might consider, is probably a person whose arguments can be trusted. At the least, we should expect an initial presumption in favor of such a person.

But Aristotle is not just interested in the ethos of the arguer. He employs fables or narratives for argumentative ends. They can be used to illustrate a comparison or likeness between one event and another (2.20.1394a), and narratives can further be used to illustrate the questionable character of an opponent (3.15.1416a). It is in regard to this that Christopher Carey notes: "in the hands of a master, *ethos,* in the sense of dramatic characterization, may fulfil the role of argument" (1996:414).

In summary, Aristotle's *Rhetoric* offers important features and advice for the development of a more contemporary model of rhetorical argumentation. While a key difference exists in that Aristotle is concerned with training speakers to speak, it is not hard to develop his ideas to further include the producers of general argumentation, verbal or written. And, again, while the Aristotelian enthymeme is by nature brief, more extended arguments, themselves comprised of simpler pieces, can be brought under the rubric of rhetorical argumentation.

Aristotle gives us a model of contextual argumentation, with a deep appreciation of audiences and a highly original concept of "argument." Rhetorical argumentation deals with what is possible, not with what is necessary, concerning itself with what "could be other than it is." It thus involves judgment, decision, and action. Its ethical dimension is evident from the kinds of issues it addresses and the roles played by pathos and ethos. Each of these concepts will be important as they are revised and developed in the pages ahead.

The sense of "rhetoric" that emerges from this discussion and that will guide me in what follows is not, then, that associated with abuse or exploitation, but is surprisingly contemporary. It is, to borrow Richard Andrews's observation, rhetoric as "'the arts of discourse' with all the associations of discourse embedded in social contexts" (1995:30).

8. Contemporary Views

One point that is clear so far is that a rhetorical model of argumentation involves more than just an evaluation of the PPC products of arguing; it also concerns the understanding of those products. Or, to sharpen the focus further, the evaluation of argumentation must include understanding, and this understanding involves looking beyond the product to the context in which it arises and to its rhetorical features. Aristotle's "context" had three principal constituents; later rhetoricians have added other factors like "message" and "common code" (Kennedy, 1991:47).

A theory of argumentation that deals only with the isolated products will be inadequate. Wenzel reveals as much when he writes: "[L]ogical evaluation is constrained by the possibilities of rhetorical analysis. In other words, the rhetorician must clear the way . . . for the logician" (1987b:107–8). This is not to suggest that rhetoric has priority over logic (or dialectic), but it is to insist again that the most comprehensive theory of argumentation will situate the latter two within a rhetorical casing. To completely grasp an argument requires an understanding of its actual rhetorical context, and this appreciation should survive even in situations where the context may not be fully recoverable. We look for the makeup of the arguer and the audience, their respective backgrounds, their relationship, and their expectations of each other, all of which may influence our interpretations of the arguments involved. And we set this in a social and temporal context, against the background of relevant events. In fact, as I will argue later, relevance is a key consideration in unpacking this network of involvements. What should go into a contemporary consideration of "context" is the primary subject addressed in chapter 3.

As the work of Wenzel indicates, the question of rhetorical argumentation has not been completely marginalized in the move to develop informal logics and to recover dialectical argumentation. More generally, the relationship between rhetoric and philosophical argument has received considerable attention in the essays of Henry W. Johnstone Jr. (1978), where the importance of the rhetorical is stressed.

Don S. Levi (1995) offers a defense of rhetoric in the sense that it provides a better understanding of what it means to think critically about an argument than does logic. Through looking at the rhetorical context of an argument, particularly the identity of the audience, he argues that "rhetoric" involves more than just rhetorical effectiveness. While the account that Levi offers is somewhat preliminary and wants for good illustrations, it indicates an awareness that at least a basic sense of "logical" correctness can be reconciled with a sense of rhetorical context.

More elaborate, and noticeably Aristotelian, is the account offered by Thomas Farrell. His three constituents of rhetorical argument echo the insights of the *Rhetoric:*

> i. The complicity of an audience in argumentative development;

> ii. The probable relation between rhetorical argument and judgment;

> iii. The normative force of knowledge presumed and created by rhetorical argument. (1977:142)

In his discussion, Farrell adds a contemporary nuance to each of these, speaking throughout of a "rhetorical validity." For example, in light of the first point; which we saw in the *actively engaged audience* of rhetorical argument, some of Hitler's reasoning (culled from *Mein Kampf*) can be judged "invalid" since it fails to "address and include an appropriate audience" (145). And with respect to the third point, he proposes that "the actual premises of rhetorical argument may be regarded as valid, based upon their relation to the social knowledge attributed to specific audiences" (147).

Not everyone would be comfortable with rhetorical argument appropriating the term *validity,* but we need to be clear about what it entails and how far it extends. As I have already suggested, rhetorical argument is not a replacement for logic, nor does it do its work. William D. Harpine, for example, responds to Farrell that "the dialectical and rhetorical perspectives cannot serve the purposes of logic" (1985:97). *Effectiveness* is not soundness, Harpine insists. Perhaps not, in the sense that logic confers on that term. But our discussion of the *Rhetoric* has served to show that there is more to rhetorical argument than effectiveness and that it possesses a strong sense of reasonableness with far greater application than formal validity. It is not so much whether rhetoric and dialectic can serve the purposes of logic, than whether they can each be clear about their own purposes, and whether logic should dictate the terms of reasonableness in the way that the tradition has encouraged. Harpine (109) further complains that Farrell's criteria are irrelevant to nonrhetorical arguments. In one sense, he is correct, and I would be surprised if Farrell contested it. But in a deeper sense, as I propose in the chapters ahead, all arguments that matter, whether or not they solely seek action, are rooted in rhetorical contexts. Whether those contexts are uncovered and their components elevated to play a role in an argument's evaluation is what is at issue here.[11]

Of all the contemporary models available to us, Chaim Perelman's (1982) rhetorical model of argumentation recommends itself for a number of its features and insights. What is essentially rhetorical about it is its unrelenting interest in audiences, far beyond anything that Levi indicates. While this focus is also the source of criticism, and may indeed make for an unbalanced account, such criticism can be met, quite often from within Perelman's own writings. In the chapters ahead, I will make a number of references to Perelman's model. I don't propose a thorough adoption of his ideas, but a development and adaption of a number of them within a rhetorical model of argumentation that meets the challenges experienced by contemporary argumentation theory.

A principal thesis of *The New Rhetoric* is that "argumentation is a function of the audience addressed" (Perelman and Olbrechts-

Tyteca, 1969:44). Two audiences are offered for theoretical analysis: the particular or specific audience of the actual situation and the universal audience developed out of the first audience. With this tandem, the account addresses the primary challenge confronting argumentation theory as recognized by Habermas: the demand for an account that provides *both* specific criteria of evaluation relative to the occasion *and* objective criteria that avoid a thorough relativism.

The goal of all argumentation according to this model is not the deduction of conclusions from premises or just the resolution of disputes, but the creation or strengthening of the adherence of the minds of the two audiences to the claims presented for their assent.

There is also a second, less explicit, goal that recommends the rhetorical perspective as the groundwork for the synthesis. I have already emphasized the interest placed in the whole person, both of the arguer and the audience. Out of this develops a model of the arguer and audience as "reasonable," a model characterized by its concern for people. This is particularly important given the traditional conception of rhetoric as advocating the exploitation of audiences to achieve its ends, of making the weaker argument appear stronger and thereby deceiving the audience. Perelman's rhetorical model rejects argumentative strategies based on manipulation (Golden, 1986:293; Crosswhite, 1995). And what begins to emerge is a model of argumentation concerned not just with the adherence of minds to claims put forward but also the improvement of those minds.

In relation to this, Aristotle's proposal in the *Rhetoric*, as I have already discussed, is noteworthy for the sense of invitation that is extended to the audience. The audience is invited into the argumentation to become a part of it, where argumentation is an act of reciprocal involvement. This is a view of argumentation that sees it create an environment in which the "self-persuasion" of the audience, as it were, can take place. Rather than being exploited, or aggressively persuaded, the audience is given the opportunity to complete the argumentation and to evaluate arguments in terms of the reasoning involved. The sense of autonomy this grants to the audience (noted by McCabe [1994]) suggests an important sense of reasonableness that in turn can meet the concerns raised by critics of the "rational" tradition, particularly the charge that argumentation is essentially adversarial.

One can still talk about persuasiveness and conviction under this model, but not in the traditional sense. The audience is persuaded by the argumentation, not by the arguer (hence not by any "rhetorical tricks"). The audience is complicit in the completion of the argumentation. With its background, beliefs, and so forth, it is part of the context that comprises the argumentation. Hence, the key sense that the audience, when it is persuaded, is persuaded by its own reflections on the argument it has drawn from the arguer's speech.

9. Outline of the Study

In what follows I intend to show how both of these goals may be brought to fruition in a theory of argumentation based on the rhetorical perspective that captures the strengths of the alternative perspectives while avoiding their problems. But in the opening chapters it is important to look at what those alternative approaches have to offer. Thus, I turn first to the logical perspective, in both its formal and informal incarnations, and assess its strengths and weaknesses as a foundation for a model of argumentation. Chapter 2 submits the dialectical, and particularly the pragma-dialectical, perspective to a similar investigation, and concludes that, while the dialectical understanding of argument is a welcome advance on the logical, it too is not sufficiently complete.

Chapter 3 begins to develop the exposition of a rhetorical approach to argumentation indicated in this introduction, and this is continued through chapter 4. Outlining and developing the essential insights of Perelman, including his central idea of the universal audience, I situate these items within a larger discussion of argumentative context with key features of locale, background, arguer, mode of expression, and audience in general. To this I add the key criteria for developing and assessing argumentation, particularly the criterion of relevance with its attention to the cognitive environments of audiences, and the role that the universal audience plays in the criterion of acceptability.

With the principal features of a rhetorical model discussed in chapters 3 and 4, the subsequent chapters provide the opportunity for demonstrating, fine-tuning, and further developing the model. This is done first through two case studies in chapter 5, and then by assessing from the rhetorical perspective two topics of continuing debate in contemporary argumentation theory. These include problems surrounding the nature of "fallacy" (chap. 6), and the problem of rationality and its critiques from postmodernism and feminism (chap. 7).

Wenzel (1989) backs his call for a synthesis of the three perspectives by indicating the kinds of relationships he sees implied by such a synthesis. At root, argumentation is rhetorical, but when rhetorical argumentation is brought under some deliberate procedural control, the situation becomes dialectical (although still with a rhetorical demand for creative and effective utterance). Logic enters the fold as the PPC structures are drawn from the discourse by arguers or critics, who remain alert to its rhetorical and dialectical features. This "natural history of argumentation," has an intuitive appeal to Wenzel. "If it is accurate," he writes, "then the naturalization of logic requires attention to the rhetorical origins of argument as well as to its dialectical organization" (1989:94). In this book, I hope to contribute to the project that Wenzel advocates, tracing argument to its rhetorical origins and developing from there a model that integrates it with the other two perspectives.

Chapter 1

Argument as Product: The Logical Perspective

The logical orientation in argumentation itself enjoys different strains. In this chapter I explore the common root of these strains and indicate the importance of a rhetorical base to the logical perspective.

The logical approach focuses on argumentation as a product. That is, its central concern is the collection of statements comprising a conclusion and one or more premises (PPC) called an argument, and the determination of such arguments as valid or invalid, strong or weak. Traditionally, the product approach is seen in the systems of formal logic, but since a number of recent "informal" logics incorporate some formal elements, we will also need to look at the relationships between formal and informal logic.

1.1 Formal Logic and the Classical Root

Classical logic, and the theories based on it like modal logic or set theory, as well as rival logical theories, all find their bases in the idea of logical consequence (Read, 1995:36). On the traditional view, a good argument is a valid one, and validity is a matter of form. One proposition is a logical consequence of another only if together they match a valid pattern. Validity itself is determined in these forms according to a notion of truth-preservation. Valid arguments cannot have true premises and false conclusions. The model implied in this truth-preserving system is that of mathematics. As Stephen Read puts it:

> The aim of logicians at the turn of the twentieth century was to axiomatize mathematics—to find a finite set of axioms, or at least a finitely specifiable such set, from which the whole of mathematics could be derived, and only that. (1995:45)

This ambition is strikingly similar to the one held by Aristotle. As noted in the introduction, Aristotle's work allowed for the current rich treatments of argumentation under the rubrics of Logic, Dialectic, and Rhetoric. But in his vision of logic as a formal science comparable to geometry we see the first move in a development that was to stress the logical over the other approaches throughout subsequent centuries.[1]

Aristotle saw himself living in an ordered, intelligible universe that lent itself to being understood. And, fortuitously, human beings naturally desire to understand their surroundings and are equipped with the reasoning capacities suitable to the task. Aristotle strove to reveal the basic structure of reality by grasping the primitive, immediate, principles and by demonstrating what must follow from them (*Posterior Analytics,* bk. 2). By means of the syllogism—"a form of words in which certain things are assumed and there is something other than what was assumed which necessarily follows from things' being so" (bk. 1, chap. 1, 24b:17–19)[2]—Aristotle sought to develop a formal system of inferences that would reveal the structure of reality. In applying themselves through such rigorous reasoning humans would come to know the world and *by virtue of doing so,* or *in the process,* actualize their full potential as knowers. That is, they would fully become the rational creatures that human beings essentially are.

This highly ambitious but intensely human project has been judged overly optimistic (Lear:1988) and criticized for reducing human nature to the capacity of reason (Nye:1990). I will discuss the latter type of criticism in chapter 7. With respect to the former, Jonathan Lear poses the problem as follows:

> Aristotle's logic reigned as the unquestioned paradigm of logic until the end of the nineteenth century. But it is not sufficiently sophisticated to realize his dream. If Aristotle is to present a unified and coherent logical theory without giving an analysis of the concept of following of necessity, it is essential that all deductions, non-formal and formal, be systematically related to the perfect syllogistic inferences. (1988:228–29)

This Aristotle did not do. But his logic as discussed here is a theory of demonstration or proof. It is not itself presented as a theory of argument, although when argument is introduced it is related to this logical foundation.

... so too with arguments—both deductive and inductive proceed in this way; for both produce their teaching through what we are already aware of, the former getting their premises as from men who grasp them, the latter proving the universal through the particular's being clear. (And rhetorical arguments too persuade in the same way. . . .). (*Posterior Analytics,* bk. 1, chap. 1, 71a:5–10)[3]

Thus the tradition of relating argumentation with formal systems is long-standing, finding its suggestion in the ideas of Aristotle. But this is not necessarily to equate "argument" with the limited model of argument in formal logic, as has become the fashion in the twentieth century. As Jaakko Hintikka notes, "this traditional conception of logic and deduction has been rejected with a rare unanimity by recent theorists of human reasoning and argumentation" (1989:3). The informal logician Ralph H. Johnson (1987a) is a point in case, arguing that, for many, logic itself became synonymous with formal, deductive logic (FDL). This involved a reconceptualization of logic as a body of necessary truths, which had been involved in its history, but only as a part of it. Johnson (1987a:50) traces the shift to Frege and to his interests in rigorous proof. Frege was not interested in argumentation per se. But his influence, like that of Russell and Whitehead, was substantial, and not only did FDL become synonymous with logic, but "argument" itself became synonymous with deductive argument. A rich tradition of interest in argument as rational persuasion, traceable to Aristotle's own discussions, was left by the wayside.

Beyond this shift of emphasis, the story against formal logic itself is that it is inadequate for the analysis of everyday argumentation. However, two things in its defense merit noting here: (1) It is not clear that it *has* ever been advanced as an adequate model for treating everyday arguments (see van Evra, 1985); and (2) That it does not serve as a complete model for dealing with everyday arguments does not mean it cannot contribute to their analysis. Michael Scriven has observed: "The syllogism was probably nearer to reality (though not to comprehensiveness) than the propositional calculus, but not near enough to make it useful in handling the average editorial or columnist today" (1976:xv). The appropriateness of this comment may depend on what we understand "average" editorials to involve. Most everyday arguments do not fit patterns of the categorical syllogism or propositional logic; but some do (Govier, 1987:201). It overstates the case to propose that these argument

forms are not useful. They are useful, if they are understood within
a theory of argumentation that captures the full range of relations
between arguers and audiences, rather than just the products of
those relations.

1.2 The Toulmin Transition

Stephen Toulmin's seminal text, *The Uses of Argument* (1958), is
a precursor of the kind of critique of FDL that Johnson develops. And
Toulmin's work is instructive for its detailing of a wide divergence between methods of professional (formal) logicians and those of everyday arguers. While it may be the case that formal logicians have
never claimed everyday arguments as their domain, Toulmin still ac-
cuses them (1958:126) of advancing a model of argument that they
expect other types of arguments to emulate. In distinction to the kind
of hierarchy that he sees proposed by formal logicians, with the for-
mally valid argument at the pinnacle, Toulmin (14) identifies a diverse range of arguments specific to different fields, which cannot be
assessed by the same procedure and by appeal to the same standards.

Toulmin calls the syllogism an unrepresentative and simple sort
of argument and traces many of what he terms the "paradoxical
commonplaces" (146) of formal logic to the misapplication of this pattern to arguments of other sorts. His own account of argument introduces new technical terms like *Warrant* and *Backing*. "Warrants"
are statements that act as bridges between data (D) (or evidence: the
ground that we produce as support) and the conclusion (C). These
bridges act to authorize the step taken. What justifies a move from
D to C? His answer is that C follows from D since W. By example:
Harry was born in Bermuda (D), so Harry is a British subject (C),
since a man born in Bermuda will be a British subject (W) (99). Warrants themselves require assurances that authorize *them,* and these
Toulmin terms *Backing* statements (B). In the example already provided, the warrant that "a man born in Bermuda will be a British
subject" is authorized by backing statements that refer to the appropriate statutes and to other legal provisions (105). This is a very simplified explanation of some of Toulmin's basic terms. He takes pains
to distinguish backing (B) from data (D), as well as backing (B) from
warrant (W). Even so clarified, the account has received considerable
criticism (Johnson, 1981; Freeman, 1991; van Eemeren and Grootendorst, 1992a:4).[4] What is of importance to the current discussion
is the way in which Toulmin presents his account in contrast to the
tradition he challenges.

He still speaks of arguments being valid or invalid, but not by virtue of form or consequence. In the argument pattern D; W; so C, the elements of the conclusion and premises are not the same. Nor is the validity of the argument a consequence of its formal properties.

> . . . a (D; B; so C) argument will not be formally valid. Once we bring into the open the backing on which (in the last resort) the soundness of our arguments depends, the suggestion that validity is to be explained in terms of "formal properties", in any geometrical sense, loses its plausibility. (1958:120)

Different fields of argument will employ different standards of assessment as warrants, data, and backing come into play in different ways. The criteria of formal logic are, Toulmin claims, field-invariant. Thus they cannot deal adequately with the nuances of argument specific to different fields. Toulmin's criteria are field-dependent and will adapt themselves to the specifics of the field in question.

Toulmin's model of argument is what he terms a *jurisprudential model,* in contrast to the mathematical or geometrical model. But on the terms discussed so far it is still a logical model. It still focuses attention on the products of argumentation and what should count as appropriate criteria for validity and soundness. Thus, many would call Toulmin an informal logician. He eschews attention to form, but not to arguments as products.

1.3 Informal Logic

It is far easier to distinguish between formal and informal logics than to give a clear definition of what informal logic involves. Writing in 1980, two of the pioneers of informal logic, J. Anthony Blair and Ralph H. Johnson, found that the field was too undeveloped for a clear definition to be possible (1980:ix). Fourteen years later, while noting maturity in the field in the quality and quantity of contributions made to it, they still believe that there is no distinctive methodology, paradigm, or dominant theory for informal logic (Johnson and Blair, 1994:4). In fact, some authors doubt that it is a logic at all, seeing in "applied epistemology" a more appropriate label for the field (Battersby, 1989; Weinstein, 1990, 1994). Nevertheless, the rudiments of its central components can be gleaned from a series of developments in recent decades.

The pioneering work of John Woods and Douglas N. Walton (1982, 1989), particularly in reevaluating the traditional informal fallacies straddled any divide that might have been thought to exist between formal and informal logic. Woods answered his own question "What is Informal Logic?" with a terse *nothing*. Assuming that the principal content of informal logic was the fallacies, Woods concluded that "the theory of fallacies is not only at its best as a formal theory, it is difficult to see how the suppression of its formal character could leave a residue fully deserving of the name theory" (1980:62). The character of the Woods and Walton approach to the fallacies remained true to this sentiment.

At the same time, Blair and Johnson were identifying a more expansive range of components integral to the "informal logic point of view" (1980:ix–x). These included a focus on natural language arguments and serious doubts about whether deductive logic and standard inductive logic could model them; a view of argumentation as a dialectical process; and a conviction that there were standards and norms of argument evaluation beyond the categories of deductive validity and soundness.

Each of these has been a recurring theme in subsequent models of informal logic, and the last has prompted a set of evaluative measures adopted by many of its practitioners. There has also been a gradual equating of informal logic with the logic of argumentation. Jurgen Habermas prompted such thinking in writing:

> The logic of argumentation does not refer to deductive connections between semantic units (sentences) as does formal logic, but to nondeductive relations between the pragmatic units (speech acts) of which arguments are composed. Thus it also appears under the name of "informal logic." (1984:22–23)

Such a perspective is endorsed by Johnson and Blair (1994:11) and by Chaim Perelman (1989b:11), who calls informal logic the logic of argumentation, and by Douglas N. Walton, who equates informal logic with "critical argumentation" (1989:ix).[5] In fact, Walton has traveled so far from the early work on fallacies with Woods that he can write: "Only recently has it become more apparent that a pragmatic approach is absolutely necessary in order to make sense of informal fallacies" (1990:419).

Interestingly, Walton's "informal logic" has a distinct pragmatic quality. When he argues that "generally the theory of informal logic must be based on the concept of question-reply dialogue as a form of interaction between two participants, each representing one side of an argument" (1989:x), he is exhibiting the kind of dialectical orientation that would place him among the pragma-dialecticians to be discussed in the next chapter.

This dual character to Walton's writings should not come as a surprise; it will also be seen in the work of others. While isolating the three perspectives on argument in order to study them, I have not suggested that they actually *work* in isolation. Accounts of argument typically include aspects of the three in their makeup, and we will find this to be the case when we turn to the dialectical and rhetorical. The issue for us has been which perspective *grounds* the theory, or, from another approach, what role the rhetorical plays in a theory.

Thus Walton's identification of informal logic with a pragma-dialectical account of argument announces one possible outcome of developments in these fields. In fact, Johnson uses such an association of the two to highlight those features that constitute an informal logic (IL). That the idea of "informal logic" has achieved some kind of general account can be seen in the confidence with which he identifies four central characteristics. Informal logic is text-based (rather than speech-based), focuses on an argument (rather than on a critical discussion), involves criteria (rather than rules), and is product-oriented (rather than procedure- or process-oriented) (1995:237).

It is this final point that most bears upon our current discussion. "IL," writes Johnson, "envisages a finished (to some degree) *product,* where the arguer is typically absent" (238–39). This leaves us with a set of premises supporting a conclusion. Other logicians with an "informalist stripe" (a myriad of them, we are told) are said to share this view, and among them Johnson counts Jonathan Berg (1992:104–5, 111); Leo A. Groarke (1992:114–15); C. L. Hamblin (1970:228); and Michael Wreen (1988:93).[6]

If both formal and informal logics are grounded in the same basic product-orientation, then what distinguishes them is the criteria by means of which arguments are evaluated.

In the classical tradition discussed earlier, the strongest claim that can be made about a premise's relation to its conclusion is that the premise entails the conclusion. But as a number of researchers have pointed out, formal validity is no guarantee of a good argument. Robert C. Pinto (1994, 1995) makes the point particularly well when he argues that entailment is neither a necessary nor a sufficient condition for the premises and conclusion of an argument being suitably linked.

Not sufficient, because an argument of the form "P, therefore P" meets the criterion of entailment but is hopeless as an argument. Not necessary, because there are innumerable inductively strong arguments in which premises do not entail conclusions. The abstract structures that classical logic studies just don't coincide with the factors that make *arguments* logically good. (1995:277–78)

In place of validity and soundness, informal logicians speak of strength and cogency and evaluate arguments with criteria like relevance, sufficiency, and acceptability (some accounts may add or substitute criteria like truth or consistency). Furthermore, just as form and evaluation are related in formal logic, so evaluation in informal logic is related to the structure of arguments and informal logicians adopt diagramming techniques as a principal tool in their evaluations (Freeman, 1991, 1994). In these ideas, a common core of what constitutes informal logic has evolved, and the field has matured from inchoate confusions to a fully formed discipline, with a recognized content and methodology.[7] We can further conclude that Toulmin, as a nonformal but product-oriented logician, fits within the informal ranks.

1.4 Problems of the Product-oriented Perspective

Many of the problems of the product-oriented account as they arise in formal logic are remedied or ameliorated by the advances of informal logic. But two that still warrant attention can be discussed under the general headings: (1) adaptability, and (2) relevance. To begin this, we return to Toulmin's critique.

Adaptability

As we have seen, formal logic lacks adaptability to different fields. The seriousness of this failure is seen in Toulmin's charge that the field-dependence of logical categories is an essential feature because there are irreducible differences between the sorts of problem arguments can tackle. Having determined the kinds of problem appropriate to a particular case, one can "determine what warrants, backing, and criteria of necessity are relevant to this case: there is no justification for applying analytic criteria in all fields of argument indiscriminately" (1958:176). Toulmin has expanded this notion of "field of argument" in terms of the problems that are said to be addressed by them. Thus the geometrical argument is a field in which we are faced with geometrical problems. A moral argument is called for by a moral problem, and the need for a prediction calls for an argument with a predictive conclusion. Setting aside problems associated with defining fields in this way, Toulmin's point is to show how unadaptable formal arguments are when we attempt to apply them across the range of such problems in fields. In a word, they lack the practical application that a theory of argumentation requires from its components.

This criticism applies more to the strict sense of validity constraining formal reasoning than it does to its interest in arguments as products. But the types of arguments produced in such systems are not context-sensitive. Which is to say that in their formulation they do not take account of the diversity of situations from which such patterns are abstracted nor of nuances in the ordinary language statements that they translate.

Problems associated with translation are widely known and, for students of formal logic, experienced. But it bears repeating that even to test a simple argument of the *modus ponens* variety (if p then q, p /q), there is often indecision as to whether the "p" of the first premise and the "p" of the second premise (or the "q" of the first premise and the "q" of the conclusion) symbolize exactly the same expressed terms or statements. Ordinary language arguments, rife with essential ambiguities and nuanced meanings, rarely lend themselves to such exact translations. Too often we find ourselves testing sanitized forms where allowances have been made in translation that belie any claim to be dealing with real-life arguments.[8]

Meaning is just one feature of context that formal logic mistreats, if it deals with it at all. Generally, its treatment of the argument produced and the relations between statements within it is conducted without reference to the background—the circumstances in which it arises, including the occasion and consequences; the arguer and her or his intentions in arguing; and the audience, with its background of beliefs and expectations. Toulmin anticipates many others when he criticizes the freezing of "statements into timeless propositions before admitting them into logic" (1958:182). Attention must be paid to the time and place of an utterance, and questions about the acceptability of an argument must be "understood and tackled *in a context*" (185). This, the purely formal logician omits from the account even before beginning.

Informal logic fares better in these respects. While critiques of logic may tend to cast their nets around both formal and informal varieties, informal logic has the adaptability to respond to such critiques in a way its formal counterpart cannot. Govier refers to a wide range of criticisms (particularly from feminists) delivered at both types of logic. One such case in point is:

> Those who propose standards for evaluating inferences and arguments are not sufficiently sensitive to the situation and context in which arguers and arguments appear. (Logic should be more *particular* and case-by-case.) (1995:198)

Such a case-by-case adaptability is exactly what Toulmin's account claimed to offer and what informal logicians have striven for in the formulation of their standards. Govier, for example, notes how the PPC structure of arguments "represents only the core of the argument" (200), implying that other features beyond the premises and conclusion exist as *part of the argument*. This is an important, albeit vague, observation. Govier's surrounding discussion remarks on the social, practical, and textual contexts and the backgrounds of non-argumentative discourse. Insofar as informal logicians address themselves to such features of the "argumentative context," they are expanding their accounts beyond the core of the product to accommodate dialectical and rhetorical aspects. Johnson (1995:242), we recall, exhibits just such an attitude by including the process of arguing and the arguers along with the product. Elsewhere, with Blair, Johnson suggests that "an argument understood as product . . . cannot be properly understood except against the background of the *process* which produced it—the process of argumentation" (1987:45).[9]

Missing here is any explicit reference to the audience of the argument. This is a common omission that characterizes the general state of informal logic. Josina M. Makau has observed of texts in the field that although some of them pay attention to contexts, "none of them teach students to fully consider the role *audience* plays in argumentative invention or evaluation" (1987:378–79). She expresses surprise at this situation given the 1980 overview provided by Johnson and Blair, where Perelman and L. Olbrechts-Tyteca's *New Rhetoric: A Treatise on Argumentation* (1969) is counted among three significant monographs. Makau remarks: "Yet given the nature of informal logic textbooks, it appears that Johnson, Blair and other informal logicians have overlooked the *central* thesis of this seminal work . . . its focus on the audience-relative nature of argumentation" (379).

Informal logic's basic sets of criteria, like relevance, sufficiency, and acceptability, allow for a more comprehensive assessment than validity and soundness. Acceptability *can* involve considerations of the contexts in which arguments arise, and relevance, as we will see in the next section, takes us beyond judgments of entailment.

Likewise, informal logicians' attention to the dynamics of argumentative discourse, to the ambiguities and vagueness and emotional ladenness of statements that serve as claims and premises, allows for a greater sensitivity to the "ordinariness" of everyday argumentation. Informal logic offers procedures for dealing with language problems in the standardizing of arguments (setting out the premises and conclusions) and further addresses them in the evaluation-criterion of acceptability.[10]

On the other hand, the use of diagrams serves to emphasize the orientation on product. Reasoning is abstracted from its contexts and attention is focused on supports within the argument. Some questions of evaluation, especially with respect to premise acceptability, may take us back to the context. But there is no guarantee that this will happen and premises can be assessed as acceptable according to whether or not they are known to be true to the evaluator. Despite this, however, we can conclude that, in general, and with the serious omission of attention to the audience, informal logic offers product-oriented models of argumentation that are context-sensitive and therefore richer in their evaluations and practical applications.

Relevance

Formal entailment captures the idea of "guaranteeing" or "following from." A premise entails a conclusion if, given the truth of the premise, the conclusion must also be true. But entailment is not strictly a notion of relevance in any way that might be useful. While truth, in these terms, is a *property of* statements, relevance is a *relation between* them. And entailment does not express the same type of relation. A typical textbook can give an inference like "New York is in New York. Therefore New York is in New York" to illustrate entailment. But for a premise to be relevant to a conclusion in any useful sense, it must act as *a reason* that increases our acceptance of, or convinces us to accept for the first time, the conclusion (Blair, 1989). Intuitively we recognize that a proposition may not be relevant to establishing a claim even though it is true. "Wayne Gretzky is clean-shaven" is not in any obvious sense relevant to the truth of the claim that "Wayne Gretzky is one of the premier hockey players in the world." However, in certain deductive systems, the rules governing logical implications (and all logical implications are also entailments) may well allow us to derive the one from the other.

When Read (1995:56) notes that truth-preservation in the classical account of formal logic endorses inferences in which the premises are irrelevant to the conclusion, he indicates a need to incorporate relevance into the criteria of logical consequence. This same need has been recognized by a number of logicians who have grappled with the problem of relevance.

In classical propositional logic, connectives like "&" and "v" allow us to construct complex propositions. We can discover the truth value of these connectives and the propositions they relate by constructing truth tables; these allow us to assess the validity of arguments—where the conclusion is true in every case in which the premises are also true. What becomes interesting, then, are valid inferences in classical propositional logic that are deemed shocking or astounding (Anderson and Belnap, 1968; Jeffrey, 1981). With an inference like "B/A>B," many substitutions for A and B give strange results. For example, "It is snowing. Therefore, if the sandwiches taste fishy, it is snowing." On the face of it, there seems to be no relationship between the sandwiches tasting fishy and it snowing such that the first necessitates the second. But with respect to the material conditional, such an inference is valid. If B is true, then "A&-B" must be false. Hence, "A>B" follows from the truth of B.

This concern over the material conditional was what prompted Alan Ross Anderson and Noel D. Belnap to propose their relevance logic. Their use of the term *relevance* to denote their logic "picked up an informal use before that time of the epithet "relevant" to characterize a consequence relation, and an implication, which was not paradoxical in the way material and strict implication were" (Read, 1988:44). It is clear to them that to state A as true on an irrelevant assumption B is not to "deduce" A from B or to show that B implies A in any "sensible" sense of "implies." This appeal to the sensible drives their concern to reconcile notions of entailment with our intuitions. A true entailment is necessarily true; the problem cases are simply not true entailments. Therefore, while they grant that valid inferences are necessarily valid, they mandate that the antecedent in a valid conditional be relevant to the consequent. In explaining their account, they present two distinct senses of "relevance": they provide a formal analysis (giving a subscripting device, which I will not go into here) of the intuitive idea that "for A to be relevant to B it must be possible to *use* A in a deduction of B from A" (Anderson and Belnap, 1968:101). It may not be necessary to use A, but it must be possible. Secondly, they propose a formal condition for the requirement of "common meaning content" between A and B, if "A>B" is deemed to be true. Thus they propose that A and B must share a variable (103; developed in 1975). As Read (1988:119) points out, the first condition for relevance is deemed both necessary and sufficient; the second is a necessary but not sufficient condition for an entailment to hold between A and B.

Anderson and Belnap have their critics, many of whom challenge the ability of their relevant logic to salvage our intuitions about validity. For example, G. I. Iseminger argues that there is no clear sense of "meaning" in the phrase "common meaning content" (1980,199). With respect to the "use" sense of relevance, Read also points out a problem. He refers to a proof of Clarence Irving Lewis wherein contradictory premises do appear to be used to derive an arbitrary proposition. Hence, "[i]t is then incumbent on us somehow to decide on the validity of the derivation before we can tell whether the contradiction has indeed, in the relevant sense, been used to obtain the conclusion" (132).

In distinction to Anderson and Belnap, Read proposes his own Relevant Account of Validity. In the Classical Account, A entails B if and only if A cannot be true and B false. But the conjunction "and" in this account is extensional. And therein, believes Read, lies the problem. To resolve this he employs the sense of conjunction that is intensional and that he labels "Fusion" (designated by X). Hence: "A entails B iff A cannot be true and (fuse) B false" (133).

In Fusion "A × B" demands both A and B in its derivation, thus binding them together in a way that extensional conjunction does not. What is important to Read is that relevance be symmetrical. But this also results in a possible shortcoming for his account: his explanation of relevance is entirely circular, since two propositions are relevant if either entails the other. Read concedes this. But he insists that his definition highlights what is distinctive in the relevant account of entailment:

> [N]amely, the important role played by fusion in its proper analysis. Fusion binds two propositions together in such a

way that one is assured of their mutual relevance in deriving any consequence from the fused conjunction. . . . Whatever "A × B" entails needs both A and B in its derivation. Hence, the new definition has these three features:

(1) it characterizes a logical relation between two propositions with the correct formal properties;

(2) it provides an appropriate sense of derivational utility; and

(3) it respects the intuition that a contradiction is not relevant to every proposition. (134)

This goes a long way toward salvaging a sense of relevance for the formal account. But with respect to our larger project of dealing with practical arguments in ordinary circumstances, it falls short. Because of its circularity Read's fusion account must lack value for our pragmatic interests. This is the case with Anderson and Belnap's relevance logic, and there is nothing in Read's account to distinguish it in *this* respect.

In turning to accounts of informal logic, we might first consider some of the theoretical work done on relevance by Walton (1982). Following B. J. Copeland (1980), Walton points to inferences that Anderson and Belnap reject as irrelevant that do appear to share a variable and that could possibly be subscripted to meet the requirement of derivational utility that Anderson and Belnap set. While noting a value to their relevance logic, Walton offers his own relatedness logic as having greater utility.

Under stipulations of this system, "A>B" is true only if A and B are related to one another. On this account astounding inferences like "B/A>B" fail in any case where A and B are unrelated. But what exactly is meant here by "relatedness"? One proposal of Walton's is to see relatedness construed as spatio-temporal proximity in an act-sequence (Walton, 1979, 1982:35–37). This explains the relevance of antecedent to consequent in "If Socrates drinks the hemlock then Socrates takes his life"; and the irrelevance of "It is snowing. Therefore if the sandwiches taste fishy, it is snowing." However, on this proposal the same inference that was rendered valid by the classical model could be rendered invalid on the relatedness model. Walton's solution to this apparent paradox is that the inference is valid if relatedness is not an issue. But if relatedness is an issue in a particular context, then the inference is invalid in that context.

Walton expands his account with another proposal for relatedness drawn from David Lewis. Here "A is related to B" means that "A and B share some common subject matter." Taking T as a set of topics, A is related to B if and only if the subject matter of A shares at least one topic with the subject matter of B. What becomes immediately clear is that relatedness so construed is not a transitive relation and, hence, classically valid forms will in some instances be invalid. Again, an astounding inference like "It is snowing. Therefore if the sandwiches taste fishy, it is snowing" fails to be valid because of the absence of any subject matter overlap between A and B.

While not without some concerns, and recognizing the need for a more developed account, Walton concludes that relatedness logic and especially subject matter overlap of propositions works well as a kind of relevance in pragmatic contexts. While he still sees the need for other types of relevance, he believes that the fundamental concept of relevance among all types is that of propositional relevance, which is best modeled by relatedness logic. This is because, in his analysis, all forms of relevance reduce in some way to the propositional structure of the product culled from a disputation.

> The core of any argument is a set of propositions. In any disputational game, the basis of the game is a set of moves and countermoves. These moves are essentially made up of propositions. Therefore propositions are the core around which the disputational structure of argument is built. (1982:32)

But "propositional relevance" could mislead us here, since he is not just talking about propositions related to each other independent of a context. He handles the paradoxical consequences of his account (paradoxical in relation to classical models) with the suggestion that some inferences are sometimes valid, sometimes not, depending upon relevance being an issue. But in the situations that concern me (and Walton, I believe), relevance is always at issue. In effect, when Walton reduces the types of relevance to propositional relevance, what he means is that they reduce to considerations of spatio-temporal proximity in act-sequences and/or subject matter overlap; both contextual considerations.

Both "spatio-temporal proximity in act-sequences" and "subject matter overlap" may contribute to an acceptable sense of relevance in arguments, but they will not be sufficient. Consider the propositions introduced earlier: "Wayne Gretzky is clean-shaven" and "Wayne Gretzky is one of the premier hockey players in the world." We are asking whether the first is a relevant reason for accepting the second, and intuition tells us it is not. Clearly, there is a relationship between the two propositions. Insofar as I understand the points that Lewis and Walton are making, I would have to say that there is subject matter overlap here. In the form of the person of Gretzky, the subject matter of the first proposition shares at least one topic with the subject matter of the second proposition. Again, this does not seem to be a case where spatio-temporal proximity in act-sequences is helpful. Although there is, presumably, on occasions when Gretzky performs the activity of playing hockey, a spatio-temporal proximity to his being clean-shaven, we would not want to say the first is relevant to the second. It is not *clearly* a non sequitur like "I had cereal for breakfast. Therefore the sun is shining in Malta." Yet the cases amount to the same thing. This indicates that both the notion of "subject matter overlap" and that of "spatio-temporal proximity" are too extreme in that they would allow as relevant cases like the Gretzky case that apparently is not relevant.[11]

What we need to support our intuitions about the Gretzky case is a more active sense of propositional relevance. To be relevant it is not enough for two propositions to be passively related; one must act upon the other such that it affects our beliefs about that other. Such an account is offered in many informal logic textbooks, which, in eschewing or supplementing details of formal consequence, avoid the problems associated with entailment. Still, when textbooks discuss relevance, they restrict their discussions to versions of what Walton termed *propositional* relevance.[12] A premise is relevant to a conclusion if it increases (or decreases) our reasons for holding the conclusion. Trudy Govier offers a typical version of this: "Statement A is positively relevant to statement B if and only if the truth of A counts in favor of the truth of B" (1992:146). Another sample account is offered by James B. Freeman:

> If either the truth of the premise increases the likelihood that the conclusion will be true or the falsity of the premise increases the likelihood that the conclusion is false, then the premise is relevant to the conclusion. If neither of these conditions holds, then the premise is not relevant.[13] (1993:199)

Both of these accounts offer a marked advance over entailment in that they are more suitable for dealing with arguments in natural language. But even strong accounts of propositional relevance are not sufficient to deal with the full range of situations in which questions of relevance arise. Consider, as one example here, the way in which Govier and Freeman treat the fallacy known as the "Straw Man."

Both logicians deal with it without making any modification to the accounts of propositional relevance they have provided (Govier, 1992:157; Freeman, 1993:210). That is, they present it as a fallacy of irrelevance even though it does not fit the notion of irrelevance in their accounts. Govier identifies the Straw Man as a fallacy involving irrelevance and writes: "The straw man fallacy is committed when a person misrepresents an argument, theory, or claim. . . . " (1992:157). But previously she had defined "irrelevance" as: "Statement A is irrelevant to statement B if and only if the truth of statement A counts neither for nor against the truth of B" (146). How exactly is the Straw Man a case of irrelevant argument *in these terms?*

Similarly, Freeman's identification of the Straw Man as a special fallacy of irrelevance where "An opponent attacks an adversary's position by attributing to the adversary a [misrepresentation] statement S. . . . " (1993:210) does not appear to fit his definition of irrelevance.

The problem arises here because the Straw Man is not a violation of propositional relevance at all but of *contextual relevance*. The arguer has constructed an argument that fails to be relevant to the context or background as it is constituted by her or his opponent's actual argument. As many instances of the Straw Man indicate, an argument that commits this error may exhibit perfect propositional relevance *internally*. The informal logic account of relevance needs to be expanded to include features of the context, especially, as we will see, those involving the nature of the audience.

Our discussion has shown that both formal and informal logic (two models of the product-oriented perspective) fail to provide completely satisfactory accounts of relevance, although the latter offers advances over the former. In contrast, the rhetorical approach to argumentation will offer a much more comprehensive account of contextual relevance, which should underlie and supplement the ideas contained in the logical (and dialectical) perspective.[14]

1.5 Rhetoric and Logic

In closing this chapter, I wish to return to the role of formal logic and consider it explicitly from the perspective of a rhetorical account. Jaakko Hintikka (1989:3) suggests that the function of logic in argumentation and reasoning is the main currently unsolved problem in the theory of argumentation, and he notes that some scholars have turned to rhetoric rather than logic for the tools of argumentation.

Hintikka's own solution is to trace the roots of formal logic to the dialectic of Aristotle and to develop an interrogative model embracing
both argumentation and logic. While his conclusions are different,
his basic approach is quite similar to that of at least one scholar of
rhetoric, Perelman. I noted in the introduction the relation between
rhetorical argument and its dialectical counterpart, to which the
later formal logic was added. A more contemporary model developing a similar understanding can be found in Perelman's work.

Frans H. van Eemeren and Rob Grootendorst attribute to Perelman and Olbrechts-Tyteca the position that logic is a completed
whole, no longer open to new developments. As it was for Toulmin,
logic is linked with the geometrical approach to reason and so "they
automatically believe it to be inadequate and irrelevant, if not both"
(1988:277). But this overstates the case. *The New Rhetoric* (1969),
and many of Perelman's subsequent writings, exhibit a concerted effort to accommodate logic alongside, and even within, a rhetorical
model of argumentation.

Perelman and Olbrechts-Tyteca begin their account by distinguishing argumentation from demonstration. But the attitude toward demonstration is not straightforward and they will ultimately
work with formal modes of reasoning in addressing what they call
"quasi-logical arguments" (1969:13–14).

The New Rhetoric gives the now-familiar contrast between argumentation and the classical concept of demonstration, and especially formal logic that examines demonstrative methods of proof.
The modern logician, building an axiomatic system, is not concerned
with the origin of the axioms or with the rules of deduction, or with
the role the system plays in the elaboration of thought, or with the
meaning of expressions. But when it comes to arguing—using discourse to influence an audience's adherence to a thesis—such things
cannot be neglected (ibid.).

Effectively, such a contrast sets formal demonstration and argumentation into different spheres of influence. The point is emphasized elsewhere: "A purely formal identity is self-evident or posited
by convention, but in any case it escapes controversy and hence argumentation" (Perelman, 1982:60). What cannot be argued is not
pertinent to argumentation. Argumentation intervenes only where
self-evidence is contested, where debate arises about the products of
demonstration (6). In this way Perelman escapes the consequences
of Michel Meyer's observation that: "If everything is arguable, then
nothing underlies argumentation" (1986:151). For Perelman, everything is not arguable. This is made clear, in the discussion of argu-

ments from authority (*argumentum ad vericundiam*). This type of argument belongs within the realm of argumentation because it is of interest only in the absence of demonstrable proof, since "no authority can prevail against a demonstrable truth" (1982:94–95).

Unlike Descartes, who wanted to build all knowledge on a foundation of indubitable self-evidence, Perelman holds such an enterprise to be an exception in the project of knowledge-acquisition, one appropriate only for scientists. In other fields, philosophy or ethics or law, a quite different practice prevails. Here reasoning cannot be limited to deduction and induction (note, he does not exclude them: they are not adequate; but nor are they irrelevant), rather "a whole arsenal of arguments" should be used, along with a broader conception of reason that includes argumentative techniques and rhetoric as a theory of persuasive discourse (160–61).

The remarks here are ambiguous. On the one hand, demonstration in the form of self-evident truths is outside of the domain of argumentation. On the other hand, deduction is *one of* the argumentative techniques to be employed. This relationship is clarified somewhat in Perelman's treatment of quasi-logical arguments (1969:193–260; 1982:53–80), which gain their force from similarities to formal reasoning. The claim is that, at root, quasi-logical argumentation is nonformal and considerable effort has been required to formalize it.[15] The analyses provided work backward from the formal scheme to the underlying argument. Quasi-logical arguments include those that depend on logical relations (contradiction, identity, and transitivity), and those that depend on mathematical relations (connections between part and whole, smaller and larger, and frequency) (Perelman and Olbrechts-Tyteca, 1969:194). For example, and significantly, argumentation makes "considerable use of the relation of logical consequence" (230). Here the *enthymeme* is seen as a quasi-logical argument cast in syllogistic form, and Perelman further notes a wide usage of syllogistic chains in quasi-logical argumentation.

Such discussions indicate a need for studying logical form and formal techniques so as to see the quasi-logical argumentation related to them and to understand how and when they can be employed. It also allows for their adaptability to a wide range of cases. Formal logic is not being discarded as irrelevant here, but its role and relevance are being rethought in a different context. A rhetorical model of argumentation should not narrow the range of methods appropriate to it, but will accommodate a wide range of methods, rethought in relation to the underlying rhetorical perspective (Willard, 1989).

The relationship between classical logic and rhetoric is finally seen in the somewhat idiosyncratic way that Perelman distinguishes between the "rational" and the "reasonable."

The distinction between formal and nonformal reasoning can be viewed as a distinction between what is rational and what is reasonable.

> The *rational* corresponds to mathematical reason . . . which grasps necessary relations, which know *a priori* certain self-evident and immutable truths . . . it owes nothing to experience or to dialogue, and depends neither on education nor on the culture of a milieu or an epoch. (1979:117)

The *reasonable,* by contrast, is that which is consistent with common sense or conventional wisdom; it owes everything to experience and dialogue. The "reasonable person" is guided by the search for what is acceptable in her or his milieu. The vision of the "rational person" separates the reason from other human faculties, and inaugurates a being who functions as a machine, insensible to her or his humanity and to the reactions of others. The "reasonable person" locates reason as an essential component, but only one component, within the human project of discovery and understanding. In a recent work, Toulmin rails against the "decontextualized ideal" (1990:200) of rationality that was the focus of thinkers from the seventeenth century through the twentieth century, and he encourages a return to a pre-Cartesian idea of rationality. This is very much what Perelman promotes in his concept of the "reasonable."

Importantly for the model of argumentation Perelman develops, the rational and the reasonable must coexist in a mutually supportive relationship. Should one dominate the other, we risk losing advances in thought based on scientific principles, or the guidance of reason to choose between systems (Laughlin and Hughes, 1986:188).

So there are a number of senses in which Perelman's texts include logic in his argumentative project. While it is not adequate for a theory of argumentation, it does contribute to one.

Perelman's model of argumentation will be considered further in later chapters, where it will often serve as an example for the perspective under discussion. It is rooted in the rhetorical, recognizing a foundation that the logical perspective alone has not shown. Given that our arguments cannot be "proved" completely, they must be submitted for the judgment of those to whom they are directed. This is the audience, the focal point around which other features of context cohere. This means that, essentially, the audience determines the argument, and that an underlying, central sense of contextual-relevance must relate to the audience. This is the case for the arguer, who constructs the argument in accordance with the audience's knowledge, background, and so forth. And it is the case for the evaluator, who critiques the argument in terms of its success in gaining the adherence of the audience for the thesis put forward.

Chapter 2

Argumentation as Dialectical

The revitalization of a dialectical approach to argumentation has emerged through a number of sources. C. L. Hamblin (1970), in his seminal work on fallacies advocates a formal dialectic that develops rules to govern philosophical disputation. In a similar vein, Nicholas Rescher (1977) has drawn on the scholastic tradition to develop a model of argument as a dialectical exchange between disputants.

There are a number of senses of "dialectical." But as the references to Hamblin and Rescher indicate, we can observe as common features the exchange of views within a dialogue, governed by rules aimed at resolving a dispute. Hence, Aristotle's interest in dialectical reasoning as a dialogue game is carried into contemporary accounts. More detailed formal dialogue models have also been developed, as in E. M. Barth and E. C. W. Krabbe (1982) and in Douglas N. Walton and Erik C. W. Krabbe (1995).

Informal logicians are not immune to the draw of dialectical argumentation. Beyond the thorough involvement of Walton discussed in the following section, we should also note the interests of James B. Freeman (1991) and J. Anthony Blair and Ralph H. Johnson (1987). For the latter, to take a case in point, "To say that argumentation is dialectical . . . is to identify it as a human practice, an exchange between two or more individuals in which the process of interaction shapes the product" (46). As will be seen, it is not difficult to adapt such a model to work with monological argumentative texts. While the reciprocity of dialogue may not be evident in such a fixed text, its involvement in the production of the text can be imagined. There should be a dialogue active in the arguer's mind as he or she anticipates moves or countermoves important for the correct development of the argument. As Maurice A. Finocchiaro observes, reflecting on his own work, "an argument is a defense of its conclusions from actual or potential objections" (1980:419). Hence, an aspect of dialogue is brought into the heart of argumentation (1995:181n.2). Accordingly, the arguer assumes certain obligations to abide by appropriate procedures for constructing the argument, for example, to allow for necessary counterargumentation.

An interesting and widely endorsed variety of the dialectical approach is offered by what is known as the Amsterdam school of pragma-dialectics, from the pens of Frans H. van Eemeren and Rob Grootendorst and from those working with them (1984, 1992a, 1994). The pragma-dialecticians share the dialectical penchant for a set of procedural rules to regulate disputes, after the manner of a Popperian critical rationalism: "This critical rationalist ideal requires the promotion of *dialectics* in the Socratic (actually pre-Socratic) sense of the word . . . the dialectic idea of having a regulated *critical discussion* is made the basic principle of reasonableness" (van Eemeren and Grootendorst, 1988:280). In North America, Walton's work (1989, 1992a, 1995a), which also owes much to Hamblin and Rescher, has led him into the pragma-dialectical fold.

Because of its growing popularity and innovative features, I will direct my attention toward the pragma-dialectical account of argumentation and treat it as a model for the dialectical perspective. It is also appropriate to focus on the pragma-dialectical position because of the claim cited earlier that "In the dialectical approach, the product-oriented [logic] and the process-oriented [rhetoric] approaches to argumentation are combined" (van Eemeren and Grootendorst, 1988:281).

Through generally reviewing the pragma-dialectical approach and examining how the rules relate to its treatment of fallacies, I intend to show that, while there is recognition of rhetorical aspects in the approach, it is not sufficiently focused, and that weaknesses in the approach can be traced to this shortcoming.

2.1 Outline of the Pragma-Dialectical Approach

The pragma-dialectical approach to argumentation is grounded in the speech act theories of J. L. Austin and John Searle and of Gricean ideas about conversational implicatures. Argumentation is viewed as a phenomenon of language usage with the focus of study being argumentative speech events. "Argumentation is a form of language usage that is part of an explicit or implicit discussion designed to resolve a difference of opinion between two or more language users" (van Eemeren, 1988:46). This requires the use of dialectics and the associated idea of having a regulated *critical discussion*. This notion of a critical discussion and the rules of conduct for the same are fundamental to the pragma-dialecticians' project. In fact, fallacies will be understood within the context of the theory (and only within such a theory) as violations of such rules, as maneuvers that disrupt and impede the resolution of disputes.

The first developed account of the approach is given in *Speech Acts in Argumentative Discussions* (van Eemeren and Grootendorst, 1984), and refinements are made to the theory throughout the middle and late eighties, culminating in *Argumentation, Communication, and Fallacies: A Pragma-dialectical Perspective* (1992a).[1]

Speech Acts in Argumentative Discussions analyzes argumentation as an illocutionary act complex that is performed by advancing a sequence of assertives and that is linked to an expressed opinion. In fact, much of the first part of the book involves investigating the relation between the illocutionary act of arguing and the perlocutionary effect of convincing (1984:47ff.). In the European fashion, the premises of an argument are referred to as the "argumentation," and the conclusion is identified as a standpoint or expressed opinion.

Argumentations are oriented toward the resolution of disputes and disputes only exist "if a language user has propounded a view and *doubt is subsequently expressed* about the acceptability of that view" (79). The defender of the standpoint is the *protagonist,* while the party casting doubt on it is the *antagonist* (both may advance argumentation during the course of the discussion). The critical discussion surrounding the dispute is presented by means of a normative model requiring four stages: the confrontation stage, the opening stage, the argumentation stage, and the concluding stage. Finally, in terms of this brief overview, the discussion is governed by a code of conduct with fixed rules. The rules are intended to enable language users to conduct themselves as rational discussants; they facilitate the resolution of disputes and the avoidance of fallacious moves.[2]

Speech Acts in Argumentative Discussions (1984) detailed seventeen rules for conducting discussions, some of them quite unwieldy. These have been refined over time, and the 1992 book contains a "simplified version" of ten discussion rules. These range from a rule (1) prohibiting parties from preventing each other advancing standpoints; to a requirement (3) that an attack on a standpoint must relate to something that has actually been advanced by the other party; to an invocation (10) against the use of vague and ambiguous language. The rules are distributed over the four stages of the discussion and cover burden of proof, the relevance of an arguer's contributions, the appropriate use of argumentation schemes,[3] the use of valid argument forms, and so forth.[4]

Joseph W. Wenzel (1985:150), in his evaluation of the early version of the pragma-dialectical theory, emphasized the fact that the variety of argumentative situations indicates that there are purposes requiring argumentation beyond the resolution of disputes. Walton addresses this in his identification of different types of dialogue in which argumentation is employed. While Walton (1992a:34; 1995a:16) identifies himself with the pragma-dialectical school,[5] he is convinced that in sticking to one model of dialogue only, that of the critical discussion, van Eemeren and Grootendorst's theory exhibits a narrowness that he cannot condone.

Walton (1989:3–6) has identified as many as ten types of argumentative dialogue, although he has also been satisfied with as few as five. This shorter list includes the personal quarrel, forensic debate, persuasion dialogue (or critical discussion), inquiry, and negotiation dialogue.[6] In identifying a greater range of dialogues in which argumentation occurs, Walton widens the scope for the occurrence and treatment of fallacies to several of the other dialogue types. "In the study of informal fallacies," he writes, "the persuasion dialogue (critical discussion) clearly has a central, or even primary, place among the many contexts of dialogue. However, because of dialectical shifting, many other contexts of dialogue are important to study as well" (1991a:39). This remark leaves open the possibility that fallacies can arise in dialogues outside of the critical discussion. In "Types of Dialogue, Dialectical Shifts and Fallacies" (1992b), he pursues this idea. Here the peripheral models of dialogue are needed to identify and treat fallacies, and he illustrates this by showing how the *ad hominem* and *ad baculum* can be used in dialogue shifts to quarrels or negotiation dialogues. This divergence from van Eemeren and Grootendorst culminates when fallacies are related to different dialogue types (1995a:9) and when the importance of dialogue shifting is confirmed (258).

Still, in central agreement with van Eemeren and Grootendorst, Walton promotes the persuasion dialogue (critical discussion) as "the single most significant type of dialogue" since it represents a normative model for good dialogue (1989:9). Thus, he adopts rules and the stages of discussion that correspond with those of the established pragma-dialectical account.

2.2 Misunderstandings and Qualifications

Several criticisms have been advanced against the pragma-dialectical perspective. But many of these are founded on misunderstandings or on a failure to note qualifications made about the theory.

The first point to note is that the model for critical discussions put forward by van Eemeren and Grootendorst is normative rather than descriptive; in its essential features it is an *ideal* model. The extent to which a particular dialogue approximates the model is something decided at the time of reconstruction. They are not *describing how* disputes actually take place, but how they *should* be performed if the optimal chance for their resolution is to be achieved, or, rather, since they recognize the fact that many disputes are too deep to be completely resolved, if disagreement between the parties is to be minimized (van Eemeren and Grootendorst, 1988:286). Van Eemeren notes: "A normative reconstruction in the dialectical sense does not mean that every form of usage is automatically regarded in toto as a critical discussion, but that we look to see what happens if the analysis is carried out as if it were a critical discussion" (1988:47).

A related misunderstanding is the belief that the pragma-dialectical perspective is concerned only with verbal dialogue. Among many North American and British argumentation theorists the practice has been to study written texts, and the pragma-dialectical interest seems removed from this. Such a concern is expressed by Alan Hajek who, in a review of a book by Walton, makes the following comment about the pragma-dialectical approach: "It seems excessively restrictive to locate all slippery slope arguments in the context of a dialogue. Surely one can use such an argument in private thought. And even when the argument is presented publicly, need there be a respondent?" (1992:23).

In fact, the pragma-dialecticians believe that their approach easily accommodates such Anglo-American practice. While suggesting that the dialogue approach best reflects the behavior of language users, they also submit that monological arguments can be treated as involving implicit dialogues (van Eemeren and Grootendorst, 1984:12–14). Elsewhere Grootendorst describes the ordinary language situations for which the pragma-dialectical theory is appropriate as including "a discursive text in a newspaper, a conversation in a cafe or a debate in some kind of meeting of a more formal nature" (1987:336). In addition, van Eemeren, when talking of reconstructing speech events, notes that this applies not only to ordinary

conversation but also to "more formal discussions, editorial comments, policy documents, scholarly polemics, and so on" (1988:47). Finally, they insist that a discursive text can always be considered part
of a discussion "real or imagined by the arguer, in which the arguer
reacts to criticism that has been or might be levelled against his
point of view" (1992a:13;fn). Argumentative discourse, even when
presented in a monologue, is deemed essentially dialogic. This is
demonstrated later in the 1992 book through an analysis of a letter
to a Dutch newspaper. The standpoint of the author (protagonist) is
identified, along with the opposing standpoint of the "missing" discussant. The text of the discussion is then organized into the four
identifiable stages of the dispute, from the confrontation to the concluding stage (93–94).

   A final qualification to note is that van Eemeren and Grootendorst's pragma-dialectical approach, like the dialectical approach in
general, restricts itself to the resolving of disputes. This is a limitation, and frequently acknowledged as such: the norms provided by
the rules for critical discussions apply only where the discourse is
actually aimed at resolving a dispute (105). Grootendorst, in allowing that the dialectical approach is neither perfect nor final, anticipates problems because of this requirement. Although it is often
obvious or reasonable to assume that a discussion is aimed at resolving a dispute, it is also recognized that "sometimes that is not at
all the purpose of a discussion, and sometimes this may not be clear"
(1987:340). In a later footnote he submits that "[t]his reason might
be seen as an indication that besides a dialectical approach there is
also a need for a theory to cover situations other than those in which
the chief issue is the resolution of a dispute" (341n.20). Such a development of the program is apparent in the more recent work of
Douglas Walton.

2.3 Pragma-dialectics and Fallacies

   A further point that the pragma-dialecticians are anxious to emphasize is that their theory gives rise to an account of fallacies that
remedies a number of problems associated with the so-called Standard Treatment of fallacies identified by Hamblin (1970). The notion
of "fallacy" and its role in a rhetorical model of argumentation will
be given a detailed examination in chapter 6. But an account of fallacy is so integral to any elaboration of the pragma-dialectical perspective that an extended discussion here is unavoidable.

In an oft-reported line, Hamblin defines a fallacious argument as "one that *seems to be valid but is not so*" (1970:12). He then provides a coherent tradition of fallacies conforming to this definition and stretching from the modern textbooks back to Aristotle.[7]

Taken at face value, the Standard Treatment has been criticized by recent commentators as inadequate and simplistic (see Goodwin, 1992). Of particular weight here have been the charges of the pragma-dialecticians. They interpret Hamblin as asserting that central to the Standard Treatment is the dual notion that a fallacy is an *argument* that is in someway not *valid* while appearing to be so. And yet, throughout the tradition, from Aristotle to Locke to Copi, the Standard Treatment contains fallacies that are not arguments at all and others which, while being arguments, are not invalid (Grootendorst, 1987:331).

Hamblin found the Standard Treatment superficial and criticized it for lacking rigorous analyses of the informal fallacies, but he felt the traditional divisions worth preserving (Walton,1991b:335). The same attitude is carried over into Walton's work; he has tried to redefine the traditional categories of the informal fallacies within a pragma-dialectical account, to provide a coherent theory for a tradition that was no more than "*ad hoc* commentary based on time-worn examples" (360).

As noted earlier, the parent pragma-dialectical theory of argument effectively *restricts* fallacies to the violation of rules for conducting a critical discussion. "Fallacies are speech acts intended by the speaker to make a contribution to the resolution of the dispute but often in fact obstructing the way to a resolution" (van Eemeren and Grootendorst, 1984:151). Hence, van Eemeren and Grootendorst regard as a *fallacy* "every violation which may result in the resolving of the dispute being made more difficult or even impossible" (182).

While I have characterized this approach as restrictive, van Eemeren and Grootendorst see among its merits that it is a wider notion of fallacy than is usual, especially in the Standard Treatment. It is wider because it does not link fallacies solely to the argumentative stage of the discussion. Fallacies of ambiguity and the "Straw Man," for example (neither of which need be arguments—something the pragma-dialectical account makes possible) can both be identified at the first stage of the confrontation and speak to misunderstandings that can affect the dispute. This particular merit is further evidenced in a case like the *ad hominem:* it "is a good illustration of a fallacy whose analysis presents considerable difficulties if fallacies are linked exclusively to the invalidity of the arguments expressed by the protagonist in his argumentation at the argumentation stage of discussion".

Among other merits claimed for the pragma-dialectical account of fallacies is that the approach is better able than others to account for the large and eclectic group of so-called informal fallacies that creates problems in the Standard Treatment (Grootendorst, 1985:161). Such problems, as we have seen, are traced to traditional attempts to have fallacies cohere around notions of argument and invalidity. But fallacies like "Many Questions" or "Ambiguity" need not be arguments, and the *Petitio principii* need not be invalid. A systematic account that treats these as violations of rules for rational discussion avoids such difficulties.

The account in *Argumentation, Communication, and Fallacies* matches twenty-six traditional fallacies, informal *and* formal, to one or more of the ten *rules* of conduct, to one or more of the four *stages* of the discussion, and to either or both of the two *parties* involved in the discussion. "Denying the Antecedent" (van Eemeren and Grootendorst, 1992a:212–15) for example, is a violation by the protagonist of the rule that a party may only use arguments that are logically valid at the argumentation stage (17 of the 26 fallacies occur at this stage, 15 of them exclusively so). The *argumentum ad misericordiam* is a violation by the protagonist of Rule 1 that parties must not prevent each from advancing standpoints at the confrontation stage.

2.4 Walton's Functional Account

Walton returns to the source of the Standard Treatment and unearths a pragmatic concept of fallacy that differs significantly from that of van Eemeren and Grootendorst.

His account begins by dividing fallacies into two paradigm cases: the sophistical tactic type of fallacy and the error of reasoning or incorrect inference type. At one point he distinguishes them thus:

> The sophistical tactic type of fallacy will be defined as a deceptive tactic used by a participant in argumentative dialogue to block or frustrate the legitimate goals of the dialogue by breaking or subverting rules. The error of reasoning type of fallacy, by contrast, involves no essential reference to a context of dialogue. (1991a:215)

The difference between the two types is that an "error of reasoning" is a matter of whether propositions follow from others and thus it does not require any essential reference to context. Throughout the history of logic, "fallacy" has always had these two meanings, but in modern times the notion of fallacy as an error of reasoning, what Walton calls a monolectical fault, has been dominant. Hence the emphasis on this in the Standard Treatment. The sense of fallacy as sophism and involving deceit, a dialectical fault, has been "expunged" from the history (219).

Walton (1991a) identifies traditional fallacies with these two types, categorizing the "*ad*" arguments among the sophistical tactics and labeling things like affirming the consequent and the post hoc and causal fallacies as errors of reasoning. But elsewhere his account identifies a new category of fallacies *between* the two paradigm types and assigns the post hoc to this middle class since it is initially a failure of inference, "but one that can only be understood as a fallacy when its dialectical context is taken into account" (1992a:239). What distinguishes the "middle ground" is what has essentially characterized the sophism: the appeal to context. Eventually, for Walton (1995a:273), all fallacies belong here and this comes to dominate his "new" pragmatic theory of fallacy.

Countering the emphasis of the tradition, Walton exposes the neglected sophistical tactic that underlies it in Aristotle's work. And it is a distinguishing feature of Walton's pragma-dialectical account that it relies so heavily on a reading of Aristotle. Walton traces the Standard Treatment's interest in "seeming validity" to the "appearance of successful refutation" in Aristotle, where successful refutation is contrasted with sophistical refutation. While successful refutation uses a method of argument in an appropriate way, sophistical refutation uses it inappropriately (Walton, 1992a:265). In Aristotle's account "the arguer uses . . . sophistical techniques of contentious argumentation in order to convince an audience that these arguments have validity and plausibility as genuine reasons for accepting a conclusion" (267). From this arose the idea that a fallacy is an argument that seems valid but is not.

Walton returns to this ancient root of fallacy as sophism, but without completely surrendering to it. Like Hamblin, he believes that a sophistical tactic type of fallacy need not involve intentional deceit. Fallacies lie in "the text of discourse of an exchange in dialogue, not in the motives or intentions of the arguer" (1991a:220). Fallacies, generally, come to be viewed as unfair argumentation tactics deployed in the context of a dialogue. This constitutes a conceptual shift from a semantic to a pragmatic view of fallacies (224).

It is understandable, then, that Walton should praise van Eemeren and Grootendorst's notion of a fallacy as "a violation of a code of conduct for rational discussants." He calls this conception "light years ahead" (1992a:265) of the idea of seeming validity, and considers it the first big step in making possible serious research on the fallacies (1991a:217). It means that a critic can cite an argument as fallacious if it violates a normative rule of dialogue that applies to a context of argumentative discussion understood by the participants. Being context-dependent, it accounts for the effectiveness of fallacious arguments since they are, in fact, forms of argument that in other contexts would be appropriate and not considered fallacious. On this reading, the fallacy lies not in the argument type itself but in its use.

Yet in an important way Walton finds the van Eemeren and Grootendorst conception of fallacy wanting and his own notion goes beyond it. On Walton's reading a fallacy is more than just a violation of a rule of reasonable dialogue. Or, rather, not all violations of rules may be fallacies. Blunders or other sorts of errors may occur that are not so serious as to constitute a fallacy, and van Eemeren and Grootendorst have failed to distinguish "fallacy" from "blunder" (Walton, 1995a:9). We may criticize someone's argument because it is incomplete or based on assumptions that have not been well supported. These criticisms are distinct from charges of "fallacy" and so, concludes Walton, it may be appropriate to speak of arguments that are simply weak or inadequately supported. "These arguments may violate rules of reasonable dialogue, or at least not live up to these rules adequately, without being badly enough off to merit the term "fallacies'" (1991a:217–18). Rule violation alone does not go far enough; it does not pinpoint or identify the fallacy.

Walton's principal concern with the van Eemeren and Grootendorst notion of fallacy is that it does not sufficiently capture the Aristotelian sense of sophistical refutation. Simply put:

> Aristotle's conception of fallacy is even more deeply pragmatic than one that equates a fallacy simply with a violation of a rule of dialogue. Aristotle sees the seeming validity and plausibility of arguments that are used fallaciously as deriving from a covert and illicit dialectical shift by one participant in a dialogue toward a use of quarrelsome or contentious reasoning that is unfair and uncalled for. (1992a:267)

This appeal to Aristotle suggests that in one of its essential features, Walton's pragmatic theory is not as "new" as he claims. But it fully illustrates the substantial break between the two version of pragma-dialectics. Since the Dutch model is moored to the critical discussion dialogue, dialogue shifting does not play a role. But this is the very feature, recovered from Aristotle, which highlights Walton's version. It is the shift from one dialogue to another within an exchange that accounts for why a fallacy may seem valid when it is not (1995a:258). Because, for example, the tactics appropriate in a negotiation dialogue or in a quarrel might be fallacious in a critical discussion (272). But since the participants are aware of the legitimacy of the tactic in another context, they may be deceived by the shift. (Dialogue-shifting is not necessary for fallacies to occur; other types of hindrance include moving ahead too fast in the dialogue or, as we will see in the next section, browbeating one's opponent.)

This does not mean that deceitful moves are necessary for fallacies to take place, and elsewhere this point, which is quite significant, is made explicit: "A fallacy doesn't have to be used in a particular case as a deliberate attempt to deceive an opponent in dialogue, but it does have to be a serious misuse of an argumentation technique that is a bad enough error . . . that it is subject to serious censure" (1992a:267). While we can challenge many arguments in a critical way, requiring them to be modified or supported further, in the case of fallacies, once they are revealed, the argument ought to always be completely abandoned (1991a:225). Fallaciousness always involves strong refutation. These points are drawn together in Walton's most substantial definition—that of his "new" pragmatic theory:

> A fallacy is (1) an argument (or at least something that purports to be an argument); (2) that falls short of some standard of correctness; (3) as used in a context of dialogue; (4) but that, for various reasons, has a semblance of correctness about it in context; (5) poses a serious obstacle to the realization of the goal of a dialogue. (1995a:255)

No explicit mention is made here of rule violation, although the whole package defines an implicit violation of the Gricean "rule" of cooperation (Grice, 1989:26). Still, it is a strange realization that while pragma-dialectics is a rule-based model, Walton's version should have traveled so far from the focus on rules.

2.5 A Critical Evaluation

I have already noted some concerns that have been raised about the pragma-dialectical approach. I want to look more closely at some of the problems related to the treatment of fallacies and the procedural rules for regulating discussions.

John Woods (1988a; 1994) raises several complaints against the pragma-dialecticians' account, but these are balanced by a grudging respect for what the account achieves. On the positive side, a unitary notion of the concept of "fallacies" is contained in the idea of rule violations. To the extent that violations of the rules are recognized and categorized, then the extension of "is a fallacy" is captured (1994:82).

Against this are two related concerns that have to do with the relationship between the pragma-dialecticians' "new" concept of fallacy and the traditional fallacies. Under the new formula, a fallacy is a violation of one of the rules. Can we turn this around and say that a violation of each of the rules is a specific fallacy? From one perspective, it seems that we can. To violate Rule 1, for example, means the prevention of either party from advancing standpoints or casting doubts on standpoints. Since this can be achieved by advancing an *ad baculum,* or an *ad hominem,* or even an *ad misericordiam,* then, Woods points out, these fallacies are all "the same fallacy— infelicities all against Rule 1; whereas their Standard Treatment descriptions recognize that they are different fallacies" (1988a:11). The same is true for other groupings of fallacies. In *Argumentation, Communication, and Fallacies,* van Eemeren and Grootendorst cross-list the fallacies under the ten rules, but they do not resolve the ambiguity that Woods has identified: that a traditional fallacy is a fallacy both by virtue of violating one of the new pragma-dialectical rules and by virtue of its own traditional conditions. This is a serious criticism. As we will see, this dual set of criteria for judging fallaciousness haunts the analysis of cases presented by van Eemeren and Grootendorst. But Walton has come to share Woods's misgivings on this point (1995a:295) and thus pays more mind to fallacies as uses of argument (15) and even *as* arguments themselves, where no corresponding "correct" form exists (199).

The lesser but related concern raised by Woods is that van Eemeren and Grootendorst's characterizations of the traditional fallacies are "as half-baked as anything one would find in the Standard Treatment against which Hamblin protested" (1994:82). Be that as it may, the pragma-dialectician might respond that the strength of the model lies in the shift of attention away from the traditional fallacies to the new unitary notion of rule violation. In fact, van Eemeren and Grootendorst have taken their analysis beyond twenty-six traditional fallacies and identified eight further "categories for resolving disputes . . . that should be considered as fallacies" (1992a:216). These include "Declaring a standpoint sacrosanct" and "Falsely presenting something as a common starting point." Thus the "rule violation" concept of fallacy can be said to accommodate more than its predecessors.

On the other hand, such a defense loses some of its force when we realize that in the shift to the new concept the pragma-dialecticians appear to bring the old criteria of the traditional fallacies with them. Or at least, at certain key junctures their account appeals to the traditional ways in which argument schemes break down. I will look at this problem in due course, as it relates to what I take to be the most serious criticism that can be leveled against this dialectical account—a confusion over the existence of objective criteria for judging arguments.

This major complaint requires more attention. We begin with the apparent freedom given to participants in the discussion to decide what they will or will not allow toward the resolution of their dispute. In its most extreme statements, this attitude seems to eschew any kind of objective criteria for judging fallaciousness. Sometimes van Eemeren and Grootendorst speak this way; other times they refer to conditions external to the discussion that may override the parties' agreements. To a certain extent this is Woods's concern back under a different guise: can the arguers remain locked *within* the code of conduct rules for a critical discussion (rules that are supposed to ensure the rationality of the participants), or must they give foremost attention to other criteria transported in from without (e.g., the conditions of traditional fallacies)? One is reminded here of Perelman's remark: "the agreement of another is not sufficient to guarantee objectivity or even universality, because it may be only an opinion common to a milieu or even a given epoch. The test of objectivity and universality must be constantly renewed" (1982:35).

Grootendorst, in discussing appeals to experts, stresses the intersubjective. Whereas in other approaches the expert's expertise is an objective verifiable fact, in the pragma-dialectical account "it is regarded as the intersubjective agreement of the discussants" (1987:339). The discussants will decide who will count, who is acceptable, as an expert. To a certain degree this attitude can be extended to other apparently fallacious moves, because fallaciousness is conditional on the context of the argument.

A number of people have drawn attention to the problem in this. With respect to Walton's work, Hajek writes:

> We can imagine situations in which even *modus ponens* . . . is used fallaciously—its appearance in a "fallacious" slippery slope argument might be such a situation. Conversely, an argument form that is fallacious in the traditional sense, such as affirming the consequent . . . could be used nonfallaciously . . . for example, by a discussant who sincerely believes that it is valid and makes no attempt to trick his opponent thereby. (1992:23)

But if van Eemeren and Grootendorst are sufficiently tied to their "violation-of-the-rules" criteria for fallaciousness, Hajek's scenarios might simply be strange but acceptable results of a radical revision in fallacy theory. John Biro and Harvey Siegel's (1992) observations deserve a less complacent response, however.

Here the issue becomes at what cost the resolution of a dispute should be desired. Participants might abide by the code of conduct and resolve their dispute but do so in quite "unjustified" and irrational ways. Again, if justification and rationality are internal to the code of conduct, the pragma-dialecticians may not be so concerned. But Biro and Siegel provide two cases that show the potential for problems. In the first, disputants may agree at the start of their discussion that handsomeness is the key criterion on which a candidate for election to political office should be judged, but they disagree about which candidate is the handsomest. At the end of their discussion, following the rules, they agree that it is candidate C. In the second case, the discussants agree "*in their argumentative practice* that only arguments with an even number of premises are valid or that whoever argues the loudest has the best argument*" (91). In each case the resolution would seem to be unjustified or irrational and Biro and Siegel believe the problem lies in making good argumentation dependent on proceeding according to rules agreed to by all disputants. As J. Anthony Blair and Ralph H. Johnson have pointed out, saying that a piece of argumentation is counterproductive when the resolution of a dispute is the goal is *not* the same as saying that there is something wrong with the reasoning in the argumentation (1993:189). Beneath the surface concern of dispute-resolution is a quite traditional interest in what Walton has labeled the error of reasoning sense of fallacy.

Woods does not think that the pragma-dialecticians would be completely susceptible to Biro and Siegel's criticisms. He believes that implicit in their account is "*some* kind of standard of objective correctness or adequacy" (1988a:13). And, indeed, as much is implied. But what exactly such a standard would involve is far from clear. Some attention to discussions in *Argumentation, Communication, and Fallacies* will illustrate my point.

In the chapter assessing "Fallacies in Utilizing Argumentation Schemes," van Eemeren and Grootendorst discuss the argumentation scheme "argument from analogy." Here they make remarks likely to fuel the concerns of Hajek and Biro and Siegel. For example:

> Whether this argumentation scheme is allowed to be used in a discussion, *depends on whether the protagonist and the antagonist can agree on the conditions for its use.* [italics mine] If they cannot and the protagonist nevertheless goes ahead using it, or if these conditions have not been fulfilled, he is guilty of one of the variants of the fallacy *wrongful comparison* or *false analogy.* (1992a:161)

Note first that the protagonist is not found guilty of the fallacy of violating a particular rule, but of the fallacy of wrongful comparison or false analogy. Secondly, here the existence of the fallacy depends partly on the agreement of the discussants. But referring to "conditions" for the use of the argumentation scheme suggests an alternative (secondary?) means of evaluation: "The argumentation scheme has been used correctly only if certain correctness conditions have been fulfilled" (1992:162). These correctness conditions involve the asking of certain "critical questions." For example, with the argument from analogy one of the questions to be asked is "whether the comparison is really justified or whether there are crucial differences. If the comparison is defective, the argument from analogy is used incorrectly and constitutes a fallacy of *false analogy*" (ibid.). Here, we seem to find traditional criteria for judging arguments from analogy transported into the pragma-dialectical account. And yet, the decision as to whether or not the conditions are adequately fulfilled still rests with the discussants. What if they do not recognize an argument as fallacious? Or does its fallaciousness really *depend* on their *recognition* of it? Furthermore, whether the conditions are adequately fulfilled actually depends not just on the discussants individually, but on their joint *agreement.*

Consider one of the examples that van Eemeren and Grooten-dorst provide. The case involves a dispute (imagined) between Neil Lyndon and Julie Burchill. It comes from one of Lyndon's contributions to *The Sunday Times* (9 December 1990). Lyndon quotes Burchill from *Time Out:*

> A good part—and definitely the most fun part—of being a feminist is about frightening men. American and Australian feminists have always known this, and absorbed it cheerfully into their act; one thinks of Shere Hite julienning men on phone-in shows, or Dale Spender telling us that a good feminist is rude to a man at least three times a day *on principle.* Of course, there's a lot more to feminism . . . but scaring the shit out of scumbags is an amusing and necessary part because, sadly, a good many men still respect nothing but strength. (cited in van Eemeren and Grootendorst, 1992a:163)

In order to show, not that feminism is Nazism, but that "the language of vulgar intolerance is readily transportable," Lyndon attempts what Trudy Govier might call a "Refutation by Logical Analogy" (1992:269–71) by substituting certain key terms for those in Burchill's discourse.

> A good part—and definitely the most fun part—of being a Nazi is about frightening Jews. German and Austrian Nazis have always known this, and absorbed it cheerfully into their act; one thinks of Ernst Rohm julienning Jews in the ghettos, or Goebbels telling us that a good Nazi is rude to a Jew at least three times a day *on principle.* Of course, there's a lot more to Nazism . . . but scaring the shit out of the scumbags is an amusing and necessary part because, sadly, a good many Jews still respect nothing but strength. (cited in van Eemeren and Grootendorst, 1992a:163)

Now the question is, is this a good move in an argument? Does it depend on Burchill's agreement in the imagined dialogue? Because, if it does, we can probably write it off as a false analogy *for that reason alone;* in the heat of a dispute, Burchill is unlikely to allow it. Nor should Lyndon expect her to. But surely this is not enough. Van Eemeren and Grootendorst recognize as much, I think, as is indicated by the following: "If disputes are to be resolved, false analogies must be avoided, but these examples illustrate that it is not always clear when an analogy *is* false. For distinguishing false analogy from correct analogy, unequivocal criteria are badly needed" (164).[8] These unequivocal criteria must be objective, but what are they, and more importantly, *can they override any agreement made (mistakenly) by the discussants* (or force an agreement where it does not exist)? Once we answer yes to this, as we must, we have firmly placed our hopes in objective criteria for deciding fallacies and not in the intersubjective agreement of discussants. Yet toward the close of their discussion of fallacies and argumentation schemes, van Eemeren and Grootendorst are still reluctant to cede the point.

> The protagonist and antagonist can only try to find a common criterion for weighing the advantages and disadvantages against each other and then decide about whether or not to allow this type of argument in their discussion. If they cannot reach an agreement, the protagonist should not use it. (166)

One has to believe that the upshot of this will be that perfectly good arguments will be dismissed because they do not contribute to resolving disputes.

One possible place to look for assistance is the work of Walton and his interpretation of the traditional fallacies within a dialectical, context-based account. I will look at how that account treats a traditional informal fallacy, and for comparison and contrast recall the way in which van Eemeren and Grootendorst handle it. The *argumentum ad verecundiam* or "appeal to authority" serves as a suitable example.

For van Eemeren and Grootendorst the argument from authority is an argumentation scheme that may be used to provide expert support for the acceptability of some proposition. But in order for the protagonist to use the argumentation scheme it is necessary that the antagonist recognize it as sound. "If the protagonist chooses it even though he knows that this is not so, he is guilty of a violation of Rule 7 known as *argumentum ad verecundiam*" (1992:161). Rule 7 involves the *correct* application of the appropriate argumentation scheme. Grootendorst (1987:339) distinguishes four ways in which the incorrect application can arise and, as noted earlier, emphasizes intersubjective agreement in determining the expert's expertise that is treated as "an objectively verifiable fact" in other accounts.

Walton also talks about the correct application of an argumentation scheme. In his case there are six critical questions all of which must be satisfied for the appeal to authority to be reasonable. An argument from authority may be regarded as weak or unreliable if any

of the questions are not posed or wrongly posed. But such an occurrence does not constitute a fallacy; the fallacy arises with the attempt to *silence* any of the questions. When "the proponent tries to
close off the dialogue prematurely in his own favour by browbeating
the respondent to yield to the authority of revered experts"
(1989:196), then the fallacy occurs. Again, the argument from authority is a fallacy when it is a fallacy "because it is a form of browbeating" (1992a:259). Thus it fits as an instance of the general
functional definition in the sense that we have the *hindering* of
the legitimate goals of argument through the *misuse* of an argumentation scheme that can be appropriately used elsewhere. The
protagonist introduces an authority but misuses the argumentation
scheme by suppressing any critical questioning of that authority.
In Walton's approach the traditional conditions of the argumentation
scheme have been incorporated within this functional account of the
fallacy.

Thus there are objective conditions, a set of criteria identified
with a particular type of argument (or argumentation scheme). But
the application of such conditions is deemed to be entirely context-
dependent. In retrospect, it may be charitable to see van Eemeren
and Grootendorst depending on a similar point. But there are several things to note about the pragma-dialectical view of fallacies as
we see it in Walton.

One point involves an ambiguity that still remains concerning
Walton's notion. Perhaps this is a consequence of the bivalent nature
of his concept. Although he insists that his notion of fallacy is best
seen as a univocal concept that falls somewhere short of the sophism
and beyond the error of reasoning, the fact remains that these two
distinct features do not wed happily or easily. (I will return to this
point in chapter 6.)

The appeal to authority is fallacious not, as in the Standard
Treatment, when a nonexpert is used, or a biased expert or an expert
in the wrong field of expertise, but when the proponent prevents such
things from being ascertained by the opponent by browbeating that
opponent. The fallacy is in the browbeating. Here it seems that
whether or not the appeal to authority is itself good is not an issue,
a proponent may browbeat in either case. Whether he has a strong
expert to support his case or an inappropriate one, he may still
choose to browbeat, to hinder the dispute from being resolved legitimately, and his argument will be judged fallacious because of his
browbeating. But Walton also insists in a number of places that arguments are effective as fallacies because they are legitimate else-

where. This implies that the fault lies in the nature of the argument, that the distinction is between instances of the same argument *type,* not between usages of the same argument.[9] The difference is between errors of reasoning and sophisms. The traditional informal fallacies have not themselves changed, but they are now subject to evaluation in sophistical contexts, and what once made them fallacious now makes them weak or unreliable.

Appearing in this light they bring with them their objective conditions and their evaluation on *this* front cannot be purely a matter of intersubjective agreement between protagonist and antagonist. At least, Walton gives much less weight to such an idea. In discussing fallacies related to various argumentation schemes he repeatedly talks of the need to "examine the sequence of questions and replies put forward by both participants in the discussion" (1992a:254). Here something, namely the correct use of the argumentation scheme, is being decided not by the participants but by a third-party evaluator. For Walton, by implication, there is a difference between the successful resolution of a dispute as a pragmatic event and the correct application of logic as a theoretical feature. What is interesting is how his account attempts to integrate the two.

The search for objective criteria in the pragma-dialectical account returns again and again to the agreement of the discussants and the rules that govern their behavior. As has been noted from the outset, it is these rules (or the observance of them) which guarantee the *reasonableness* of the proceedings. So perhaps all along we have only needed to recognize these rules as the necessary objective conditions.

In fact, this is the best answer we get from the pragma-dialecticians. "For dialecticians who maintain a critical outlook, reasonableness is not solely determined by the norm of intersubjective agreement but also depends on the external norm that this agreement should be reached in a valid manner" (6), that is, according to the rules. I take the quotation marks around the "external" to be alerting us to some qualifying sense of the word. This norm is not completely from the outside because the discussants have some say in its application.

Elsewhere van Eemeren and Grootendorst appeal to a two-part criterion of validity—problem solving and conventional: "This means that the discussion and argumentation rules which together form the procedure put forward in a dialectical argumentation theory, should on the one hand be checked for their adequacy regarding the resolution of disputes, and on the other for their intersubjective acceptability for the discussants" (1988:280). That the same explanation is repeated in subsequent texts indicates this to be a fundamental and continuing feature of the account (1995a:129). The rules should be adequate for resolving the dispute *and* be acceptable to the discussants. How do the two parts of this criterion work together? How is the agreement of discussants not, in fact, the resolution of the dispute? Or must the dispute only be resolved by the rules? This last question is answered in the affirmative. The rules should have priority over the agreement of the discussants.

> . . . the rules indicate when participants intending to resolve a dispute are entitled, or indeed obliged, to carry out a particular move. They must observe all the rules that are instrumental to resolving the dispute. Any infringement of a discussion rule, whichever party commits it and at whatever stage in the discussion, is a possible threat to the resolution of a dispute and must therefore be regarded as an incorrect discussion move. (131)

At least three comments are appropriate here:

1. The rules govern the discussants. But, as we have seen, some rules depend upon the argument scheme (as with analogy) being acceptable to the discussants. In such instances the discussion rule does not so much govern the agreement of the discussants but cede authority to it.

2. Discussants are required to observe all the rules instrumental to resolving the dispute. Which rules are at stake are presumably recognized by the discussants. One might take from this that the failure to observe a rule is an "infringement of a discussion rule," which in turn is "an incorrect discussion move." As we have seen elsewhere, such an infringement (violation) constitutes, by definition, a fallacy. So one might take from this that there is a fallacy of omission: the fallacy of not observing a rule—*any* rule. But this would not be a fallacy like any other in the account since it is not, strictly speaking, a *violation* of *a* rule.

3. Finally, the soundness of the argumentation is decided by its adequacy in resolving a dispute *and* its "intersubjective acceptability to the discussants" (1988:280; 1995a:129). Thus, the acceptability of the argumentation to both of the discussants *is* a determining factor in deciding its validity. On this ground, it seems that the discussants can reject good arguments. Is it enough for the argument to

resolve the dispute without both discussants' agreement? Presumably not, since the dispute (between the discussants) can hardly be considered resolved if they cannot accept the reasoning instrumental in resolving it (unless that judgment is made by a third party). Now, in this *normative* model it might well be prescribed that the discussants should accept argumentation that resolves the dispute. But the practical application of this begs to be clearly demonstrated. Besides which, it hardly makes sense to place so much importance on the agreement of discussants if the rules constrain them in how they can and cannot respond.

I can begin to demonstrate what I take to be the underlying problem in all of this by returning to *Argumentation, Communication, and Fallacies*. In the chapter on "Fallacies in Choosing the Means of Defense" the authors address argumentation that plays on the audience's emotions and more particularly the usage of the *ad populum*. Now the reader might well wonder: from where did the audience come? Van Eemeren and Grootendorst have been very clear in *restricting* their analysis to the dialectical interest in the resolving of disputes between protagonist and antagonist, to reach agreements or to minimize disagreements. And fallacies have been linked to discussions *between* the two parties involved only. "[M]anipulating the emotions of those present" (1992:134) does not fit happily into such a scenario. In fact, the entire text (and pragma-dialectical program) has been set up to be *resolution-oriented* and not *audience-oriented* (dialectical and not rhetorical) (1992:7–8). It is this bias that is starting to suggest difficulties in the account.

In fact, van Eemeren and Grootendorst have an answer in *this* instance. "Generally speaking, the *argumentum ad populum* thrives best in discussions on a broad scale, in which many people consider themselves involved" (1992a:135). So the audience in question is one that considers itself a *participant* in the dialogue, a party to be persuaded to accept a standpoint. Although certain difficulties are suggested by such a "pluralistic" discussant, I will not address them here but will proceed to a more substantial, and concluding, point that has been suggested by this turn in the discussion.

2.6 Rhetorical Elements:
Audiences, Readers, and Third Parties

In talking about the rules governing an Aristotelian dialectical exchange, Hamblin makes the poignant observation: "Bystanders or audience are understood to know these rules and to be capable of intervening to enforce them if necessary, and to be the ultimate adjudicators" (1970:62). In a review of the merits of dialogue-rules in argumentation, James Crosswhite takes the observation back to Plato: "It is interesting to recall that in Plato's dialogues, the judges and enforcers of the rules of dialogue . . . are the members of the audience" (1993:389). Now, it appears, the pragma-dialectical perspective obscures, but still depends on, this same foundation.

The audience-as-participant has an overt place in the pragma-dialectical perspective and will require, one assumes, some consideration of rhetorical features. But the audience-as-spectator is also involved in the perspective, although left in the background. Bringing it to the foreground will not only indicate its underlying importance (because what the audience-as-spectator brings with it is the demand for clear objective criteria) but also require considerations of further rhetorical features.

The audience-as-spectator, onlooker, and implicit judge, is hidden throughout the texts of the pragma-dialecticians as is evidenced by the reference to audiences, readers, and third parties.[10] Consider some comments from two of the main texts. In *Speech Acts in Argumentative Discussions* we find "[the first two variants of the *ad hominem*] are not directly *addressed to* the other party (though they are of course directed *against* him), but to a *third* party consisting of spectators. These are *rhetorical* rather than *dialectical* tricks" (1984:191). In *Argumentation, Communication, and Fallacies,* in a discussion of the "Straw Man" fallacy, we find that "the manoeuvre is more likely to succeed with an audience not entirely sure exactly what the other party has asserted than the opponent himself. In the case of a polemic in a newspaper, for example, the readers will rarely be able to lay hands on the article they need. . . . " (1992a:126).

Walton (1991a) talks of the critic, of someone who judges. And he makes the most explicit reference of any of the dialecticians when he admits a third party into the picture to judge the rules of the dialogue.

> This third party is, in a way, external to the dialogue. She presides over it, so to speak. Her function is to shape and enforce the rules as they apply to the moves of the participants. . . . The judge or referee is not a direct participant. . . . She is a kind of overseer who regulates the sequence from a higher level. Accordingly, we could say that this third party is not a part of, or component of the dialogue itself. (1996:185)

While this judge or referee is a welcome addition to the account, Walton tells us no more about her. We are left to speculate how this role is adopted and fulfilled in anything but the ideal case.

Walton's "critic" (1991a) has a burden of proof to show that a fallacy is committed. This may be difficult because such things "tend to seem reasonable to the uncritical evaluator" (1991a:221). The uncritical evaluator here, like the critic, is not a participant in the dialogue for whom the resolution of a dispute matters, but is a consumer of arguments, an appraiser of them, for whom fallacies are at issue. To such an individual the existence of fallacies will not depend on intersubjective agreement, or at least, that aspect of the traditional informal fallacies that concerns their conditions of correctness, formerly identified as their fallaciousness in the Standard Treatment, now identified as their unreliability or misapplication by van Eemeren, Grootendorst, and Walton. That aspect is still there, still matters, and still requires an evaluator's attention. The pragma-dialecticians have clothed the traditional informal fallacies in a "coherent theory," but no longer calling them fallacious does not change in them what other argumentation theorists have found and will continue to find interesting.

Our inquiry has taken us outside the dispute to a silent audience who is expected to play some role of adjudication. In the final quote that I will offer, that role is made explicit.

In the chapter on "Fallacies in Concluding the Discussion" van Eemeren and Grootendorst write:

> If they cannot agree on this, the dispute continues. As an unbiased third party will often be in a better position to decide who has won, to an outsider it may, meanwhile, be perfectly clear what the outcome is, but this does not really solve the problem.
>
> A joint discussion by protagonist and antagonist as to who has won the discussion is usually impossible if the discussion is implicit, as in the case with many written texts. Of necessity it is then up to the reader to decide for himself whether the protagonist has provided a conclusive defense of his standpoint. (1992a:184–85)

So this is how we would be expected to deal with the Burchill/Lyndon dispute: thrown back on our own resources. The final arbiter for so many of the argumentative texts that we encounter and the dialogues in which the disputants cannot agree will be the audience/reader, and this audience/reader will of necessity use objective criteria to decide the rationality of the arguments concerned.

One of the merits of the pragma-dialectical approach had been its combination of the logical and rhetorical perspectives. Hence the recognition paid to some "rhetorical tricks." But the dialectical approach was preferred because argumentation was deemed to be resolution-oriented and *not* audience-oriented. Now it seems that it is far more audience-oriented than was first allowed. Discussing the rhetorical approach of Chaim Perelman and L. Olbrechts-Tyteca, van Eemeren and Grootendorst note that its notion of success in argumentation depends on the audience accepting it. It offers "a rhetorical concept of reasonableness in which soundness is equated with effectiveness" (1988:277). This is rejected by van Eemeren and Grootendorst because it is too relative a standard of reasonableness. But that standard now appears to underlie important aspects of the pragma-dialectical program. In fact, the reader who must decide and the unbiased third party are reminiscent of the objective standard served by Perelman and Olbrechts-Tyteca's universal audience.

Finally, we must ask whether *all* argumentation must be essentially dialogic rather than monological. Van Eemeren insists that when a protagonist anticipates a discussion, even though it may never be verbalized, "the moment he argues, the very fact of his argumentation testifies to the legitimacy of a dialectical approach to argumentation" (1986:2). By contrast, in her early assessment of the pragma-dialectical perspective, Sally Jackson suggests that "S *[speaker] may construct an argument not for the sake of L [listener] but for the sake of some audience,* either real or imagined. S may make an argument with no expectation or intention of convincing L" (1985:133).

There is a distinction implied here that is worth noting. It may be a matter for debate as to whether I can make an argument with no intention of convincing, as Jackson proposes, but it is certainly a suggestion that I operate quite differently in relation to two different audiences: one who is a *participant* (real or *imagined*) in my argument, and the other who is a silent spectator. The silent audience is the one I invite in to read (or hear) my monological investigations, working through a problem for myself. On another occasion, I may argue the results of that monological inquiry and *then* arm my audience with all kinds of counterargumentation tools to further the effectiveness of my appeal. The pragma-dialectician may insist that in each case a dialogue is involved, but, if so, it is not the same kind of dialogue or audience. The one who silently stands behind my private reasoning is not one to be convinced but one who *represents* objective standards of rationality against which I judge the merits of my own thought. It is this representation of objective standards that is never given sufficient space in the pragma-dialectical account and that needs to be developed. But such a development must play down the emphasis on the dialectical and give more attention to the logical (Pinto, 1995:284) and, particularly, the rhetorical perspectives. What those objective standards should be is the central subject of chapter 4.

All of this, then, is not to eschew dialectical rules or the approach that relies on them. What is called for is an integration of such rules in a rhetorically based account. Rules for effective argumentation must, in the first instance, reflect the general rules of effective communication. Something along the lines of Grice's Cooperative Principle becomes important here and we will have recourse to it in later chapters. As a conventional social practice, argumentation shares the mutual goals of cooperative communication, where each participant recognizes "a common purpose or set of purposes, or at least a mutually accepted direction" (Grice, 1989:26).

Even a hostile audience, completely unsympathetic to the position of an arguer, recognizes, if they are reasonable, that that position is best challenged if it is understood, and best understood if it is presented in a relevant, honest, informative manner. Likewise, the arguer recognizes the importance of these elements if the audience is to be convinced. Thus the nature of argumentation itself dictates that certain obligations be acknowledged by arguers, obligations that serve the interests of both arguers and audiences. Grice captures these elements in basic maxims: "Be informative"; "Be truthful";[11] "Be relevant"; and "Be perspicuous" (26–27). The rules provided by van Eemeren and Grootendorst and by other dialecticians extend and supplement such basics in important ways. Put at the disposal of a rhetorical account, such rules become available to test that dialectical obligations have been met whenever the context indicates such obligations arising. But these rules are not the end all of any analysis and they invite additional criteria. How such criteria grow out of rhetorical considerations is the subject of the next chapter.

Chapter 3

Contexts and Arguments:
An Introduction to the Rhetorical Perspective

Sections of the introduction uncovered the model of rhetorical argumentation to be found in Aristotle's *Rhetoric* and, together with points raised in chapter 1, these indicate how the separate traditions of "argument" and "rhetoric" have lost sight of this common root. Aristotle's rhetorical argumentation was characterized by its interests in ethos and pathos and by its concept of rhetorical argument, which included the paradigm and the enthymeme. The enthymeme of the *Rhetoric,* as has been clarified, is a notion of probable, everyday argument, free from more complex chains of reasoning, and requiring the *active* involvement of the audience—perhaps to complete the reasoning, certainly to assess it. On these terms, rhetorical argumentation is a cooperative venture, intended to involve both arguer and audience in its development and outcome.

The argumentative perspective here differs from that of the dialectical model proposed by Douglas N. Walton and perhaps by other pragma-dialecticians. In Walton's persuasion dialogue *both* parties have a thesis to prove to the other party (1989:6; 1995a:19, 232). Rhetorical argumentation, as developed here, has as its primary concern the attempt by an arguer to gain or increase the adherence of an audience for a thesis. The audience is not passive in this, as we have seen. But nor is the audience conceived as actively promoting its own thesis, as in the persuasion dialogue. The audience does not strive to persuade, but to grasp, consider, and evaluate. In this sense, our interest extends beyond the verbal exchanges of interlocutors and the "speeches" that consume the *Rhetoric* to include written texts that embody the position and strategies of an arguer and that comprise a central part of the argumentation in that context. At the same time, the audience does persuade, in the sense that it persuades itself (or not) of the legitimacy of the reasoning involved, rather than being persuaded by the speech of the arguer.

Beyond its origins in the *Rhetoric,* rhetorical argumentation has a contemporary exemplar in the new rhetoric of Chaim Perelman, and it is by considering ideas associated with this model that we shall begin to explore the rhetorical perspective on argumentation.

3.1 The New Rhetoric

Unlike demonstration, argumentation expects a meeting of minds: "the will on the part of the orator to persuade and not to compel or command, and a disposition on the part of the audience" (Perelman, 1979a:11).

The new rhetoric is a model of argumentation that collapses Aristotle's distinction between rhetoric and dialectic (Arnold, 1982:ix) and, as we have seen, further embraces logic. Fundamental to this rhetoric are fluid concepts of audience, argument, and adherence; concepts constantly modified by the demands and practices of argumentative communities (Perelman and Olbrechts-Tyteca, 1989:44).

Argumentation has an aim other than the deducing of consequences, and that is "to elicit or increase the adherence of the members of an audience to theses that are presented for their consent" (Perelman, 1982:9). And this involves transferring to the thesis the adherence that an audience already holds to certain ideas (23).

This aim of argumentation is not purely intellectual adherence, but includes the inciting of action or creating a disposition to act, which in turn involves attention not to the faculties (intellect, will, or emotion), but to the whole person. Arguers attend to this with great adaptability: "depending on the circumstances, their arguments will seek different results and will use methods appropriate to the purpose of the discourse as well as to the audiences to be influenced" (13).

Here again we see the thrust of the reasonable over the rational, as Perelman conceives them. The rational, detached from context and stripped of passion; the reasonable, embedded in the lives of historical beings.

This interest also embodies Perelman's own motivation for his adoption of a rhetorical approach. Having studied justice without seeing the importance of rhetoric (1963), he derived deeply unsatisfying conclusions—that judgments of value could not be justified, that all value is logically arbitrary (1979a:8). In response, he turned to studying the ways in which people reason about values. Ten years of such analysis, jointly conducted with L. Olbrechts-Tyteca, led to the recovery of forgotten areas of Aristotelian logic, revived under the rubric of the "new rhetoric."

Thus the motivation is both practical and ethical. The new rhetoric emerged in Europe at a time of tremendous physical and intellectual upheaval. Positivism with its method of inquiry had detached itself from the immediacy of human experience and was unable to meet the moral vacuum of the postwar years. The problem here, or a principal one detected, was the separation at the heart of Objectivity, which removed the assertion from the person who made it (Perelman and Olbrechts-Tyteca, 1969:59). Lost in this separation is a sense of commitment. Thought that leads to action is different from the statements in a scientific system because it moves the person to modify the self on the basis of that thought.

> Since rhetorical proof is never a completely necessary proof, the thinking man who gives his adherence to the conclusions of an argumentation does so by an act that commits him and for which he is responsible. (62)

James Crosswhite gives a spirited defense of Perelman's project in light of such motivations. Significantly, he notes that Perelman's approach to argumentation elevates the values of human freedom and participatory political life.

> Perelman's work in rhetoric is not incidental to his work in law or in the Belgian resistance; it is the culmination of it: a philosophical response to a postmodern Europe shaped by systemic (and systematic) violence and unconstrained fragmentation. (1995:137)

In effect, Perelman's claims about argumentation in life mirror his life in argumentation. He epitomizes the model of reasonableness at the heart of the theory: the arguer as actor and reactor, immersed in an intersubjective network of rhetorical contexts. In fact, as James Crosswhite phrases it, our fate as humans "is bound up with our relation to rhetoric" (1995:140). In such a light, Crosswhite's earlier observation that *The New Rhetoric* is not the usual sort of theory of argumentation (136) seems to be a classic understatement.

3.2 Emotion and Argumentation

Attention to the human experiences that motivate rhetorical argumentation and the emphasis on reasoning with the "whole person" evokes the problem of philosophy's traditional separation of reason from emotion. ("Traditional," that is, if we ignore the *Rhetoric.*)

The dominant rationalist viewpoint of this tradition (to be discussed in chap. 7) excludes emotional considerations as irrational and strives for objectivity and impartiality. Emotional appeals are viewed as "at best diversionary tactics" (Brinton, 1988a:78) and "always suspicious, if not outright fallacious" (Walton, 1992c:67).

Recently (Brinton, 1986, 1988a, 1988b; Damasio, 1994; Nehamas, 1994), however, serious attention has been given to how reason is related to feeling. Much of the impetus for this, at least on Alan Brinton's part, is the recovery of the importance Aristotle gave to emotions in rhetorical argumentation. While the first chapter of Book 1 of the *Rhetoric* warns against the tendency to overemphasize emotional appeals in rhetorical treatises, the next chapter elevates pathos to the same level as logos and ethos. And while commentators are divided on how to interpret this apparent ambivalence, a cautionary reading recognizes a legitimate role for pathos in argumentation when appropriate conditions are observed (see Nehamas, 1994; Frede, 1996).

For Walton (1992c:68), once we break free from the deductive paradigm of valid argument, we find numerous legitimate contexts for emotional appeals in argumentation. Invariably, these involve situations that require an agent to act upon what is argued, and these are just the kinds of circumstances which, as we just saw, motivate the argumentation of the new rhetoric. Of particular note there, of course, was Perelman's overriding concern with the matter of "justice."

In discussing the reasonable grounds for feelings of emotions given by Aristotle (*Rhetoric* 2.9.1386b), Brinton (1988a:80) shows how emotions like anger, indignation, and pity share an essential reference to *justice*. This in turn is linked to good character (ethos), since we *ought* to react appropriately to what is unjust (1988b:210).

This certainly challenges the idea that reason's relation to justice is based on impartiality and objectivity. Interestingly in this regard, the neurologist Oliver Sacks notes the case of a judge who, as the result of frontal lobe damage, was totally deprived of emotion. Rather than excel at his profession, he removed himself from the bench, "saying that he could no longer enter sympathetically into the motives of anyone concerned, and that *since justice involved feeling, and not merely thinking,* he felt that his injury totally disqualified him" (Sacks, 1995: 287–88; italics mine).

However, the role that emotion plays in argumentation cannot be arbitrary and without structure. Brinton in his work takes great pains to recognize emotions as *reasons* and to organize the appropriate accounts under terms like the *pathotic argument* (which consists in giving reasons or drawing attention to the reasonable grounds for passions, emotions, or sentiments [1988a:79]); and the *Argumentum ad Indignationem* ("the form of pathotic argument which consists in giving good grounds for the angry emotions" [81]). Consequently, Brinton's concern is not just with the effectiveness of such types of argument, but primarily with their legitimacy (1988b:209).

As Brinton points out, if we know what counts as reasonable grounds for an emotion, then we can think in terms of evaluating the type of argument that has a kind of emoting as its intended "conclusion."[1] Martha C. Nussbaum (1994:82–83) also recognizes that, for Aristotle, emotions can be created and removed by discourse and argument.

A key distinction in Brinton's account is that between *evoking* an emotion (arousing it in others) and *invoking* an emotion (appealing to an emotion as a basis for action). The characteristic required for either to play a legitimate role in argumentation is that a kind of rational assessment is possible. For example, the *evoking* of an emotion,

> ... might or might not be "reason-giving." If it is reason-giving, then it treats the emotion (or the proposition that you ought to undergo the emotion) as a conclusion. If you ought to feel grateful for reason A, B, and C, then my presenting you with A, B, and C is no less appropriate than my presenting you with reasons for doing *x* when you ought to do *x*. So much for the question of the *legitimacy* of the appeal to emotion in the *first* sense: it can be a legitimate kind of argument. Of a given attempt to evoke we may ask, "Is it reason-giving? Does it proceed by giving *grounds* (by way of cognition, that is)?" If the answer is "Yes," then we may proceed with an assessment of the particular case. (1988b:212)

Brinton ties pathos to ethos because, for Aristotle, having the appropriate feelings is itself an aspect of good character. Ethos was another key element in Aristotle's account of rhetorical argumentation and it should characterize any modern account. Here we are concerned with the role of character in argumentation.[2] For argumentation that appeals to or represents character in some way as to lend credibility, to (or detract it from) a claim, I shall adopt Brinton's (1986) term *Ethotic Argument*. Walton (1992c:248) restricts ethos, as per Aristotle's treatment, to political argumentation (cf. also, Murphy, 1995), but Brinton's usage is more expansive.[3] Again, he is interested in the legitimacy of ethotic arguments more than in their effectiveness, and with the preexisting impressions of character rather than just what arises in a discourse.

Using character appeals to support or to weaken a claim has obvious association with both the *ad verecundiam* (appeal to expert/ authority) and to the *ad hominem*. In fact, Christopher Carey indicates a direct relation between two of these insofar as "[h]ow one makes a case against an opponent (*ad hominem*) reflects on one's own character (*ethos*)" (1996:409). But ethotic argument has a wider sense than each of these. Appeals to authority involve some specific expertise or knowledge that a person, group, or source is alleged to possess.[4] But having a good character, such that one is deemed trustworthy, is a more general feature (it may indeed be a precondition for some appeals to authority). In Aristotle's terms, the exemplar of such a character exhibits practical wisdom, excellence, and goodwill.[5]

As such, the character of Socrates stands as a time-resistant case to illustrate such an exemplar. Were Socrates to advise us to do something, would that be a *reason* for doing it? To Brinton (1986:251), the answer must be yes. While Socrates' approval or disapproval does not *make* the act noble, his status as a deliberator and judge of extraordinary perceptiveness is so much beyond our own that our reasons for doing the act are increased. It may not suffice as a reason for doing the act, but Socrates' ethos provides us with a specific sort of reason for doing it.

Where ethotic arguments of this sort are well-grounded, that is, where the character invoked or represented is of high quality and known to be so, and where the individual's character is being appealed to in a relevant way, that is, where the issue is one where advice from a person of good character could carry weight, *then* such arguments are legitimate and not fallacious. This holds for the forms of ethotic argument represented in *ad verecundiam* or *ad hominem* reasonings, which, of course, have their own additional conditions governing their legitimate usages.

Ethotic argument plays an important role in rhetorical argumentation and evaluations thereof. I will make reference to this feature in the chapters ahead, but the types of moves involved in such reasoning will be particularly scrutinized in the second case study of chapter 5.

3.3 Context

At the heart of the rhetorical perspective is the attention to audience. This has been viewed as both its principal merit (Scult, 1989) and as its greatest weakness (van Eemeren and Grootendorst, 1995a). Before looking at the centrality of the audience for Perelman, I want to first take a more general look at what is at stake when we resort to context. The first substantial model of rhetorical argumentation given, by Aristotle, understood context in terms of the relations between logos, ethos, and pathos. Since then, as we saw earlier, other features like the "message" and the "common code" have been added.

A merit of the revival of the tradition of argumentation, has been the general attention paid to the contexts in which arguments occur. Even the product-oriented approach of informal logic shares this advance, looking beyond the core structure of PPC. Yet there is room both for a wider inclusion of contextual features that should count as relevant for argumentative purposes, and for the further development of argumentation from the perspective of its contextual components.

In chapter 1 we saw Ralph H. Johnson (1995) address argumentation as a complex sociocultural activity, a view he shares with the pragma-dialecticians. The root context of our inquiry is a social context (Billig, 1987:87); argumentation is a feature of social relations and shares in the complexity of those relations. Michael Billig describes the basic aspects of the context of argumentation as justification and criticism. He trades on Perelman's insight that this tandem is central to rhetoric, where "a question of justification ordinarily arises only in a situation that has given rise to criticism" (1979a:33). Such criticisms of what is held or established, be they norms or values, always occur, claims Billig, within a social context. This does not mean that we are drawn into a study of culture or sociological relations. For our purposes, it must only alert us to the importance of the first element of context: locality.

1. *Locality.* By this term I understand the time and the place in which the argument is located. Depending on the issue, such considerations can vary from being peripheral to playing a central role in the recognition and assessment of arguments.

Where and when people live affects the nature of their thinking and therefore their arguments. How often have we seen writers (or heard speakers) criticize authors of antiquity for failing to think with the clarity that centuries of subsequent development have made possible for those same writers (or speakers)? This is more than a lack of charity on such people's part. It is a failure to recognize that reasoning takes place within the milieu familiar to the reasoner. The challenge is to try to see the problem *from the perspective* of the author, despite the vast distance between us. To imagine what the world looked like for Plato, is to think in terms of the assumptions and traditions that to a certain extent constrained his thinking. Then one can begin to assess his reasoning *on its own terms,* not on ours. It is one matter to decide that Plato's *Republic* (once we understand it) would not work in modern contexts. It is quite another matter, and an unfair one, to criticize it for failing to anticipate decidedly modern concerns.

Part, then, of argumentation assessment is interpretation. In the fields of history, anthropology, even sociology, this is widely understood. But the lesson is often missed for argumentation in general. Particularly, as a social exchange of ideas and reasons, the assessment of argumentation *between* societies or cultures will face problems not experienced when the argumentation is *within* one society. This is part of what makes argumentation such a richly fascinating area of study: that we can be brought to consider the reasoning of someone fundamentally distinct from us in terms of the period of history in which he or she lived, with its norms and attitudes.

Intracultural argumentation can also make demands on our interpretative skills. But at least we share the same place and time, even if we do not agree on *how* we share it.

2. *Background.* Related to locale, as the previous remark suggests, is *background.* Few argumentation theorists ignore this term and it is often taken as synonymous with (and to exhaust) context itself. By background we understand those events that bear on the argumentation in question. That is, those that are instrumental in understanding it: the occasion of the exchange/discourse; prior argumentation on the issue and/or between the arguer and audience; current social/political events that give clarity or urgency or, even, irony to the argumentation in question; and the consequences for the participants of the outcome of the argumentation. Billig captures the importance of background in the following remark:

... we cannot understand the meaning of a piece of reasoned discourse, unless we know what counter-positions are being implicitly or explicitly rejected. In the same way, we cannot understand the attitudes of an individual, if we are ignorant of the wider controversy in which the attitudes are located. In other words, the meaning of a piece of reasoned discourse, or an expressed attitude, does not merely reside in the aggregation of dictionary definitions of the words used to express the position: it also resides in the argumentative context. (1991:44)

A telling example of the consequences of missed background, also related by Billig (1987:91–92; 1991:45), comes in the reaction first made to Bishop Whately's *Historic Doubts Relative to Napoleon Buonoparte* (1819). The argumentation in this text is in support of the position that Napoleon never existed. Or so it would appear. Napoleon was presented as the invention of the British press in order to boost sales. Neither Whately nor any of his acquaintances had actually *seen* Napoleon. And so on. The argumentation was well developed and itself had a contemporary currency (it would fool few today). The book was very popular, going through several editions. But many readers missed the point, which depended on the background of a recent debate. The argumentation, while directly supporting the position of Napoleon's nonexistence, was indirectly intended as support for a position countering Hume's skepticism on miracles. Whately was subjecting an "obvious fact" to the same scrutiny as Hume had miracles, thereby putting in question Hume's enterprise. Without the full background, the reader not only misses the point but loses the opportunity to assess a quite fascinating exercise in counterargumentation.

3. *Arguer.* An essential component of any argumentation is the source—the intelligent originator of the meanings inherent in it. While locale and background contribute to the source, the arguer is its principal constituent. Usually an individual, the "arguer" can be a group, as with the source of an advertisement, advocacy statement, or political speech.

Like the audience, as will be discussed in the next section, the arguer is one of the principal, if not the principal, agents of the argumentation. In a slightly different context, Jonathan Potter (1996:151–58) provides several examples from science and media reports of cases where descriptions are constructed so as to present

facts or evidence as having an agency of their own. The experimenter
or reporter, with their perspectives and decisions, disappear behind
a discourse that has the appearance of being neutral and objective.
Potter's insight can easily be transferred to the common presentation of arguments, especially in the FDL tradition with its context-
free products.

Where the argument-as-product is considered important, we
often find the argument treated as having its own agency. The arguer
and audience are forgotten and their actions are transferred to the
product, which lies "complete" in its particular structure, and "acts"
upon us. In such cases, we may be told things like: "the argument
shows, . . . " "the premises support, . . . " "the evidence warrants . . .
(or speaks for itself)," or "the conclusion claims, . . . " How does
the argument, premise, evidence, or conclusion do so much? Because
with the arguer and audience, the *communicators,* dismissed and the
context ignored, there is no one and nothing left to account for
the activity at the core of argumentation. The tendency in such cases
is to lend the argument-as-product an authority of its own, to insu-
late it from the kinds of questions that might otherwise be raised.

Recovering the context in such cases requires that we look carefully at the real agents involved. To overlook the point of view of the
arguer is a serious failure (Vorobej, 1992). It plays a role not just in
deciding how the content of an argument should be interpreted, but
also in determining the type of argument-as-product involved in the
argumentation. Mark Vorobej, for example, presents a psychological
account of deduction, defining it in terms of the arguer's intentions.

> An argument is deductive if, and only if, the author of the ar-
> gument believes that the truth of the premises necessitates
> (guarantees) the truth of the conclusion. (1992:105)

This is placed within a general discussion of the importance of
psychological considerations in argument reconstruction. Identifying
suppressed components, for example, requires attention to an author's beliefs: "it is inappropriate to add any premise to an argument
if there is reason to believe that the author of the argument would not
accept that premise" (111). Of course, if deduction can be defined in
terms of an arguer's beliefs, then so too can other types of arguments.

Yet talk of an arguer's beliefs or intentions raises a number of
critical concerns. In fact, much of the negative attention paid to contexts often relates to the difficulty of ascertaining the arguer's intentions. Three principal complaints are raised: (a) the intentions

behind a text can rarely be fully recovered (especially when the author is deceased or otherwise absent); (b) the meaning of a text can be considered quite independently of any intentions an author might have had (a criticism courtesy of literary theory); and (c) even speakers do not always know what they mean. Unlike rehearsed speech (which is on par with the written text), spontaneous speech, so much a part of ordinary arguments, is not "prethought," the speaker does not know what she will say before she says it and so "hears" it at the same time as her audience. We have all found ourselves in situations where, when asked what we mean by something we have said, we respond "I'm not sure; let me think about it."

Of course, given the importance of the arguer to our enterprise, accepting these criticisms will significantly undermine our endeavors. Nor can we ignore them by citing the many examples (perhaps even the common case) where recovery of the arguer's intentions is not a problem. I will briefly address each of these criticisms in turn.

a. If it is the case that an arguer's intentions are not always clear, then this points to the importance of placing the arguer in her or his locale. It also further emphasizes the evaluator's role as interpreter. Context in its widest conception is the laboratory of the argumentation theorist. We consider, examine, test, and arrive at the best and most comprehensive reconstruction of the argumentation that is commensurate with those parts that are clear. Which is to say that what we know about the locale, background, and audience can cast light on an otherwise shadowy arguer.

b. That a text can have meanings independent of any intended by an author is not in question. To recognize this is to recognize the richness of our social relations and the ambiguities of discourse. Multiple meaning shifts attention beyond the arguer alone to, principally, the audience. In fact, given such problems of translation (Davidson, 1984) it may be a truism that meanings attributed to an argument will differ from what the author intended.

An important observation registers here. Once looked at from the dual perspectives of audience (with diverse members) and the ambiguities of language, the argument (i.e., the traditional PPC set) loses its fixedness. What the logician sees as *the* argument becomes *one* within a group of contextually legitimated arguments, and is therefore *a part* only of the argumentation. Members of an audience may read an argumentation, in its broadest sense, differently, understand different meanings to key words or phrases (or gestures), and thereby recognize different arguments. The argumentation theorist will see the multiple meanings *as part of* the argumentation. If rhetoric teaches us anything here, it is the difficulty of trying to fix *a* meaning for an argumentation (while not precluding this possibility). Argumentation theorists (like scientists with their hypotheses) work with all plausible meanings. Plausible, that is, in light of other aspects of the context. Working with context requires us to consider how a text has been and could be understood.

Of course, in this light, that meanings exist independently of an author does not preclude the author's intentions, where clear, constituting *a* meaning. But what it might require, on occasion, is that the meaning attributed to the author is not given priority. We will see later that the *logician*'s sense of argument can still be elevated *if* it is the argument of the universal audience, because both the logician's argument and the perspective of the universal audience should reflect what is reasonable. In this way we can salvage logic's core argument-as-product, but we do so *from a rhetorical base*.

c. Not all argumentation is related to spontaneous speaking. Much, perhaps most, has at its core a rehearsed "text." But much everyday argumentation is linked to the spontaneity of speakers, tumbling helter-skelter from mouths (and minds) in the give-and-take of conversation (Willard, 1989:93–98).

Instances where we do not rehearse our speaking puts us on par with the audience—we are part of the audience for that argument. But if the aim of argumentation is to gain the adherence of an audience for a thesis, then an argument must be more than just spontaneous speaking. As the speaker considers what she is saying, she refines, repeats, and focuses her ideas in order to make her point. Where she fails to do this, we cannot say that an argument is involved. Not all speaking is a part of argumentation.

These criticisms, individually and together, serve to emphasize how important it is to take account of context. We must pore carefully over the context before deciding on the arguer's position, even when a first glance might have suggested that position to us. And once we have recovered it, we cannot assume that the arguer's position is the sole or even the primary meaning of an argumentative text. The context will often offer others. It has a depth that a simple search for a premise-conclusion set never begins to uncover.

4. *Expression.* Important to the construction, identification, reconstruction, and assessment of arguments are the ways in which they are expressed: the utterance involved and the force of its expression; what is said and what is left unsaid; the mannerisms of the arguer (when present); and the medium used to convey the argument, along with the conventions of that medium.

Much attention has been paid to the speech act model as one suitable for treating argumentative utterances. The pragma-dialectical theory of Frans H. van Eemeren and Rob Grootendorst, for example, is grounded in a speech act account. The term *pragma-dialectical* derives its name from the verbal exchanges of a critical discussion seen as an interaction of speech acts (1992a:7). Argumentation is an illocutionary act complex that can be understood within the framework of "the 'standard version' of *the* speech act theory" (italics mine) started by J. L. Austin (1962) and developed by John Searle (1969). Since Searle is seen to be developing Austin's theory, it is not surprising that most of their discussion concerns the former's more elaborate, rule-based, depiction of the model (van Eemeren and Grootendorst, 1984:19ff.). In fact, Grootendorst is explicit about this: "When I refer to speech act theory, I mean the standard version developed by John R. Searle" (1992:672n.1).

An examination of how argument has been treated within a speech act framework is conducted by Scott Jacobs, who singles out the van Eemeren and Grootendorst model for its success in offering a descriptive framework for analyzing argumentation as well as a normative framework for establishing standards of procedure (1989:349). But despite this acknowledgment, there is a problem:

> This sort of analysis, like speech act analysis in general, locates the structure and function of argumentative intentions in the unit of the isolated act (Schegloff, 1988). It therefore suggests a constancy of structure and function across a broad range of contexts and patterns of expression (which is, of course, part of its appeal) . . . close examination of the actual circumstances in which arguments get expressed reveals that arguments do not always submit to this kind of analysis. Instead of an isolable and homogeneous speech act, one finds a family of act types that vary in function and pragmatic logic depending upon the context of their use and the form of their expression. (350)

Jacobs supports the existence of a family of act types by analyzing complaints; hypothetical arguments, including devil's advocate arguments where the speaker is not committed to believing the claim asserted; indirect arguments; and bargaining arguments. In each case, there are different pragmatic preconditions and a different illocutionary force at work. Jacobs concludes: "the notion of argument as a stable, homogeneous class of utterances definable by a common force and a common set of felicity conditions does not fare well when tested against actual language uses" (360)[6]

An even more decisive critique of the "Searle/Austin view" and its developments as a suitable frame for argumentation is delivered by Charles Arthur Willard. He notes the common criticism of the paradigm case in speech act theory, which sets aside the nonliteral, nonserious, ambiguous, and so forth. Everyday human discourse, including argumentation, is characterized by the very things that have been excluded here. "Communication is thus reduced to a speaker's intentional literal utterances plus a hearer's reactions in unambiguous contexts" (1989:70). Clearly, this is too restrictive given the various means, direct and indirect, by which arguers communicate their arguments. Like Jacobs, Willard is able to explore several significant cases of argumentative communication that do not conform with the speech act theory criteria for making an argument. Significantly, these include two cases that depend, for their full argumentative understanding, on the silences of an utterer (96): where what is not said combines with what is said to complete the arguer's position. A further example, which Willard allows as a case of interaction based on dissensus, consists purely of eye contact and gestures with no expressed utterances. A homeless man is refused entry to a warm hotel lobby by the stares of a police officer. The man makes his case by hugging his torso as if cold and by looking into the lobby. The police officer makes his case through a constant impassive stare. The homeless man shrugs, and moves on. "A request is made; a reason is given. The request is denied; no reason need be given. . . . The request and refusal both depend upon 'what everybody knows" (97).

In general, I am in full agreement with these criticisms of the speech act model. As it has been developed, it is not adequate for treating the wide range of situations in which arguments arise that a rhetorical approach to argumentation recognizes. But it is worth noting here that the model that fails is, at root, that of John Searle. The common assumption of a natural progression from Austin to Searle not only overlooks Searle's principal deviation from the path that Austin was taking, but it also misses the ways in which Austin offers promising insights into the importance of context.

Searle's model is founded on criticisms of Austin, and the former considers his own work to "provide us with the beginnings of a theory of speech acts" (1969:131), something that Austin had failed to do *on Searle's terms*. Austin's interest in speech acts had to do with describing how we experience these acts; Searle proposes formulating theoretical rules for them.[7] Two very different models emerge from this divergence: Austin's is a concrete speech act drawn from experience; Searle's is an abstract speech act, formulated and imposed on experience.

Searle speculates that some people might believe that there are two distinct semantic studies, one the study of the meanings of sentences, and the other a study of the performances of speech acts. In fact, according to Searle, these are not two separate areas of concern but the same study from different perspectives. This is because every meaningful sentence can be used to perform a particular speech act, and "every possible speech act can *in principle* be given an *exact formulation* in a sentence or sentences" (1969:19). I emphasize certain words here because they indicate that the notion of a speech act that supports Searle's unified study is an ideal one. He is interested in what can "in principle" happen in "possible" speech acts, and he believes that an "exact" formulation in a sentence can be given of each speech act. While there are repeated references to the context of utterance in Searle's work, it is clear that he is involved in an activity far and above the mere description of total speech acts that characterized Austin's work.

Austin's *How to Do Things with Words,* as it develops, defends a shift from analyses of propositions to analyses of what he calls "the total speech act in the total speech situation" (1962:52). This indicates a conception of the speech act as part of the situation. If the speech act is to be understood, it is not sufficient to understand the propositions involved; it must be examined in light of the situation in which it arises. This is because the situation conditions it, and situations will vary in their "pragmatic preconditions," to borrow words from Jacob's critique of what it now makes more sense to call the Searlean theory of speech acts. It is still legitimate to wonder whether the "total" speech situation could ever be recovered, and to recognize that appropriate conventions would be part of that situation. But a development on Austin's terms would replace the rule-based abstractness of Searle's shift with a context-based description of utterances. A descriptive program allows for the diversity of context. It does not exclude what does not fit a predefined theoretical framework.[8]

While Austin gives no comprehensive inventory of the "total speech situation," we can gather from his principal text that it will include such things as the "I" who is doing the action (1962:61); gestures, pointings, shruggings, and so forth, which may accompany utterances or serve without the utterance of any words (76); the conventions that explain acts like arguing (102–3); and, of course, the consequential effects produced upon the "feelings, thoughts, or actions of the audience, or of the speaker, or of other persons" (101).

In total, Austin's early musings on context anticipate the variety of modes of expression that capture the rhetorical perspective's broad sense of "argument." Outside of limited professional areas, arguers are not first and foremost logicians; they are first and foremost communicators. And in this respect:

> arguers, like all communicators, use any or all of the communication vehicles available to them: serial predication, claiming, and reason-giving, as well as proxemic, paralinguistic, gestural, and facial cues. Once we have an argument, *anything* used to communicate within it is germane to an analysis of how the argument proceeds and how it affects the arguers. (Willard, 1989:92)

This necessarily broadens the extension of "argumentative text." Films, newsreels, humorous anecdotes, fables, and other narratives, even the juxtaposition of headlines with photographs on a newspaper's front page may promote a point of view for which an audience's adherence is sought, or may be used in that promotion. In each case the "text" can be analyzed on its own terms, according to its particular conventions, for example, humorous anecdotes, quite apart from its nature as argumentation. What will characterize each one as having an argumentative aspect is the common denominator of involving an attempt to gain or increase an audience's adherence for the position proffered. Which brings us to the last and most important contextual consideration: the audience.

3.4 Audiences

At the heart of the rhetorical perspective is the consideration of audiences. Walter R. Fisher suggests that audience is "the decisive and most fundamental concept in Perelman's new rhetoric" (1986:86). To focus on audience is to view argumentation from the perspective of its effectiveness, its power to move and to change the world. Because there is no discourse without an audience, there is no argumentation without rhetorical effect.

Given the primacy of audience for Perelman, I will draw on several of his insights. Following his lead, a general sketch of the importance of audience can be given on four fronts.

First, audiences are complex. The audience is defined "for the purposes of rhetoric" (Perelman and Olbrechts-Tyteca 1969:19), and "for the development of a theory of argumentation" (Perelman 1982:14), as *the gathering of those whom the speaker wants to influence by his or her arguments*" (Perelman and Olbrechts-Tyteca 1969:19; Perelman 1982:14). Of course, an argumentation, particularly in the form of a written text, may reach a wider audience. Consequently, we must distinguish the audience for the argumentation from those who happen to come under its purview or be influenced by it. The complexity lies in the diverse makeup of potential audiences. For Perelman, the audience may range from the private reflections of the arguer up to the "universal audience" of all competent and reasonable people. And the competence of audiences can vary from those who know only premises of a very general nature (termed *loci* [Perelman and Olbrechts-Tyteca 1969:83]) to the knowledge of specialists. Most perplexing, are composite audiences comprising members who ordinarily do not agree (Crosswhite, 1989:165). In such cases, the model of the universal audience is particularly helpful.

In addition to their complexity, or as a further aspect of it, a second point to note about audiences is that they change, even in the course of argumentation. In fact, the very conception of audiences, like that of arguments or adherences, may "always be modified" (Perelman and Olbrechts-Tyteca, 1989:44). This may be seen to refer only to the composition of the audience. A further remark concerns the audience's attitudes: "We must not forget that the audience, to the degree that speech is effective, changes with its unfolding development" (Perelman 1982:149).

The emphasis on change in the audience indicates the third point, one that is stressed in the Aristotelian account. The rhetorical audience is not a passive consumer of arguments, as some logicians seem to think; it plays an *active* role in the argumentation. The nature of the audience sets the terms of the premises, which are formulated in light of theses accepted by those to be addressed (21). The audience contributes assumptions to the reasoning, as we saw with the rhetorical enthymeme. And the audience can interact with the argumentation in the mind of the arguer or in dialogue with the arguer. Here "audiences can . . . take these arguments and their relation to the speaker as the object of a new argumentation" (49).

These three aspects of audiences point to the fourth and major point: that arguments are judged successful and evaluated not directly in terms of their internal logical support, but in terms of their impact on the audience.[9] The aim of argumentation is the adherence of audiences to its theses. It will be judged strong or weak according to the degrees to which this is accomplished. But this leads us quickly to two stumbling blocks: since success is viewed only in terms of the audience accepting a thesis, then it would appear that *anything goes* in persuading an audience; and, connected with this, that the model of argumentation involved is thoroughly relativistic. Both of these objections are addressed in the remainder of this chapter and in the next. I will prepare the groundwork for that discussion by indicating exactly how Perelman's model gives occasion for such concerns.

In fact, Perelman does not believe that "anything goes" in persuading an audience. This hints too much of the traditional philosophical objection to (sophistical) rhetoric, viewed as the ability to make the weak argument *appear* stronger.[10] Perelman addresses this concern with the fundamental distinction between the particular audience and the universal audience.

Even here, the distinction is not as clear as perhaps we would like. Allen Scult suggests that the universal audience is not vigorously defined by Perelman because it is not a logical or strictly philosophical construct. Furthermore, and paradoxically, "attempts to define it obscure its meaning" (1989:154). However, without a clear meaning attached to it, Perelman's universal audience risks being sidelined in even greater obscurity.

As we have seen, there are a number of audiences recognized in Perelman's texts (Perelman and Olbrechts-Tyteca 1969:30). But he makes an important distinction between the particular audience being addressed and the universal audience somehow lying within, or framed by, or participating in, that particular audience. I use the term *participating* quite deliberately to invoke a similar problem of relationship, that between Plato's Form and its instantiations in the world. It is a relationship that has occasioned considerable debate over its exact nature, and a similar controversy surrounds the ambiguous relationship between Perelman's universal and particular audiences. Scult, in the end, offers the best interpretation:

> Validation of your argument lies in the securing of the adherence of both, i.e., your construct of the universal audience and the actual audience you are addressing. One checks the other. The particular audience keeps your concept of universal audience from becoming an abstract irrelevancy—simply a handmaiden to the eccentricities of your thinking. The universal audience conceived of as the community of minds competent to judge your argument keeps you from submitting to

the temptation to persuade the particular audience you are addressing at any cost. (1989:159)

Indeed, as we will see in the next section, this is how Perelman *uses* the construct of the universal audience as an imagined tool of the arguer. As such, the universal audience gives a fixedness to the structure of an argumentation that reclaims the core of the product previously offered by logicians. But it does this now from the under-lying rhetorical base. That is, while an argumentation is susceptible to a range of interpretations according to the composite makeup of particular audiences (all of which are considered in the evaluation of that argumentation), an agreement of the universal audience can fix one meaning as its core. Furthermore, the agreement of the univer-sal audience takes us beyond the recourse to an agreement between discussants favored by the dialectical approach.

In elaborating upon the structure of the universal audience, we will need to address the criticisms brought against it. As a concept, it is deemed to be riddled with inconsistencies (Ray, 1978; Ede, 1989), or even unnecessary for Perelman's (and Olbrechts-Tyteca's) own project (Johnstone, 1978:105). Again, while it "cancels out the sub-jectivism associated with the idea of audience . . . it ceases to be an operational concept since it can only be understood as a metaphor" (Meyer, 1986:133).

3.5 The Universal Audience

To a certain extent, Perelman must share some responsibility for criticisms laid against his notion of the universal audience, insofar as those criticisms may be based on misunderstandings. Perelman is a writer who will often discuss ideas or views without clarifying his attitude toward them. Only in a subsequent discussion do we realize that an idea he has been explaining is not one he is endorsing, or at least, not one he is endorsing in the way it has been explained.

Thus, some charges that the universal audience is too ideal or hypothetical a concept (Ray, 1978; Ede, 1989) stem from the follow-ing passage:

> Argumentation addressed to a universal audience must con-vince the reader that the reasons adduced are of a compelling character, that they are self-evident, and possess an absolute and timeless validity, independent of local or historical con-tingencies. (Perelman and Olbrechts-Tyteca 1969:32)

This passage, and the extensive discussion from which it is taken has led to a lot of criticism and confusion. Simply put, *it is not* Perelman's view. What he is outlining here is the traditional conception of a universal audience to which philosophers have long appealed. It is *against* this conception, and more generally the conception of certitude in philosophy it characterizes, which Perelman's new rhetoric is reacting. His reason for rejecting the traditional conception is simple: "[It] links importance to previously guaranteed objectivity and not to the adherence of an audience, rejects all rhetoric not based on knowledge of the truth" (Perelman, 1989a:244). Elsewhere he calls it a "supraindividual and antihistorical conception of reason" (1967:82). So, at the start, we must recognize at least two notions of the "universal audience." That employed in the tradition being rejected, and the modification proposed by Perelman. At stake are two distinct conceptions of reason. Perelman is clear on this:

> But my conception of reason differs from the classical conception. I do not see it as a faculty in contrast to other faculties in man. I conceive of it as a privileged audience, the universal audience. (ibid.)

The failure to recognize when this distinction is being invoked accounts for some of the criticism being leveled against the new rhetoric, particularly those that charge Perelman with inconsistent usage (Ede, 1989:147).

Perelman wants to separate the traditional philosophical values of guaranteed objectivity and a rhetoric based on the "knowledge of truth" from his approach to argumentation. Philosophers must broaden their conception of reason and, hence, argument (1982:161).

Crosswhite, in his apology for Perelman's concept, distinguishes the universal audience from the ideal audience and criticizes the latter. On Crosswhite's thinking, argumentation addressed to ideal audiences must be couched in the most abstract and formal terms. "The agreements such audiences are capable of reaching never concern the concrete and substantive kinds of issue such audiences were designed to deal with" (1989:161). This contrasts markedly with Perelman's universal audience, which is designed to consider concrete issues addressed in arguments directed across times and cultures.

At the same time, audiences are not given, but made. Perelman (Perelman and Olbrechts-Tyteca 1969:19) views all audiences as such, even the particular ones. This makes sense in light of our experience as arguers. When we attempt to understand our immediate audience we construct a model of their beliefs. In such cases, as with Perelman's universal audience, the model's features can be checked against real people. Still, it is the universal audience that is addressed by the philosopher. There is no choice between the particular and universal: the work of the philosopher has elevated the specific features of the particular audience into universal dimensions.

Thus there is an important connection between the immediate, particular audience and the universal model drawn from it. Perelman begins with a particular audience and then looks at *its* universal features. Constructing these universal audiences involves defending one's conception of universality. The philosopher addresses the universal audience as he or she conceives it (1989a:244). As Crosswhite points out, this move is particularly useful in dealing with composite audiences: "when an actual audience consists of a number of different particular audiences who ordinarily do not assent to the same arguments, one can construct from them a universal audience, and aim one's arguments at it" (1989:165).

Perelman likens this universalizing to that of Kant's categorical imperative (1967:82; 1989a:245), and not to the general will of Rousseau's small political community, as John W. Ray (1978:366) had proposed. The philosopher attempts to universalize the specific features of the situation and solicits general agreement for them in this way. Only arguments that can be universally admitted are judged reasonable. This does not preclude arguments about what constitutes the universal audience for a specific case. Dialectical exchanges may ensue where opponents disagree on this. This is, after all, an essential feature of what is at stake in argumentation. Here agreement on the universal audience must be achieved through dialogue before the stage of appealing to that audience (Perelman 1982:16–17).

The universal audience is not an abstraction, then, but a populated community. It derives from its conceiver, conditioned by her or his milieu (1989a:248). "There is always something empirical in it, something which comes from the experience of the author and the traditions of a culture" (Crosswhite,1989:166). The universal audience is a concrete audience that changes with time and with the speaker's conception of it (Perelman and Olbrechts-Tyteca 1969:491). It is far from being a transcendental concept borne out of a rationalism (Ray, 1978). But although the universal audience will change, the test of universality goes on—*it* transcends a milieu or a given epoch.

As we will see in the next chapter, universal audiences can be constructed from particular ones by universalizing techniques that imaginatively expand audiences across cultures and time and apply notions like competence and rationality. What results is an audience that can assent to concrete propositions and not simply formal proofs and empty platitudes. But the starting point, here and in all argumentation, has been a fully conceived audience, real or imagined, which listens, reads, and reacts. The universal is fully grounded in the practical requirements of the real. Perelman stresses this when he indicates the need for the philosopher (arguer) to guard against errors in her or his argumentation by testing theses through "submitting them to the *actual* approval of the members of that audience" (1967:83; italics mine).

So the universal audience, it transpires, is the distillation of the concrete audience, comprised of the common features as imagined by the arguer (speaker). For an argument to be strong it should elicit the agreement of this universal audience, insofar as the arguer determines it. Put another way, a convincing argument is one whose premises are universalizable (1982:18).

There is, though, a further, important distinction to make. We are left, on the terms explained so far, with the prospect of "universalizing" thoroughly disagreeable audiences/arguments: the discourses of the racist and the intolerant of all shades. This is one of the things the demand for objective standards in argumentation is most concerned with handling. And this problem, in turn, evokes the specter of the *ad populum* argument, which is usually considered fallacious. Douglas N. Walton's discussion of this argument-type appropriately relates it to the need for universal standards, and even to Perelman's universal audience. The traditional concern over the *ad populum* argument is that it is directed only to a specific group of respondents. Walton's response is to locate this within the parameters of a critical discussion, the primary sphere of the pragma-dialectician. *There* it is reasonable for one party to attempt to resolve a dispute by utilizing the commitments of the other party. Consistent with his account of dialogue types and shifts, Walton allows that the *ad populum* could be fallacious in contexts like, say, the scientific inquiry, but is legitimate in a critical discussion. As he recognizes in a comment appropriate also to rhetorical argumentation[11]: "If the goal is to convince the group by reasoned persuasion, then the commitments of the group must be taken as the starting point from which to select the arguments' premises, if one's argumentation is to be successful" (1992c:71).

Interestingly, a need for wider validation *is* recognized, and this is provided for by the rules governing the dialogues. Of further interest is how Walton proceeds to prefer these rules to Perelman's universal audience. As we saw in the last chapter, however, these pragma-dialectical rules are themselves suspect when an attempt is made to employ them as an objective criterion for validation. And Walton's reasons for declining Perelman's model are not convincing:

> It may be that all persuasion dialogue argumentation in natural language presupposes a narrative and historical context of background presumptions and unstated premises that can be understood and accepted only by a specific audience or readership, even if that audience cuts across historical epochs and cultures.
>
> Thus, it would not seem to be necessary to require a universal audience for argumentation in persuasion dialogue. Knowledge-based interactive reasoning would only be necessary and useful if all the participants in the dialogue shared the same (universal) knowledge base. (72–73)

This "knowledge base," we can happily grant, the specific audience does not share, as will be discussed in chapter 4. But what the comment overlooks is that point I have been stressing in this discussion: that there is a universal audience for every specific audience and it represents not so much a shared knowledge base as a shared conception of what is reasonable. Whether it is "necessary to require" the universal audience in a particular context depends on that context itself. But it remains a tool for both the arguer and the evaluator to consider.

As Crosswhite emphasizes, Perelman has within his model distinctions with which to address the problem of universalizing intolerant, or otherwise problematic, audiences:

> The philosopher, on the other hand, says Plato, cares about what is good—that is, cares about whether an audience *should be* persuaded by an argument or not. This is exactly what Perelman cares about, and this is why he distinguishes between effective arguments and valid ones on the basis of a distinction between particular and universal audiences. (1989:162)

Not all rhetoric can be reduced to an argumentation aiming at the universal audience. Perelman distinguishes between a philosophical discourse, that makes an appeal to reason via the universal audience and thus aims to convince, and an efficacious discourse that seeks to persuade a particular audience only. A young man trying to persuade a woman to marry him, or a priest speaking to church faithful, are examples of discourses that Perelman views as aiming at efficacy (1989a:247). This speaks to a distinction introduced early in the *New Rhetoric* with a view to heading off the traditional criticism that rhetoric is satisfied merely with persuading an audience by using any means: "We are going to apply the term *persuasive* to argumentation that only claims validity for a particular audience, and the term *convincing* to argumentation that presumes to gain the adherence of every rational being" (Perelman and Olbrechts-Tyteca 1969:28). One must be concerned, then, with determining *whether* an argument is addressed to a universal or a particular audience (perhaps using the universal as the default audience where the arguer's intentions are unclear).

The philosopher, we know, is always concerned with addressing the principle of reason inherent in the universal audience. But many arguers may not share such a concern. In *constructing* their arguments, they will devote their attention to the audience they would persuade. But insofar as we are called upon to *evaluate* those same arguments, we should judge their reasonableness principally in terms of whether they would be acceptable to a universal audience (as we conceive it for that argumentation). Thus the universal audience encourages a "rhetorical criticism model" (Golden, 1986:292) that promotes universal values over simple effectiveness.

Put in other terms, a rhetoric worthy of the philosopher deliberates before a reasonable decision. And such is founded not on a prior truth as it was for Plato, but on what is justified to the audience by the arguments provided. Hence, the "reasonable" *will* vary in time and space, and "what is reasonable for a particular audience may not be so for a universal audience" (Perelman, 1989a:248). Hence, furthermore, "reasonable" in a philosophical discourse affirms the agreement of the universal audience, as conceived by the philosopher rooted in her or his time and place. Hence, lastly, the pluralism in philosophy and the absence of an incontestable truth.

While being a hypothetical construction, then, the Perelman model is not, on this reading, an ideal model. What this allows us to do is to keep our focus on the immediate audience with its particular cognitive claims, while recognizing a standard of reasonableness that should envelop that audience and that it should acknowledge whenever recourse to the universal audience is required. In this way we can understand Perelman's repeated insistence that the strength of an argument is a function of the audience, and that in evaluating arguments we must look first and foremost at the audience.

One can appreciate from the preceding discussion of the universal audience why critics might be moved to charge that Perelman espouses a relativism. As van Eemeren and Grootendorst explain it, Perelman reduces the soundness of argumentation to the determinations of the audience. "This means that the standard of reasonableness is extremely relative. Ultimately, there could be just as many definitions of reasonableness as there are audiences" (1995a:124). Introducing the universal audience as *the* principle of reasonableness to mitigate this problem only shifts the source of the concern to the arguer. Since the universal audience is a mental construct of the arguer, now there will be as many definitions of reasonableness as there are arguers.

While we have seen Perelman to be suggesting more than this, something of these criticisms sticks. In the next chapter I will set out criteria for argument evaluation and construction from the perspectives of audience and context. In doing so, while I depend upon an elaboration of Perelman's principal ideas, I will need to develop these ideas and adapt them beyond Perelman's own discussion, and to add further considerations (e.g., relevance). In this way, the criticisms of useless abstractness (universal audience) and relativism will be further addressed.

Chapter 4

Audiences and the Conditions for Adherence

The universal audience is often discarded as irrelevant or unhelpful because it is considered simply an idealization with no concrete application. In this chapter, I will discuss how a developed notion of the universal audience, understood generally in the way in which Perelman introduced it, can be used in the construction and evaluation of argumentation. To gain the adherence of an audience in a *reasonable* way (unreasonable, exploitative, ways of gaining audience-adherence for a thesis can be seen in the counterside of what is discussed), the argumentation must be contextually relevant (i.e., relevant to the audience in its particular context) and comprise premises that are acceptable to the particular audience *and* to the universal audience formed from it. The process involved will be demonstrated later. A proficient use of the notions of relevance and acceptability at work here requires an understanding of the *cognitive environment* of the audience, a further idea to be explored in this chapter.

4.1 Perelman's Relativism

Is Perelman committed to a relativism, and is this more generally characteristic of any rhetorical model of argumentation? It might help to avoid a direct answer to this question for the time being and ask instead about the nature of any relativism in question and what is unpalatable about it.

Frans H. van Eemeren and Rob Grootendorst write of the Perelmanian account:

> The consequences of this sociologically oriented approach is that argumentation that is sound in one case need not be so

in another. Its soundness depends on the criteria employed
by the audience that carries out the assessment. This means
that the standard of reasonableness is extremely relative.
(1995a:124)

It is not clear that this consequence need follow. Granted, the
quality of the argumentation will vary from context to context. This
is the consequence of a context-oriented model. But to insist that
"what is sound in one case need not be so in another" overlooks the
uniqueness of cases. If, quite hypothetically, two cases were identical
(in context: audience, locale, etc.) *then* the argumentation *would be*
sound or not in both. If the criticism is that the soundness should in-
here in the argumentation (presumably the PPC product) and not
the case, then we are no longer speaking about a rhetorical model.
Should the concern be that *bad* reasoning will be accepted in one case
and not in another case, then this overlooks the role of the universal
audience to reject bad reasoning in any case in which an appeal is
made to it.

Beyond this, there seems to be a deeper misunderstanding. To
charge that the "*standard* of reasonableness is extremely relative"
(italics mine) ignores the distinction between *the* standard of reasonableness in the model and the individual applications of that
standard. The standard of the universal audience as a standard of
reasonableness will be invoked in different ways for different audiences in different contexts. But the *exercise* of universalizing and
basing judgments of acceptability on the universalization remains
the same.

The aim of argumentation in this model is not the uncovering of
Truth (whatever might be meant by this term) but the eliciting or
strengthening of an audience's adherence to theses presented in the
argumentation. Even legal argumentation displays this characteristic, despite the presumption that its interest is in truth. Legal trials
determines not the truth, but which side has the most evidence in its
favor to overturn or to uphold the presumption of innocence assumed
under law (Oddie, 1991).

At the same time, we have seen that Chaim Perelman does not
eschew all notions of truth. Truth, on his terms, relates to the determinations of audiences; it is a product of argumentative situations,
open to scrutiny and to challenge. To proceed this way is to break
with any notion of an objective Truth that is the goal and condition
of argumentation. Such a notion of Truth demands the cessation of
argumentation.

In a lively defense of a relativism more extreme than that found in Perelman, Derek Edwards, Malcolm Ashmore and Jonathan Potter associate the maintenance of truths deemed certain with a religious domain rather than with a scientific one: "Truths become sacred objects, unfit for profane and corrosive inquiry, to be celebrated by incantation and propagated by conversion to the faith" (1995:40) Let's examine this idea further.

A striking case that serves to illustrate their point arises in the form of the so-called Rushdie affair and the *fatwa* proclaimed against the British author after the publication of his novel *The Satanic Verses* (1988). Deemed offensive to Muslims because of the way in which it portrayed the prophet and his wives, and even how the title invoked the lines allegedly expunged from the Qur'an after it was revealed to Muhammad that they were inspired by Satan, the novel set off a debate that disclosed the real distance between two major world cultures.

Rushdie is condemned because he has been judged to criticize what is held to be inviolable, the core of the Muslim faith. At stake is a Truth that will suffer no insult to its authority. This appears as an instance of Truth as "an evil idea" (Willard, 1989:121), where the tyranny of Truth prompts people to suppress and kill any who devalue it. But the case is more complex. The Rushdie affair is the occasion for a conflict of ideologies so alien to each other that there seems to be little ground on which to build a bridge of understanding.

"For Muslims, the very stability of society rests on the maintenance of proper belief and practice" (Easterman, 1992:98). But no less is the case with Western culture. Saturated in the "religion" of Liberalism, the foundations of Western societies cohere around values alien to the Muslim world. And Western behaviors and practices extend from those central values just as much as the Muslims' do from theirs. The Muslim lives out of an established Truth and moulds her or his behavior to conform to it. Individuality is not a value to be recognized or promoted. Free speech leads to an erosion of faith and is harmful. In the West, individualism and freedom of speech are the values that drive the machine toward a secular, scientific notion of Truth that is not preestablished.

The debate, then, is between two conceptions of Truth that cannot be recognized as instances of the same thing. Their similarity is only homonymous.[1] The debate is so explosive because it does not speak to incidental features of these cultures but to the very identity of their members. They understand themselves in terms of the societal values that define them.

The debate indicates the dangers inherent in a term like *Truth,* which can give expression to such dissimilar concepts. It serves further to indicate the importance of a rhetorical model of argumentation which, if it is to have any success, requires its proponents to understand such differences of concept as arise from the different audiences involved. The Rushdie affair was the occasion for considerable argumentation that did no more than repeat the doctrines of one or other of the two camps without ever penetrating the worldview of its (opposing) audience (see Appignanesi and Maitland, 1989). For rhetorical argumentation to be effective, it must *begin* from assumptions accepted by the audience, and this necessitates a prior appreciation of one's audience and the viewpoints involved.

There are respects, this suggests, in which relativism as a perspective is desirable. But relativism (like Truth) means different things to different people. This is particularly evident from the criticisms leveled against it.

There are a number of versions of relativism with corresponding critiques, not all of which are relevant here (cf. Margolis, 1990). At its most extreme it involves the questioning of *all* truths as claims, since the line "between the objectively and the constructedly real, between rocks and quarks, furniture and fascism" (Edwards, Ashmore, and Potter, 1995:39) is extremely unclear. The most serious criticisms are those that attribute an inconsistency to the relativist's position. I will consider three here.

Chief among the criticisms is the charge of total subjectivism captured in Protagoras' thesis that "man is the measure of all things, of the things that are, that they are so, and of the things that are not, that they are not" (*Theaetetus* 152a3–5). It is this sense of relativism that informs van Eemeren and Grootendorst's complaint against Perelman. What the thesis denies is the validity of objective truth. While Plato uses it to examine the relativity of perceptual impressions in the search for knowledge, it also expresses the rhetorical position that people will assess cases in different ways and do so reasonably, despite their differences (Billig, 1987:42). Simply put, it does not preclude agreement on what is the case. People from different perspectives can dispute the reasonableness of their judgments. The rhetorical perspective on argumentation facilitates this. As long as any position is assumed to hold the truth (even if that position has yet to be determined), the exercise of reasonable disputation is undermined. Criticism directed from a position of truth, or expected truth, will not value the strengths and weaknesses of people's proposals. Doctrines of the kind that envision Absolute Truth as Plato did may endorse this critical approach, but rhetorical models will not. Michael Billig makes just this point:

> On this earth we must conduct our measuring through argumentation, rather than hope to capture the silent vision which will end all argument. Plato may have dreamt of an end to argument, but in Protagoras' philosophy there is no escape from rhetoric. (1987:44)

A second, related, criticism is the charge that for relativists "anything goes," that they have no commitments, and were they to acquire any, they would be violating their own position. Often expressed as "naive relativism," anyone holding such a view would certainly appear to be naive. But the criticism takes on the appearance of a Straw Man. No relativism can escape the context of its deliberations (including the relativist thesis) and this context forms a natural constraint on what "goes." In this sense, relativism is not a denial of all "truths," since the context forms an underlying truth (cf. Feyerabend, 1987:79). What is at issue, again, is the terminology. If the objectivist or realist owns the only concept of "truth" that can have any currency, then the relativist does appear to be inconsistent, even self-refuting. The mistake is in assuming that "truth" has only this one sense. "Universalists then assume that self-proclaimed relativists are speaking within this absolute connotation of truth-talk" (Code, 1995:197).

A third criticism, appropriate to consider here given Perelman's motivations, is the charge of moral or political quietism. Unable to choose between equally "valid" perspectives, with everyone's views on par, the relativist is thought to be frozen in motion. On the contrary, given the diversity of opinions that can be put forward on a position, the relativist insists that the relative merits of each position also be put forward. The relativist's position advocates justification through argumentation. "Far from ruling out the possibility of justification of a particular view, relativism *insists upon it*. . . . Rather than merely defending relativism against accusations of moral dissolution, we assert its *moral and political strength*" (Edwards, Ashmore, and Potter, 1995:39).

Perelman's work particularly counters the third criticism. James Crosswhite (1995:140) defends Perelman's model against van Eemeren and Grootendorst's invocation of the "hobgoblin" of relativism by appealing to the deeply ethical motivations behind the new rhetoric. On one level, van Eemeren and Grootendorst may be right: people have the freedom to construct quite wild and useless universal audiences. But, as Crosswhite notes, "what claims do such private conceptions of universality have on anyone else?" And he continues:

> This is where the question of "relativism" might more appro-
> priately arise, and this is where Perelman's rhetorical theory
> of universality tries to establish the possibility of reason-
> ing—where people must imagine new ways of being audi-
> ences for one another's reasoning (more universal ways) in
> order to avoid violent fragmentation. This kind of moral
> imagination is the opposite of arbitrary choice. (141)

A charge that "anything goes" has no force against Perelman's position, and van Eemeren and Grootendorst's concern that the po-sition promotes undue subjectivism is misplaced. Nor, it should be clear, is Perelman's a position of quietism. The arguer who appeals to the universal audience shaves away the arbitrary and rests her or his case on the common concerns of actual communities. In the ap-peal to the universal audience, suggests Billig, Perelman's "practice of argumentation forbids any thorough-going relativism, for to enter argumentation is to leave absolute indifference behind. Only the complete sceptic would not bother to argue" (1991:26).

For Perelman, the reasonableness of an argument is not bound up in the truth or falsity of its conclusions. He recognizes the fact that human communities have, as a matter of common practice, ad-hered to theses that time subsequently proved to be wrong or in need of substantial revision. But this does not mean that the arguments that prompted the adherence to such theses were unreasonable. In the time and place of their occurrence, with the evidence available, such arguments were well-grounded and reasonably accepted. In fact, a rhetorical model of argumentation would have refused to take these theses as the Truth, no matter how well grounded, but would have held them open for scrutiny and revision.

Philosophical reasoning, Perelman reminds us, is by nature con-troversial. It is free from coercive constraints and thus implies the philosopher's freedom and responsibility. Thus, the criteria, values, and norms of philosophy are not absolute values and truths, but ex-press the convictions of that free individual "engaged in a creative, personal, and historically situated effort: that of proposing to the uni-versal audience as he sees it, a number of acceptable theses. . . . Aware of his limitations, the philosopher knows his efforts will not produce a definitive and complete work" (1967:85–86).

The philosopher proposes acceptable theses, and in doing so looks to justify those theses or to show that no justification is required. We need to consider, then, the notion or notions of "acceptability" at work in a rhetorical model. To gain the adherence of the audience for the theses, the argumentation must be acceptable. This involves both the particular audience, who occasions the discourse, and the universal audience constructed from it—the concern of Perelman's philosopher.

In order to explore acceptability, we must first look at the more basic criterion of adherence that underlies it—that of relevance. We must examine here the sense of contextual-relevance that elsewhere I call audience-relevance (Tindale, 1992, 1994). The argumentation must be relevant to the particular audience. Insofar as this is the case, the argumentation will also be relevant to the universal audience, since the latter is drawn from the particular audience. That is, as has been stressed, the universal audience is the universalization of the particular *in its context*.

4.2 Relevance and Cognitive Environments

In chapter 1, I drew a distinction between two types of relevance important to argumentation. The first is what can be called premise-relevance. Discussions of relevance in informal logic textbooks are invariably restricted to this sense. It involves the relations of relevance that exist internally among the components of an argument-as-product in its PPC structure. For example, a premise (P) is relevant to a claim (C) if it acts upon the claim so as to increase or decrease our reasons for holding that claim.

The second sense, which I illustrated through examining informal logic treatments of the Straw Man argument, I called contextual relevance.[2] It involves the relevance of the PPC product to its underlying context.

Joseph Wenzel W., discussing relevance from a rhetorical perspective, views it "as a pragmatic relationship between the materials of argument and the situation, that is, to the complex of persons, events, objects, relations, exigencies, and constraints that an arguer seeks to encompass" (1989:89). This is very much what I have in mind in what follows, where the "materials of argument" are understood in a broad way to refer to content and structure. In fact, the sense of contextual relevance that I identified in chapter 1 would be further designated as topic-relevance. It involves the relation of the argument to the topic or issue. Hence, we can see how the Straw Man falls within the domain of topic-relevance (and *not* premise-relevance). But topic-relevance does not exhaust contextual relevance. Of greater significance, and setting the conditions for a full understanding of the other two (premise- and topic-relevance) is what I shall call audience-relevance. This involves the relation of the information-content of an argument, stated and assumed, to the framework of beliefs and commitments that are likely to be held by the audience for which it is intended. In concentrating upon this third type of relevance, I will eventually show how it underlies the other two.

Some of the recent work that has concentrated upon or had implications for a theory of relevance in argumentation (e.g., Blair:1989; Berg:1991; and Woods and Hudak:1989) has indicated that it is appropriate to look beyond the argument-as-product when making judgments about its relevance. J. Anthony Blair's work, to focus on one of these projects, with its developed interest in relevance warrants, is particularly useful in showing this. He refers to relevance as a function of a premise's relation to a premise set (1989:72), and then, more importantly, its relation to an audience. This last point is not as explicit as it might be, but arises from a number of the comments made. Relevance warrants, for instance, are directed at audiences; designed to demonstrate the relevance of premises that have been challenged. When trying to convince others of a claim an arguer "will often supply (among other things) sets of premises which she believes the audience will find relevant" (77). Later the importance of extrastructural matters in judgments of relevance is further indicated when Blair writes that the relevance of a consideration will vary according to circumstance or may be relevant on one criterion but not another "depending on the beliefs of the reasoners" (80). All of this moves us further from simply looking at the relation of premises to conclusions within an argument. A final example given illustrates what interests us here. When "Hetta is a woman" is offered as a premise for the conclusion "Hetta should not get the job," then if the job is driving a taxi, the premise is relevant to the conclusion if the job is in Saudi Arabia, where women are prevented from driving, but irrelevant in Canada, where job discrimination on the basis of sex is illegal.

Blair's account of premise relevance takes him beyond his announced topic of "the relevance of premises of arguments to their conclusions" and thus serves as a helpful entry for my discussion of audience-relevance. The references to the beliefs and tolerances of audiences leads us to consider the environments in which audiences assess arguments and make their judgments of relevance. To discuss these environments I will draw on a theory of relevance grounded in context. I have in mind here Dan Sperber and Deidre Wilson's notion of a "cognitive environment" as it arises in their theory of relevance (1986; Blakemore, 1992) and ways in which the ideas involved can be applied to argumentation.

While Sperber and Wilson claim not to be trying to define the ordinary English word "relevance," their attempts to provide scientific psychology with a concept close to the ordinary language notion of relevance amounts to something very similar. They are concerned with the role that relevance plays in human communication, and consequently turn to human communication to illuminate the nature of "relevance." Of interest here are the claims made about human cognition and the cognitive environment. Human cognition, they insist, is relevance-oriented (1986:46). Consequently, anyone who knows an individual's cognitive environment can infer what that individual is likely to consider. From this they can draw their main thesis: "that an act of ostension carries a guarantee of relevance, and that this fact—which we will call the *principle of relevance*—makes manifest the intention behind the ostension" (50).

Sperber and Wilson are suspicious of such catchphrases as "mutual knowledge" and "shared information," which they find vague. Although we may share a physical environment, our differences seem to preclude any further generalizations about us: we represent the world differently, they claim, and our perceptual and inferential abilities vary; we possess different belief structures through which we understand the world, and quite different sets of memories. So although our physical environment may be the same, what they call our cognitive environment would be different for each of us (38). To clarify how I am employing the notion of a cognitive environment, I offer six statements that can be made about the concept or ideas related to it. In these statements I extrapolate from what Sperber and Wilson say, but do not, I hope, misconstrue their meaning.

1. *A cognitive environment is a set of facts manifest to us.*

This is explained by adopting a Platonic analogy between visual and intellectual perception. Each of us sees in a visible environment which is the set of all phenomena visible to us. Aspects of our visible environment may go unnoticed until required in some way. Then when we are asked, for example, "what is the color of X's shirt?" or "how many people are in the room?" we can provide the information. Corresponding to this visible environment is a cognitive environment that is the set of all the facts manifest to each of us, which we can perceive or infer. "A fact is *manifest* to an individual at a given time if and only if he is capable at that time of representing it mentally and accepting its representation as true or probably true" (39). This will include both immediate perception and memory.

2. *Our cognitive environments differ.*

This is primarily because, while the physical environment is shared, our cognitive abilities, like our visible abilities, are distinct. One way in which this is important is that we will differ in our ability to infer other facts from those we directly perceive. Memory will also come into play here, since knowledge previously acquired affects our ability to work with a present set of facts. And additional considerations are the ways in which we differ in terms of interests, perspectives, and expectations. From such suggestions, it would seem that our cognitive environments are perhaps too unique to enable us to employ the idea in argumentative contexts. The fourth statement will speak to this.

3. *Cognitive environments include assumptions, which may be incorrect.*

As first defined, a cognitive environment involves manifest facts that may be represented as what is the case or what is probably the case. In extending what is manifest to cover assumptions, we are able to include what may turn out to be incorrect. Assumptions may not at first be distinguished from what is known, and may later be confirmed or deemed mistaken. It is likely that at any time we hold mistaken ideas; ones that we have not investigated fully, but for which we have sufficient evidence to hold them, ideas about the nature of relevance, for example. As Sperber and Wilson point out, "something can be manifest without being known . . . if only because something can be manifest and false, whereas nothing can be known and false" (40).

4. *Overlapping cognitive environments give rise to a shared cognitive environment (with mutual manifestness).*

The idea of a shared cognitive environment replaces that of "mutual knowledge" or "shared information." The same facts and assumptions can be manifest in the cognitive environments of two people. This is because they not only share a physical environment but also have similar cognitive abilities. However, because of such factors as their different memories, they can never share a total cognitive environment. But insofar as their cognitive environments intersect, then that intersection is a cognitive environment. And Sperber and Wilson clearly understand that such cognitive environments can be shared by multiples of people, giving as one of their examples Freemasons.

A cognitive environment in which it is manifest which people share it is a *mutual cognitive environment*. Freemasons share a mutual cognitive environment. As individuals they are essentially different, but there is an overlap in that certain facts and assumptions, within a shared physical environment, are manifest to them. They may not make the same assumptions, but it is possible for them to do so. Mutual manifestness, then, is weak in the right sense, since a claim that an assumption is mutually manifest will not be a claim about actual states or processes but about cognitive environments.

5. *The boundaries of cognitive environments are always imprecise.*

One reason for this is that there is no clear demarcation between weakly manifest assumptions and inaccessible ones. When we share a cognitive environment with others, we know what assumptions are mutually manifest to us all. This is indirect evidence, probable in nature. We do not know what assumptions people actually make unless they tell us or act in ways that clearly indicate them. Where the boundaries arise between individuals' overlapping cognitive environments is difficult to determine unless we know a lot about them and, in particular, their specific memories. But in determining and assessing cognitive environments as these relate to argumentation, we are interested in the environment of an audience and judgments we can make about that. Whether certain people belong to certain audiences, particularly as audiences grow in size, is beyond our concern at this juncture.

We can talk, for example, of a general memory without worrying about whether certain individuals share in that memory. We ought to expect people to remember major events of a local, national, or international nature: the waging of wars, the impeachment and assassination of political figures, events of human achievement, and human failure. That such facts are mutually manifest to us allows us to make determinations about cognitive environments without making determinations about any one person's mental processes. The person who denies the historical fact of the Holocaust or that human beings have landed on the moon, is a different case, though. They hold assumptions not shared by others. But we would want to say that the incorrectness of these assumptions could be inferred from the facts that are manifest to them.

6. *Our ideas about mutual manifestness clarify our ideas about common knowledge.*

In fact, they supplant them. This point follows from the discussion of Statement 5. The account of mutual manifestness emphasizes something of which most argumentation theorists are well aware but fail to accommodate in their work: that we do not know what is *known* in common by others; that we do not know what is mutually *known*. We do not even know what is mutually *assumed*. But we do know that we share environments in which facts, information, and assumptions are readily accessible. We are constantly made aware of this through the common concerns, attitudes, and restricted vocabularies that characterize the different spheres of our lives, whether they be of work, political associations, cultural groups, or national interests, to name some of the key spheres. And we can judge what people could possibly come to hold by virtue of their sharing in those environments.

In spite of what we know, we invariably use the apparent misnomer "Common Knowledge" either loosely or in ways that imply no more than mutual manifestness, but without its degree of clarity. Witness Copi: "Included in context is what is called 'common knowledge'. For example, it is common knowledge that society has not yet finally settled matters of justice and retribution" (1986:32). There is no clear way of testing whether this is commonly known, although people certainly act as if such a "fact" were not manifest to them. The same "unknowableness" haunts supposedly illustrative examples like this one from Little, Groarke, and Tindale: "Neurosurgeons earn higher incomes than high school teachers" (1989:203). Again, Govier explains that common knowledge means "if the premise states something that is known to virtually everyone . . . or if a premise is very widely believed" (1988:79).

It is closer to experience to realize with Sperber and Wilson that human beings operate in situations where "a great deal can be assumed about what is manifest to others, a lot can be assumed about what is mutually manifest to themselves and others, but nothing can be assumed to be truly mutually known or assumed" (1986:45). Our struggles with the problematic "common knowledge" also seem to be unnecessary since the adoption of mutual cognitive environments gives us all the information we need when assessing information in relation to audiences.

To summarize what has been said about this concept: a cognitive environment is a set of facts and assumptions that an individual, or, in the case of shared cognitive environments, a number of individuals, is capable of mentally representing and accepting as true (although they may be mistaken in doing so). We focus upon the environments, not upon the individuals (or audiences). And these environments tell us nothing about what people know or assume, but about what they could be expected to know or assume. As we will see, this idea of a cognitive environment is valuable for understanding audience-relevance.

In direct communication, of which arguing is a form, there is a presumption of relevance. J. Anthony Blair seems in agreement on this point. He concludes that "[p]remises are presumed relevant until challenged or questioned" (1989:81). Sperber and Wilson (1986: 50,156) make the claim explicitly, influenced as they are by Paul Grice.[3] Grice's "Cooperative Principle" clearly pertains to argumentative concerns. Arguers, as communicators, have a vested interest in ensuring the components of their arguments include all that is required to affect the desired purpose of the activity. Accordingly, relevance is a critical requirement and Grice's maxim "Be relevant" a central maxim (1989:27). Unfortunately, it is the vaguest of his four maxims.

To a great extent, the introduction of the cognitive environment addresses the difficulty of applying Grice's relevance maxim. When we present an argument to an audience, we not only attempt to alter their cognitive environments, but hope further to alter their actual thought processes: to bring them to hold what we have introduced to the cognitive environment to make manifest to them. The first intention, utilizing the cognitive environment, is a matter of relevance (particularly audience-relevance); the second intention, convincing the audience in light of the alteration of the environment, is a matter of the acceptability of the argumentation that has been used to do so. The success of the latter, however, depends upon our success in the former task: the altering of the cognitive environment. This presupposes that we have a fair idea of that cognitive environment in order to "be relevant" to it and to its content. We "are relevant" insofar as we take into consideration this environment of the audience and construct our argument so that it relates to its features; this is not inconsistent with any of the facts made manifest there, and can generally be understood in terms of what is already available to the audience.

In the context of analogical reasoning, John Woods and Brent Hudak propose that something is relevant for an arguer "when, or by the extent to which, it changes his mind with respect to some fixed issue (1989:32)." In a more fundamental sense, I would suggest, something is relevant if it relates to a cognitive environment so as to create the *possibility* of that change. To require change is too strong a demand for relevance. Unsuccessful argumentation can still be relevant, but fail to gain an audience's adherence for what it makes manifest due to the unacceptability of some of its statements. The arguer intends to make manifest a set of assumptions and must do this in a way that makes it mutually manifest to both audience and communicator that the set of assumptions is intended.

These assumptions, or any one of their number, are relevant if they modify or improve the environmental context by providing further evidence for old assumptions, or evidence against old assumptions. That is, the premises actively affect what is made manifest in the cognitive environment so as to make manifest further assumptions. This would be a relevant altering of the cognitive environment. In addition, where *new* ideas are being presented to an audience and argued for, audience-relevance would require that as much as possible of the information being given in support of those ideas be related to (relevant to) assumptions that we know are manifest in that audience's cognitive environment. This must occur even when audiences are introduced to a new body of information. When the physics professor first confronts a freshman class, she expects that certain things are manifest to the class. One of these is the professor's own authority as a knowledgeable person, the recognition of which serves as a warrant (in Blair's sense) for the relevance of the information disseminated. In addition to this, the professor assumes as manifest a set of facts that is a prerequisite for the level of study the class has reached, and tries to introduce the new ideas in relation to those facts. These facts include those with which students are expected to be familiar, although individual students may have gaps in their backgrounds that prevent them from grasping the relevance of some of the professor's remarks.[4]

Diane Blakemore, who follows Sperber and Wilson in her presentation of pragmatics, employs a number of insightful examples. In these, the inferences a hearer makes depend not on the words uttered (the propositions) but on her knowledge of the world (i.e., contextual information). Here, we might observe, contextual relevance has priority over propositional relevance. She goes on to note that "assumptions derived through direct observation are held with a very strong conviction" (1992:14–15). This is contrasted with the strength of an assumption derived as the result of the interpretation of an utterance, which depends on the confidence the hearer has in the speaker. That is, in terms I introduced earlier, the ethotic element is important here. Contextual effect, or the prompting of inferences, is strongest through direct observation, and then through the interpretation of an utterance *combined with* trust in the speaker (ethos).

Inferences are drawn where the information is relevant to the cognitive environment. That is, where it has contextual effect (Sperber and Wilson, 1986:108–9). There are three important ways to see this: (a) it allows a conclusion (contextual implication) to be derived; (b) it provides evidence to strengthen an assumption; and (c) it contradicts an existing assumption (Blakemore, 1992:30,137–38). In each case, new information may be introduced into the cognitive environment, just as each can be instrumental in causing adherence to a thesis.

Audience-relevance, then, requires this type of effect. If a premise or argument has contextual effect, then it is relevant to the audience. It seems to me now that several things can be said about relevance *in this sense:*

1. First, and most obviously, insofar as audiences share cognitive environments, then the relevance of a statement can vary depending on the audience. In these terms the relevance of a statement is literally a relation and certainly not a property of the statement. For example, if the statement "The Roman Catholic Church does not endorse the use of contraceptives" is advanced in support of a claim that "University students' health plans should not subsidize birth control pills," then it is likely to have a real contextual effect in the cognitive environment of Catholic university students, while none at all in that of non-Catholics. For the former audience we would judge it relevant: it makes manifest to them further assumptions that they could grasp. For the latter audience, we would not judge it relevant.

2. Secondly, irrelevant premises can be made relevant through the addition of premises that have contextual effect (these may involve hidden premises, which I will discuss under point 4). I believe Blair's relevance warrants can work in this way, if they clarify the relevance of a challenged premise by providing supplementary information. Consider this example from Trudy Govier (1988):

P: Children who have a long bus ride to school often arrive at school rather tired and restless.

C: We may expect that children who have a long bus ride to school will achieve lower grades than children who are able to walk to a neighbourhood school.

Given that walking can be as tiring as riding, the relation between riding and low academic performance is not obvious. Additional premises would improve the relation. "Students who walk to school are not tired and restless" would seem to be a candidate here.

Or "Children who have long bus rides get on average an hour less sleep a night than those who walk to school." It also seems that the more relevant information given, the greater the likelihood of some contextual effect taking place. In each case, of course, the contextual effect is determined according to the audience involved.

3. Associated with this is a third suggestion, although a contentious one: that premises or premise sets can have strong or weak relevance by degrees. For example, these additional premises increase the support the initial premise lends to the conclusion. On its own each of these may have weak relevance in that they introduce into a cognitive environment assumptions from which implications can be drawn. The introduction of facts may constitute a strongly relevant reason (e.g., "There is no other difference between the two groups of students"), or, in the strongest relevant sense, allow members of the audience to deduce a certain conclusion, as in the two-premise set: P1 "Children who ride the bus to school are tired and restless" and P2 "Tiredness and restlessness negatively affect academic performance."

What is contentious about this is that it does not seem to be degrees of relevance that is at stake but sufficiency of evidence. From such a point of view, relevance appears to be an all-or-nothing matter. I remain unconvinced of this, although it has plausibility. Granted, if it is just a matter of adding more information through the addition of more premises, as in a general induction, then the criterion in question is indeed that of sufficiency. Yet on the other hand, we certainly speak of some premises being more relevant than others, and behind this "way of talking" may be a genuine recognition that one premise relates to more manifest material in a cognitive environment than does another. When the physics professor uses an example to illustrate a point, the more of the audience's background material that is encompassed by the example, the greater its likely effect, and therefore its degree of relevance. A minor example making use of less background material may be less effective.

4. A fourth and final point that I want to make here concerns hidden premises.[5] Previously (with Gough [1985]), I have suggested that when we set out the structure of others' arguments we are looking not for what is missing from the discourse, but for what is hidden or unstated. But the advice given for drawing out the hidden premises, while, I think, important in its focus, is alarmingly vague. It amounts to several admonitions to check, work with, and stay true to, the context. I am now in a position to say more useful things about this in relation to what we are recognizing as a central aspect of the context.

We can begin by stressing the fact that we have good reason to state that arguers are predisposed to relevance. It seems reasonable to agree with Blair (1989) (and by implication with Sperber and Wilson [1986], and with Grice [1989]) that an arguer intends her or his premises to be relevant to the conclusion. (They may not be relevant, of course, but it is the intention that is important here.) I would go further and say that he or she intends the premises to be relevant to the cognitive environment of the audience. So the first pointer for suspecting a hidden premise would be that a stated premise does not appear relevant. We then have a framework for assessing candidates for the hidden premise. When we have some of these candidates, we need to be sure we are attributing to the arguer statements that he or she is reasonably likely to hold. Having an awareness of her or his cognitive environment (not mental processes) puts us in an excellent position to make such judgments. We know many of the facts and assumptions that are manifest to the arguer, and therefore what he or she could assume or infer. Furthermore, if we are aware of the *mutual* cognitive environment that the arguer and audience shares, then we are in an even better position for testing candidate statements for the status of a hidden premise (or conclusion).

An example of this can be drawn from an illustration used by Sperber and Wilson (1986:121). A flag seller asks a passerby to buy a flag for the Royal National Lifeboat Institution (RNLI). The passerby declines because he always spends his holidays with his sister in Birmingham. His retort could be recast in a PPC form:

P: I always spend my holidays with my sister in Birmingham.

C: I cannot be expected to subscribe to the RNLI.

For the seller to understand the relevance of the premise to the conclusion certain facts and assumptions must be manifest to her, from which the implication of a hidden premise or two would follow. Facts: (a) Birmingham is inland; (b) The RNLI is a charity. Assumptions: (c) Someone who spends his holidays inland has no need of the services of the RNLI; (d) Someone who has no need of the services of a charity cannot be expected to subscribe to that charity.

Either (c) or (d), or both, can be drawn out as hidden premises to supply the relevant link from premise to conclusion. The second of these (d), being controversial, is an important hidden premise to state. But if the flag seller is unable to grasp the context, she will not see the relevance of the premise to the conclusion. The same could hold for someone evaluating the argument.

The discussion of relevance and cognitive environments, then, helps enormously to give some form to the concept of "context" when determining an argument's hidden components. Beyond the detection of hidden argument components, this example further illustrates how premise-relevance is grounded in contextual-relevance; that premise-relevance cannot be fully determined without some recourse to the context. The logician who restricts the assessment of relevance to the relation between premise and conclusion has not told the full story on relevance in that piece of argumentation.

Audience-relevance, as I have explained it, requires that a premise or argument be related to what an individual or group's cognitive environment makes manifest. It does not demand that the individual or members of the group actually grasp what is made manifest, only that they are capable of doing so. If we recognize that communication is inherently risky, that we often fail to communicate completely (or at all), then there is less reason to expect a fail-safe procedure for determining relevance.

What does follow from the preceding discussion is that audience-relevance is prior to both of the other types that I already have identified. Topic-relevance explicitly relates to aspects of content, but these aspects themselves would be in part determined by the cognitive environments, shared or not, of those involved. Premise-relevance, in the restricted sense of whether a premise makes a difference to its conclusion, is now deeply affected by its status in a context, as a product of an arguer and a commodity for an appraiser. Premise-relevance, as the lifeboat example illustrates, is subordinate to audience-relevance if only because we do not reason in a vacuum, but also because we cannot ever fully wrestle the products of reasoning from the process (and processors). But whether a premise serves as a good reason for a claim is another matter. Relevance is only part of the story of good argumentation. To complete the picture we turn now to questions of acceptability and to the central role of the universal audience.

4.3 Acceptability

Relevance is not enough. Argumentation that is relevant to an audience bears on the cognitive environment with its (the argument's) potential to modify that environment. Argumentation that is irrelevant to the audience will leave their cognitive environment unaffected. They will not recognize the argumentation as being *for them.*

Thus, in a fundamental sense, failure to be relevant will result in a failure to be effective and the argumentation will be considered poor.

But the relevance of the argumentation to the audience does not guarantee their adherence to the claims conveyed through it. Relevant argumentation may fail to gain adherence for a thesis because the statements, say, express values recognized by the audience but not wholly endorsed by them, or they are supported by authorities that the audience does not recognize.

The provision of acceptable argumentation is complicated by the fact that the appeal is to the whole person, rather than just to the intellect or emotion. Consequently, as Perelman reminds us, depending on the circumstances, the argumentation will use methods appropriate to the purpose of the discourse and the audience to be influenced. This, as we have understood from the outset, allows for free-ranging possibilities. Although my discussion of relevance has used examples of PPC arguments, what is to be included under "rhetorical argument" cannot be determined in advance of future argumentative situations or exhaustively cataloged. The force of the rhetorical perspective can be best seen through its use in the analysis of examples and in its applications to related problems. Subsequent chapters will be devoted to filling out the perspective. Still, there is a fundamental piece of advice offered that can be explored in relation to acceptability. It too comes courtesy of Perelman: "The only general advice that a theory of argumentation can give is to ask speakers to adapt themselves to their audiences" (1982:13).

The usefulness of the notion of cognitive environments extends to the adjudication of acceptable argumentation. Just as the notion helps to determine the relevance of argumentation, so resort to the cognitive environment of the particular audience assists us in considering what that audience will accept. As a general rule, logicians are fond of pointing out that there is a presumption in favor of common knowledge.[6] As I have already discussed, "common knowledge" turns out to be a problematic idea, primarily because we cannot be sure (as arguers or evaluators) what people actually know, individually or together, and individuals can always claim that they did not know what everyone else knew. Appealing to the cognitive environment of the audience allows us to look instead at what they can be *expected* to know given the information and ideas that are readily available to them. That individual members of an audience have not "processed" what was manifest to them and formed the related beliefs is not, on this front, a problem. Given the diversity of membership possible within an audience, appeal to the cognitive environment is weak in just the right way to further the goals of argumentation. Otherwise, arguers would be forced to encumber their reasoning with layers of unnecessary argumentation covering matters which, in fact, would never be contested by the particular audience *in general*.

Billig (1987:196–97; 1991:144) prefers to speak of a community's "common sense." This comprises a community's values and maxims.

> The link between the orator and the audience rests upon more than a sharing of argumentative forms. It also comprises a common content. If orators are identifying with their audiences, then they are emphasizing communal links, foremost among which are shared values or beliefs. The concept of common-sense (*sensus communis*) might be a helpful one for discussing this communal content. The orator, in identifying with the beliefs of the audience, will be treating the audience as a community bound together by shared opinions. (1987:196)

Illustrating the point with references to Allport's tolerant American and Gorgias's appeals to Hellenic national pride, Billig observes that the arguer/orator would not feel the need to justify such beliefs to the respective audiences. There is a presumption in favor of such appeals, *if* they correctly address what is commonly believed. Knowledge of the audience, and, in our terms, particularly the cognitive environment of the audience, increases the likelihood of such appeals being correct. In such cases, it is reasonable to assume that argumentative statements expressing or depending upon such beliefs will be acceptable to the particular audience such that the burden of proof lies with any who would suggest otherwise.

Generally, then, there will be a presumption in favor of the acceptability of argumentation constructed in this way. Here the context, with the cognitive environment of the audience at its center, is a primary determinant, along with the arguer's recognition of that context.

Such recourse to audiences and to their own standards of acceptance raises not only the specter of relativism just discussed but the more serious problem of allowing what intuitively seems impermissible when we look beyond the restricted interests of specific audiences. We encountered this in the last chapter when discussing Douglas N. Walton's view of the *ad populum,* and here it needs more attention. Are we committed to finding acceptable the statements of the racist when his like-minded audience approves of them? When an audience does not see the sleight of hand involved, or raises no objections, should we allow the questionable reasoning of an arguer? These questions point to a serious problem, identified in the introduction and again in chapter 1. This is the need for objective standards. The point is itself implied by the reference to "questionable reasoning," because to whom is it questionable? If we are prepared to extend to individual audiences carte blanche authority to set the standards of acceptability, then we fall prey to the vicissitudes of popularity that have plagued argumentation theory, primarily in the form of *ad populum* arguments (cf. Chap. 3). As a response to this problem, the role of the universal audience is crucial.

In the *Eudemian Ethics,* Aristotle echoes the sentiments of Plato's Socrates in asserting that "neither need we examine the views of the many; they speak in an unreflective way on almost any topic" (1.3.1214b-1215a). If we are inquiring after something in which the many have no interest, then this can be granted; but if we are aiming to convince the many or to understand their perspective, then we ignore their views at our peril. As has been stressed earlier, the successful arguer (where success is measured by the ability to bring about an audience's adherence to a thesis) must begin with premises that are acceptable to the audience and move them, through perspicacious reasoning, to a claim that they did not hold but will now have reason to hold. To be successful, it should again be stressed, the arguer must have some idea of the beliefs likely to be held by her or his audience in order to construct those initial premises. The serious study of argumentation compels a serious interest in the doxastic states of audiences and epistemology generally.

4.4 Blair and Johnson's Community of Model Interlocutors

Before turning to the role that the universal audience plays in addressing this problem, we can benefit from the insights associated with a competing proposal mentioned earlier in the chapter. This is Blair and Johnson's community of model interlocutors. While this is similar to the universal audience in many basic ways, the main point of contrast between the two serves to demonstrate the value of Perelman's proposal.

Blair and Johnson's community of model interlocutors exists in order to generate standards of appraisal. On their thinking, argumentation, if it is to be rational, must be addressed to "the community of interlocutors who hold well-informed beliefs about the subject under discussion" (1987:50). This is to turn away from the specific and immediate audience with its prejudicial beliefs to the more ideal, hence model, audience that holds only well-informed beliefs. This model audience may in fact be nonexistent but serves as a standard of assessment in the way in which we might test a student's submitted work against a general notion of what it ought to be like to be passable.

As a theoretical model, the community of model interlocutors is highly accomplished. Its members possess the required background knowledge, are reflective and good discriminators, are open, unprejudiced and willing to modify their beliefs, and in knowing what to look for they are dialectically astute. What is particularly noteworthy about this model is surely that it works to the degree that the evaluator using it approximates its characteristics. Thus, an evaluator must decide for a particular premise how an unprejudiced open audience would judge it. To do this the evaluator needs to imaginatively adopt such a perspective.

The community of model interlocutors guides the evaluator, suggesting steps for the evaluation itself. But it is also distanced from the evaluator, its characteristics are maximums of reasonableness, and thus debates are likely to arise about the evaluations themselves over and above discussions of the premises.

The community of model interlocutors operates in a way that shows it does not have a fixed membership. A group of model interlocutors exists for each premise, sometimes admitting experts on the subject matter in question. This group will be limited in what it knows by the contexts and standards of the day. And it will contain all relevant perspectives, hence the requirement for a community. Blair and Johnson write:

> In general, then, we are proposing that a premise in an argument is acceptable without defense just in case a person following the methods and embodying the traits of the pertinent community of ideal interlocutors would fail to raise a question or doubt about it. (53)

In fact, as noted, the person evaluating the premise must judge that the ideal community would accept it. Success, then, depends on the ability of the evaluator to construct the appropriate ideal community and to make the judgment that such a community would raise no question. And this is viewed independent from (although in some cases related to) the specific audience to which the premise is addressed. All this requires a developed and sophisticated mind. And remember, when we argue we start with premises *our* audience finds acceptable in order to establish a common ground from which to reason to our claim. If the criteria for assessing the acceptability of such premises is that of the community of model interlocutors, then we may be hard-pressed to establish that common ground. For Blair and Johnson (55), the purpose of argumentation is now to persuade the community of model interlocutors to accept the claim. If I am to consider this as an arguer, then as I write for and to this ideal audience, there is a distinct possibility that I will lose touch with the audience in front of me.

4.5 The Universal Audience Again

It is probably unnecessary to note the many similarities between Blair and Johnson's community of model interlocutors and the universal audience of Perelman and L. Olbrechts-Tyteca. More instructive is the key dissimilarity. This appears in the common ground that exists between the particular and universal audiences. The universal audience is not a model of ideal competence introduced into the argumentative situation from the outside. It is developed *out of* the particular audience and so is essentially connected to it. Despite the merits and usefulness of Blair and Johnson's proposal, the gap it demands between its ideal audience and the immediate audience of the argument makes it an unattractive model for a rhetorical approach to argumentation.

As Perelman repeatedly reminds us, we cannot evaluate argumentation independent of the audience for which it was intended.[7] Understanding the particular audience takes us only so far in this task; resorting to the universal audience completes it.

In constructing the universal audience for an argument, we do not give up effectiveness. On the other hand, the universal audience, as a representation of reasonableness in the context, cannot value effectiveness over reasonableness. In this way manipulation is ruled out. Where scrutiny discovers it, the perspective of the universal audience rejects it, and the arguer who thinks in these terms will not use it.

Members of the particular audience still retain their perspectives and prejudices, but they do not let them rule what they realize is reasonable. Rather, they distance themselves from their own prejudices in judging their universal elements. Crosswhite captures what is involved in this:

> [P]ollsters have pretty well established that California voters are racist, that they vote for or against candidates on the basis of race. In constructing a universal audience of California voters, one would reject this characteristic. And my guess is that California voters would see the reason in this— they would say, yes, race is a factor in how we vote, but we recognize that in some important sense it probably shouldn't be, and that political argumentation shouldn't make appeals of this sort. (1989:164)

A key test in this is whether something can be universalized without contradiction. If it cannot, it must be rejected (or not included in the argumentation). Fallacies count as contradictions of this sort, recognized as such by the reasonable element *within* audiences. The passions of the racist also fall into this category of contradictory elements. Of course, the racist himself, as well as most of his audience, may not recognize this, but the evaluator will, and now he has a clear *reason* for why such statements should be rejected.

In all of this the universal audience is not a community of experts transported into the argumentation to adjudicate it. Rather, we are addressing the reasonableness of real people, able to distance themselves and to see beyond their perspectives.[8]

The actual construction of universal audiences from particular ones can take a number of forms. Crosswhite (1989) catalogs several *techniques* for doing so, depending upon the context and audience involved. These include bracketing out all of the features of an audience that attach to its particularity to try to reduce it to the common elements that unify its members. Alternatively, one can adopt the technique of identifying the "highest" or most reasonable elements within the audience, excluding those that are clearly unreasonable. Again, though, these things are determined in terms of the particular audience itself. Should it include members who ignore experience, or who won't allow two sides of an issue to be heard, or who cut off the opposition from responding, then these elements can be excluded, because, reason would recognize, such people would not allow others to do the same things to them.

A further technique is to imagine the audience distributed across time. For the argument whose force can be considered "timeless" has always been associated with what is universal. If something works beyond the confines of its occurrence, then this counts in its favor.[9]

Beyond assisting in the evaluation of the argumentation and acting as a check against the particular audience having free reign in deciding what is acceptable, the use of the universal audience produces several other results of significance.

1. To construct a universal audience for an argument and audience rooted in a particular context is to raise *a series of questions* against the reasoning involved. The satisfactory answering of such questions indicates the quality of that reasoning. What questions are appropriate and when will depend on the contexts involved. The case studies of the next chapter will provide opportunities for illustrating such points.

2. The universal audience sifts through the various ways of *seeing* the argument to arrive at that which is most reasonable. With this decision the particular audience would be in agreement. Argumentation is rooted in agreement, not disagreement: the arguer constructs her or his argumentation on the basis of statements with which the particular audience would agree; the universal audience is drawn in part from the agreements of the particular audience and expects to be confirmed by it; and the aim of the argumentation as developed is to elicit agreement for the theses it advances. This version of the argument that is brought forward from the various perspectives in the particular audience and their different ways of reading the argumentation amounts to the salvaging of the logicians' PPC product. But rather than reading this product onto the argumentative situation, it is arrived at from beneath, as it were, drawn from the varied views of the immediate audience and concretized in the move of reasonableness that the universal audience represents. Still, this agreement of a PPC is not a fact, but is imagined by the arguer/evaluator. Thus, as with other models, there is still room for a dispute of what constitutes *the* argument. And unlike with other approaches, alternative versions are not discarded but still held for consideration during the process of evaluation.

The goal here, it is worth remembering, is *reasonable* argumentation, not the *correct* application of *rules* in pursuit of truths. Given that the universal audiences represent the reasonableness of the argumentation, we may find debates arising about the universal audiences that are proposed and about the results of using them. Crosswhite makes just this point:

> There is another kind of deliberation in which one explores the differences between two conflicting concepts of a universal audience—for example, in the situation of a genuine moral dilemma. This kind of exploratory discourse often takes the form of a dialogue, question and answer, in which each interlocutor aims to uncover hitherto neglected agreements. Such "dialogue" can also take place in self-deliberation. The ultimate goal of this dialogue is to uncover agreements significant enough to yield a new, probably more general, universal audience. (1989:167)

3. A final point of significance to note is that constructing the universal audience involves considering the reasonable in each case, in each argumentation. We do not, to repeat, impose a conception of the reasonable onto the argumentation, but rather we look for it there. Producing and evaluating argumentation involves learning about what is reasonable, rethinking it, adding to it, and taking from it. The development of the reasonable is an ongoing project. In fact, it is the project of human development. We do not transport in a notion of reasonableness. We describe it; we do not prescribe it.

4.6 Preliminary Examples

Among the many things that concern argumentation theorists are the principal exercises of argument evaluation and construction. Preliminary examples of each will illustrate some of the principles discussed in this chapter and set the stage for the more extensive studies of the next chapter.

We might first consider the case of the Kuwaiti babies torn from their incubators by Iraqi troops after the invasion of Kuwait in August of 1990.[10] This alleged incident is considered by many to have been critical to the argumentation used to persuade the Senate and the American people to enter into a war with Iraq in January of 1991.

Those arguing for military engagement with Iraq as a means to counter the Iraqi invasion of Kuwait (and the full range of motives of such people do not concern us here) had a difficult task on their hands. They had two principal audiences to convince—the Senate and the American people, but these were connected by central interests such that to persuade the latter was to encourage the former. The general context, historically and socially, was one that did not favor the thesis to be advanced. The debacle of the Vietnam War still cast a shadow into the collective mind of the population. They were not predisposed to sending Americans to fight "someone else's" war in a distant land when no clear U.S. interests were at stake and when the costs of such a war still played upon the cultural consciousness.

The argument had to be developed on a number of fronts, including advancing the claim that a war with Iraq would not be like previous wars, that war itself had changed, had become technologized, sanitized, and that it could be fought without a great loss of life. But beyond this, the arguers had to relate the argument for military engagement to the values and beliefs of Americans, directing the argumentation at an environment in which notions of freedom and justice were prevalent, and modifying that environment to persuade Americans that given their values they *ought* to act by supporting the proposal. Here they had the advantage of a big aggressor (Iraq), which the argumentation made even bigger, attacking a small victim (Kuwait), again exploited in the argumentation. But Americans had failed to support the causes of small victims against big aggressors before (quite recently Indonesian forces had invaded East Timor). The difference in this case lay in the financial and public relations resources to which the arguers had access, and in the further characteristic that their audience possessed of being susceptible to media events, particularly those that were emotionally charged.

Thus the incident of the Kuwaiti babies being pulled from incubators by Iraqi troops played a key role in the argumentation that persuaded the American people and Senate to support the war. The incident was related to the Congressional Human Rights Caucus by an emotional fifteen-year-old Kuwaiti, propagated by then president Bush, and corroborated by the strong authority of Amnesty International, who estimated that over three hundred babies had been killed in this incident (Reuters, 1990).

From the audience's perspective this was effective argumentation, judging by the swing in popular opinion. The Senate backed the call for war, although by only five votes, and a number of senators cited the babies' case as influencing their decision. A universal audience constructed from this audience by focusing on common values, reasonably applied, would judge this good argumentation (if not sufficient to justify a declaration of war). It makes important appeals to self-defining values of justice and fairness and it includes supporting evidence from respected authorities, if not in the person of the American president, then certainly in the case of Amnesty International.

The problem with the case is seen only with subsequent revelations that it is based upon falsehood and executed with the apparent intention to deceive. Further investigation failed to corroborate the story of the babies being torn from their incubators. An embarrassed Amnesty International retracted its endorsement. And the fifteen-year-old girl turned out to be the daughter of the Kuwaiti ambassador to the United States (not in itself a mark against the argumentation except for the efforts taken to keep her identity hidden). The argumentation with this key "fictitious" event was traced back to the public relations firm of Hill and Knowlton, who received a reported eleven million dollars from a group called the Citizens for a Free Kuwait (Rowse, 1991:20).

Thus the immediate audience, with its universal construct, was persuaded by argumentation it should not have been. Subsequently, it is reasonable for it to reject the argumentation and to revise its position. To endorse a position on the basis of deceit and falsehood is clearly in contradiction with what is reasonable here and cannot be universalized. The bad reasoning lies with the arguers who have exploited the audience, presumably believing that they could not have persuaded them in any other way.[11]

For arguers directed by the principles of a rhetorical model, such moves are impermissible. Consider how we might use these principles in constructing argumentation for permitting doctor-assisted suicide in certain regulated settings in North America—an admittedly complex issue, but one that we can introduce here.

First we decide who we wish to persuade and concentrate upon that audience, considering its makeup and attitudes. There is a proportion of the general public who, media reports tell us, already favor such legislation, so we will address our arguments to those who do not.

The cognitive environment of this hostile audience (or, at best, undecided audience) is one informed by media attention to recent controversial cases of assisted suicide, doctor- or otherwise. Thus our argumentation can assume a basic understanding of the issue and only try to clarify terms or points that fall outside of such an understanding. We devote some time to creating our profile of such an audience and in particular looking at the objections they hold and why it is they hold them. Some members will have religious objections, feeling that assisted suicide involves human interference in an area that is God's alone. This must be addressed in the argumentation. Others may fear the possibility of any ensuing legislation opening up the way for the deterioration or removal of palliative care, or of focusing attention on dying at the expense of treatment. And there will be other objections. Given the cognitive environment, it can be assumed that the audience is familiar with recent emotionally compelling cases of people who have requested assistance and not received it. If sympathetic to such cases, the audience has not been sufficiently persuaded by them, so reiteration of such cases would not be a fruitful path to take.

In constructing a universal audience for this particular audience, we can adopt the technique of bracketing the unreasonable members and focusing on those who remain. These are people who care about the issue of death and severe illness and who expect their various objections to be met. But they will carefully weigh the responses to these objections and judge them fairly. In developing our argumentation along these lines, we strive to avoid contradicting the basic values and principles to which the audience already adheres, trying to couch our points in the same terms.

With such a difficult issue, involving a moral dilemma of the kind acknowledged earlier by Crosswhite (1989:167), much of our deliberation will be *about* the universal audience itself, the manner of reasonableness alive and alert in those we address. We will be prepared to enter into debate about the nature of this universal audience and modify our views as appropriate. In addition, we are anticipating the kinds of questions an evaluator would direct against our reasoning. Arguing here is a self-aware as well as audience-aware activity in ways that were not accessible for the arguers in the Kuwaiti babies' case. It has its internal checks to avoid undue subjectivism and exploitation of the immediate audience, and to prevent a particular audience accepting whatever its prejudices demand. The universal audience and the arguer's concern over it will moderate the form and manner of the argumentation. The results of arguing without attention to, or concern for, such an audience are readily apparent in the Kuwaiti babies' case.

In these examples, we have begun to suggest how the principles underlying a rhetorical approach to argumentation, with its primary interest in audience, can be applied. The two case studies of the next chapter provide the opportunity for a more developed examination of these points.

Chapter 5

Case Studies in Rhetorical Argumentation

A distinctive feature of rhetorical argumentation is that its value is most evident in the treatment of "cases" rather than in short, terse, PPC arguments (Wenzel, 1989:87). By "cases" here is understood entire bodies of discourse with a unified subject matter and purpose, promoting some specific overall position. Internally, the discourse may be directed at different audiences with various subsidiary purposes and contain a range of different argument types. The interpretation and understanding of the whole discourse must affect the interpretation and understanding of its parts.

Case studies conducted from such a rhetorical perspective on argumentation as has been presented in the previous chapters involve an integration of the logical and dialectical elements with the underlying, context-establishing rhetorical base. Together, they capture the argumentative content and purposes of the text. In the following studies, different elements of the rhetorical account are stressed according to the way in which a case lends itself to such emphases. The cases are chosen so that, in combination, they provide broad illustration of the rhetorical model of argumentation as a tool for the analysis of argumentative discourse. The first case involves a study of one specific text. The second concerns questions of personality and testimony in several related texts that bear on one issue.

5.1 Case A *Clear Thinking on Shell Oil, Nigeria, and the Death of Ken Saro-Wiwa*

The discourse of interest here is a full-page "message" from Shell International Petroleum Company Ltd., London, printed in leading newspapers across the world in the third week of November 1995.

A.1 Background and Locale

Shell's newspaper message followed the death ten days previously of the Nigerian writer Ken Saro-Wiwa and eight of his compatriots from the Ogoni region, executed by the military junta in Nigeria under the leadership of Gen. Sani Abacha. International concern over the charges of murder and their trial had led to considerable pressure being exerted on the Nigerian government not to carry out the death sentences. In the fallout following the executions, one of the principal targets of international condemnation was Shell Oil, a major multinational corporation operating in Nigeria, which was believed to be supporting the military government. If only by its presence there, it was thought to be in a position to influence the government, and yet to have done nothing. Outrage grew from statements of condemnation to calls to boycott Shell products.

Shell's image was not helped by the fact that this was the second time it had been in the international spotlight in the course of six months. June of 1995 had witnessed the "Brent Spar affair," when Shell decided to dump the oil platform of that name into the ocean. Although some experts belatedly agreed that burial at sea was the cleanest way to dispose of the Brent Spar, Shell was slow in presenting its case and suffered a public relations disaster after Greenpeace waged a successful campaign to force Shell to find an alternative, though expensive, means of disposal. Now the company faced renewed criticism after the Nigerian hangings. This came just as Shell was planning a multibillion dollar natural gas project in the Niger delta. The multinational's response was the newspaper campaign titled "Clear Thinking in Troubled Times."

This background already gives much of the atmosphere that pervades the Shell text. The locale of interest is, of course, distinctly contemporary. But it is especially so in that it involves so many current values that influence economics and politics in a world of fast communication where people can feel intimately connected with events thousands of miles away. Disapproval with despotic military regimes, a strong belief in the self-determination of peoples, and deep concerns over environmental issues are three of the major contemporary values that influence the context of this piece of argumentation. The discourse speaks to the last of these, but it pays little or no direct attention to the other two.

A.2 Arguer and Audiences

With a public relations campaign of this nature we can expect to have many hands, or minds, behind the discourse: a collective arguer. The common aim of the elements of the argumentation is to promote (or salvage) the company's interests, and it does this by attempting to gain its audience's (or audiences') adherence to several claims that are put forward, directly or indirectly. The text has been constructed with care and deliberation. We would do well to weigh the meanings of individual phrases and to follow the various directions in which they point us.

Beyond what has just been said, the *intent* of the discourse must be considered in relation to the principal components that make up the particular audience for this argumentative text. The choice of major newspapers to disseminate its message indicates a desire to reach a wide, intelligent audience. The arguers can expect a wide audience ranging from the hostile to the sympathetic to the indifferent. For these last members, generally, Shell is concerned about getting across "its side of the story." Here, the text may be merely informative. But of those it wishes to *convince,* those whose adherence to its theses it seeks, we can identify two subgroups of principal interest: the potential boycotters of Shell products (who the arguers can expect to be hostile to Shell's position), and members of the business community, particularly investors in the company, who have an economic interest in the issue (these people the arguers can expect to be sympathetic, but concerned). Of course, it is possible for an individual to be a member of both principal subgroups, and to feel the appropriate conflicts. Such different groups of the particular audience can be expected to read the discourse in light of their respective interests. Thus they may not see the same points as important, or interpret statements in similar ways.

In light of these principal audiences, or subgroups of the particular audience, we can consider the likely intentions motivating the discourse. A collating of intentions may be useful later when we interpret meanings. We can attribute to the arguers, for example, first the intent to *justify* the behavior of Shell in Nigeria, past and future. To this end, there is an attempt to promote the thesis that Shell did everything that was appropriate, or, alternatively, that everything Shell did was appropriate, in the Saro-Wiwa affair. Connected to this is the desire to *clarify* "the facts," repeated throughout the discourse. A stronger intention that can be attributed to the arguers is to *defend*

Shell, to promote explicitly the thesis that Shell was not to blame for any wrongdoing. Intentions of justification, clarification, and defense would relate to the interests of both boycotters and investors, while still being understood by the broader readership of the newspapers.

Beyond this, we can expect the arguers to intend to *reassure* the business component of its audience. A bottom-line position that permeates the discourse is that Shell has no expectation of pulling out from Nigeria. The company's future economic success in the region rests in part on convincing investors of this. At the same time, and for equally compelling economic reasons, Shell must want to *deter* protesters or boycotters from taking or continuing such courses of action. In fact, we might fairly read this as one of the foremost intentions behind the discourse. Convincing their critics that to boycott Shell products would be misguided or inappropriate is an important aim of the argumentation.[1] With these different intentions associated with different subgroups in the audience, we can expect the discourse to contain "different arguments"; that is, different groups will read *the* argument according to their relation to the discourse. All such "arguments" are part of the argumentation.

A.3 Mode of Expression

The forum chosen for this argumentation is explained by the need to reach the particular audience in a relatively economical way. Conventions of the medium are adhered to such that the case is advocated in apparently unobjectionable ways.

The utterances themselves are carefully chosen. Language is used that *constructs* a version of events that supports the position. The words *do* things in presenting events in a certain light, categorizing and judging. We will note this in the discussion of individual paragraphs, particularly Paragraphs 2, 4, and 8, each of which prepares the groundwork for the phase of argumentation that follows. Rhetorical questions are employed to effect and language creates a shift of onus in Paragraphs 3, 5, 7, 10, and 11.

With these preparatory remarks in place, I now turn to the argumentative text itself, before developing the general critique further. There are twelve paragraphs to consider.

PARAGRAPH 1

> *In the great wave of understandable emotion over the death of Ken Saro-Wiwa, it's very easy for the facts to be swamped by anger and recriminations. But people have the right to the*

truth. Unvarnished. Even uncomfortable. But never subju-
gated to a cause, however noble or well-meaning. They have
the right to clear thinking.

The opening of the discourse trades in pathos with a touching tone of
sympathy for those affected by Saro-Wiwa's death. Their reaction is
seemingly understandable. A connection with the audience is made
and then this normal reaction is transformed into a need to consider
the issue of facts, of what is "true" and based upon "clear thinking." To
observe that "people have the right to the truth," is to assert, indirectly,
that they have not been given this. And the further choice of "subjugated" suggests that this withholding of the truth has been somehow
deliberate: truth has been brought under the yoke of a cause.

In this way, Shell (as represented through the arguers) is set up
as an authority on truth, promising to reveal what has been hidden.
Furthermore, a key value in this issue is that of self-determination
and rights: the rights of the Ogoni people, and of Ken Saro-Wiwa and
his compatriots. And Shell is portrayed as a protector of people's
rights, including the right of the audience to be given the truth.

The effect of this first paragraph, then, is to situate Shell in relation to the issue in a particular way as to create a positive ethos:
an advocate of truth, a protector of rights, and in some implied way,
a victim of false information.

PARAGRAPH 2

The situation in Nigeria has no easy solutions. Slogans,
protests and boycotts don't offer answers. There are difficult
issues to consider.

Three assertions are made. None is defended. But this paragraph
stands mainly to prepare the groundwork for the reasoning in the
next. It asks readers to set aside protests and boycotts, which don't
offer answers, and to consider the difficult issues involved. On the
face of it, this is reasonable advice. But at another level it serves to
dismiss protests and boycotts as a way of responding and any case
that could be made for *them.*

PARAGRAPH 3

First, did discreet diplomacy fail? Perhaps we should ask
instead why the worldwide protests failed. Our experience

*suggests that quiet diplomacy offered the very best hope for
Ken Saro-Wiwa. But as worldwide threats and protests increased, the Government position appeared to harden. As
Wura Abiola, daughter of the imprisoned unofficial winner of
the last Nigerian presidential election said, "The regime does
not react well to threats. I believe that this is the way of showing that they will not listen to threats." Did the protesters understand the risk they were taking? Did the campaign become
more important than the cause?*

Significantly this paragraph shifts the onus from Shell to the
protestors, and it offers arguments. It is suggested that two possibilities had existed for responding to the Nigerian government on Saro-
Wiwa's behalf. One was "quiet diplomacy." The text supports an
interpretation to the effect that the arguers view this as the route
that *should* have been taken (an implicit claim), and the support for
this is the authority of Shell's own experience. This point is left undeveloped, and we are not told the grounds on which they judge this
to have been "the very best hope."

The other possible response was "worldwide threats and
protests." Clearly, this is not deemed to have been the right approach
(implicit claim) because the regime in question "does not react well
to threats." The support for this is given in the form of a knowledgeable authority, Wura Abiola, daughter of the imprisoned official winner of the last Nigerian presidential election. Thus, it is not so much
that the discreet diplomacy failed, but that the worldwide protests
failed. In fact, the text suggested, those protests precipitated the outcome. A correlation and causal relationship is suggested between the
increased protests and the hardening of the government's position.
The final shift of responsibility is accomplished if we take the two
questions at the end of the paragraph as rhetorical questions (the
text is suggestively ambiguous on this—it implies as much, but does
not state it). Thus read, the protesters *did* understand the risk, but
the campaign became more important than the cause. And so, we
might conclude, the protesters continued on a path that jeopardized
Saro-Wiwa's life. The discourse thus completes its shift of onus of responsibility for this: it is not Shell that should be blamed for failed
diplomacy, but the protesters who were at fault.

This may have the effect of reassuring investors, since Shell was
not responsible, and also to deter boycotts, since it would be inappropriate to attack those not responsible. Left unanswered is the question
why the campaign should have become more important than the cause.

PARAGRAPH 4

> *There have also been charges of environmental devastation. But the facts of the situation have often been distorted or ignored. The public—who rightly care deeply about these issues—have too often been manipulated and misled.*

Paragraph 3 closes the first stage of the discourse: absolving Shell from responsibility in Ken Saro-Wiwa's death. But the critics have gone further. There have also been charges (directed at Shell) of environmental devastation. Like Paragraph 2 in relation to 3, Paragraph 4 lays the groundwork for the next part of the argumentation. Again, the arguers adapt themselves to the audience: the public is right to care deeply about these issues. But also again, the public has been misled and manipulated. Shell, in ownership of the "facts," can remedy this.

PARAGRAPH 5

> *There are certainly environmental problems in the area, but as the World Bank Survey has confirmed, in addition to the oil industry, population growth, deforestation, soil erosion and overfarming are also major environmental problems there.*

The relevance of this paragraph to what Paragraph 4 introduced is the first thing that comes to mind. It has the immediate appearance of a red herring, with attention shifted from the oil industry (which is the contextually relevant topic) to four other "major environmental problems." Again, an authority is appealed to in the form of the World Bank Survey. This shift has the affect of diluting what amounts to an admission: that indeed there have been environmental "problems" (*devastation,* the stronger term of the charge, has been dropped and is not directly admitted). Charitably, we could allow that the diversion is a relevant one (i.e., where it returns to the appropriate topic) by reading a hidden claim here along the lines of "Therefore, Shell is not that bad," or "Shell is not the only contributor to major environmental problems." Such a charitable reading, however, serves to emphasize the admission of guilt. It is then left for us to ask whether the environmental impact of the oil industry is like that of the other identified culprits in its extent, severity and treatability.

PARAGRAPH 6

> *In fact, Shell and its partners are spending US$100 million*
> *this year alone on environment-related projects, and US$20*
> *million on roads, health clinics, schools, scholarships, water*
> *schemes and agricultural support projects to help the people*
> *of the region. And, recognising that solutions need to be based*
> *on facts, they are sponsoring a US$4.5 million independent*
> *environmental survey of the Niger Delta.*

"In fact" is how this paragraph begins, as if to set the record straight. But, *in fact,* the detailing of Shell and its partners' philanthropy, while relevant to the interests of its particular audience, is not relevant to that other important consideration of contextual relevance—the topic.

The topic in question is that of environmental devastation. The largess exhibited in the concern for roads, health clinics, schools, and so forth, is quite irrelevant to the topic. But it does contribute to the ethos underlying the argumentation. It shows the character of Shell (and, by extension, the arguers) in a favorable light.

However, if the solutions referred to in the last sentence are solutions to environmental devastation, then this statement at least is relevant to the topic. Interestingly, while the company is "spending" $100 million on environment-related projects, it is "sponsoring" the $4.5-million survey. What is contained in this difference is unclear, but it might be thought that sponsoring involves less of a commitment than spending.

PARAGRAPH 7

> *But another problem is sabotage. In the Ogoni area—where*
> *Shell has not operated since January 1993—over 60% of oil*
> *spills were caused by sabotage, usually linked to claims for*
> *compensation. And when contractors have tried to deal with*
> *these problems, they have been forcibly denied access.*

This paragraph deals more directly with the question of environmental devastation. But it does so once again by distancing Shell from the events. Shell has not operated in the Ogoni area (the region under the international spotlight) since 1993. Instead, the blame shifts to the Ogoni people themselves who, presumably, conduct the sabotage to support their claims for compensation (since the profits from the area go to the government and not to the people of the region). Indirectly, this paragraph weds the environmental issue with the political. They clearly impact on each other. If, as the discourse is later to argue (see Par. 12), the oil companies should not intervene in politics, then the environmental devastation (or, at least, over 60 percent of it) becomes a result of something in which they have no direct involvement.

PARAGRAPH 8

> *It has also been suggested that Shell should pull out of Nigeria's Liquified Natural Gas project. But if we do so now, the project will collapse. Maybe forever. So let's be clear about who gets hurt if the project is cancelled.*

Like Paragraphs 2 and 4, Paragraph 8 represents another change of direction in the argumentation, setting up the next stage. Having responded to charges of responsibility for Saro-Wiwa's death and for environmental devastation, a further charge has involved a call for Shell to pull out of Nigeria's Liquified Natural Gas project (a $3.6-billion investment[2]). A final and important appeal is made to the company's ethos, and this is developed in the ensuing paragraphs. The cancelation of the project, should Shell pull out, will cause harm. Shell would prevent that harm.

PARAGRAPH 9

> *A cancellation would certainly hurt the thousands of Nigerians who will be working on the project and the tens of thousands more benefitting in the local economy. The environment, too, would suffer, with the plant expected to cut greatly the need for gas flaring in the oil industry. The plant will take four years to build. Revenues won't start flowing until early next century. It's only the people and the Nigerian Government of that time who will pay the price.*

The cancelation will hurt thousands of Nigerians, directly and indirectly, as well as the environment (although this harm is industry-related, since without its presence there would be no oil flarings). No reference is made of the harm that would result for the company itself and for its investors.

Not only will it harm presumably innocent Nigerians, but it will fail to punish the guilty. Since revenues will not flow until early in the next century, they will not be an immediate resource for the current government. This serves to further distance Shell from the interests of the military regime. Yet the paragraph ends with an initially vague statement: "It's only the people and the Nigerian government of that time who will pay the price." What price? From the context, we can presume that this is the price of not having the revenues from the project, if it is canceled (i.e., again, the current government will not be punished, only a future one). Dialectically, this overlooks some serious counterargumentation: that the current regime stands to gain considerable status just by having the project go ahead. I will consider this in the next section.

PARAGRAPH 10

> *And what would happen if Shell pulled out of Nigeria altogether? The oil would certainly continue flowing. The business would continue operating. The vast majority of employees would remain in place. But the sound and ethical business practices synonymous with Shell, the environmental investment and the tens of millions of dollars spent on community programmes would all be lost. Again, it's the people of Nigeria that you would hurt.*

Again the ethotic element is pronounced in this paragraph. Shell is a good the absence of which would have a serious deleterious effect in Nigeria. Should Shell exit Nigeria altogether, nothing would really change *except* for the loss of sound and ethical business practice, environmental investment, and money slated for community programs. Moreover, the "bad" to which Shell stands in contrast is now the reader, "you." This is the most serious challenge to the audience so far, aimed presumably at those as yet unpersuaded by the argumentation. Guilt is shifted once again to those who would challenge, through protest or boycott, Shell's presence in Nigeria. This charge, where the arguers take the offensive, is continued in the next paragraph and is a pattern of the closing steps of the argumentation.

PARAGRAPH 11

> *It's easy enough to sit in our comfortable homes in the West, calling for sanctions and boycotts against a developing coun-*

try. But you have to be sure that knee-jerk reactions won't do
more harm than good.

Rather than adapting to the audience, this paragraph challenges the
audience to adapt. It contrasts the comfortable West with the developing world, a Goliath against a David. Not surprisingly, few would
feel comfortable being associated with the aggressor in such a
metaphor. The paragraph can be seen as an attempt to create the
emotion of shame (cf. *Rhetoric* 2.6.1383b-1385a). No one seriously
wishes to damage the welfare of a young country and to impede its
development. Nor would people be happy with the emotive label of
knee-jerk that denotes an unthinking reaction. With this term, the
arguers underline their claim to have given the factual, clear-think-
ing side of the issue.

Forgotten here is that the calls have been for boycotts against a
military government and influential companies, Shell principally,
which by their presence support the government. The harms, and not
just economic harms, done to a people by such a government need to
be weighed against the identified harms of a company like Shell International withdrawing from Nigeria.

PARAGRAPH 12

Some campaigning groups say we should intervene in the po-
litical process in Nigeria. But even if we could, we must never
do so. Politics is the business of governments and politicians.
The world where companies use their economic influence to
prop up or bring down governments would be a frightening
and bleak one indeed.

Finally, the serious question of Shell's influence on the politics of
Nigeria is considered and rejected in the logos of this paragraph. The
dichotomy indicated in Paragraph 7 between economics and politics
is made explicit. They move in mutually exclusive spheres and
should not intervene in each other's affairs. Nowhere in the discourse
is an attempt to construct a version of reality clearer than it is here.
Contrary to what is apparent throughout the world, and evident in
the cognitive environments of a wide range of audiences, here it is
claimed that not only are companies unable to intervene in politics
but, prescriptively, they should not do so. For doing so would lead
to a world that is "frightening and bleak." Presumably, no one
wants such an undesirable outcome; therefore, in general, companies

should not interfere with governments and, in particular, Shell should not interfere with the government of Nigeria. The quiet diplomacy of Paragraph 3 has been reduced to silence.

A.4 Dialectical Obligations

Chapter 2 indicated the sense in which we will understand the usefulness of features of dialectical argumentation. I take it to refer primarily to an argument's character as a dialogue with moves, real or imagined, back and forth between a proponent of a thesis and a participatory audience not previously committed to the thesis. In a text like the foregoing, the dialectical nature is the result of the arguers' imagined dialogue with their audience(s). They have put forward their thesis aware of the views held by the audience(s), and should have further anticipated countermoves by the audience(s), all this with a view to convincing the audience of the theses put forward.

The arguers acquire a set of obligations toward the audience, prompted partly by the need to communicate effectively. Thus I have recognized the general applicability of Gricean maxims as these are deemed appropriate to the context and in relation to the goal of adherence.

In this instance, we can highlight features of the analysis so far conducted by discussing violations of three dialectical rules. In addition to one of Paul Grice's rules, I will consider an Aristotelian rule and one of the pragma-dialectical rules.

Van Eemeren and Grootendorst's first pragma-dialectical rule reads: "Parties must not prevent each other from advancing standpoints or casting doubt on standpoints" (1992a:108). In a monological text such as the one currently under investigation, this rule could be violated by presenting the other party in such a negative light as to undermine that party's position in the dialogue or debate. This can be done by depicting the other party as "stupid, bad, unreliable, and so forth," or by "casting suspicion on his motives" (209). The effect of such dialectical moves, if done successfully, is to shift an advantage to, in this case, the arguers, by discrediting the other party. Hence, such a move is a violation of appropriate procedure.

The arguers of "Clear Thinking in Troubled Times" violate this dialectical rule in at least two instances with respect to that subgroup of its audience that comprises protesters and boycotters. In the first paragraph, suspicion is cast on the motives of the protesters. Truth, we understand, should never be "subjugated to a cause." Thus, the arguers depict proponents of the opposing position as valuing their cause over truth. The protesters cannot be trusted to tell the truth, so anything they might have said or say lacks credibility. This idea is continued in Paragraph 3 where the ethos of the protesters is attacked. With the campaign becoming more important than the cause, it is implied that the protesters did not really care about Saro-Wiwa.

Secondly, Paragraphs 10 and 11 involve a more concerted attack on the character of Shell's opponents. As we have seen, "you" who would protest and boycott represent the "bad" element harming Nigerians, in contrast to Shell who is helping them. The opponents are creatures of comfort (Par. 11) reacting in a knee-jerk fashion. Thus, they have not thought through the issue and tackled the difficulties as Shell has.

These violations of the pragma-dialectical rule impede any defense or counterargumentation that the other party might attempt to launch because they construct such a negative portrait of the other party. Such an unfair argumentative procedure would, if we might think ahead, be unacceptable to a reasonable audience.

An Aristotelian rule pertinent here reads "It is a good rule also, occasionally to bring an objection against oneself" (*Topics* 156[b]18). This need not be done at every turn, but an arguer is obliged to acknowledge the more obvious counterargumentative moves likely to be brought against a thesis.

Again, I shall discuss two instances where this problem comes to the fore. The most serious omissions were identified in Paragraph 9. When the arguers detail the harms that would result from Shell canceling the natural gas project, they omit any reference to the negative impact it would have on the company itself. It is not only the people and government of the future Nigeria who would be harmed, one might object, but Shell will lose its substantial investment in the project as well as even greater future revenues. In the context of the international debate, oil company profits have been a prominent topic and the arguers would be wiser to address it than to ignore it. Likewise, the claim that the current regime will not profit from the project considers only the direct financial relationship and overlooks how such a project confers status on a government and, in serving as an example of a substantial international investment, opens the door for other investments from which the government might profit. Thus, there is a key counterargument to be raised against the arguers' point.

Again, in Paragraph 12, the more controversial claim is advanced that companies like Shell cannot interfere in the politics of countries like Nigeria. In fairness, this raises an issue of such importance that it could not be dealt with in such a limited text. But the claim is so clearly susceptible to objection that such a criticism begs acknowledgment. As *The Economist* argued: "As the country's biggest producer of oil, which produces in turn 80 per cent of the government's revenues . . . [Shell] cannot pretend to have no political impact whatsoever" (1995:18). There is a difference between having a political impact and interfering in politics. But the text does not even recognize objections based on the first of these distinctions.

Questions about the application of a number of Gricean rules could be raised with respect to this text. I have already touched on ways in which the invocation to "Be relevant" has been violated, and I will return to this later. Here, I propose to introduce one of Grice's submaxims under the general rule advocating honesty. It reads: "Do not say that for which you lack evidence" (1989:27). That someone fails to provide evidence for a claim they advance does not necessarily mean that they lack the evidence. But the failure to provide evidence for a claim at least indicates a failure to meet an important dialectical obligation.

A clear violation of this rule is evident in Paragraph 3. Here alternatives are presented for dealing with the military government in Nigeria: either "worldwide threats and protests" or "quiet diplomacy." In favoring the latter the Shell arguers claim that their experience suggested that it "offered the very best hope for Ken Saro-Wiwa." This important claim is not supported. Of course, it may be the very best hope because *the only other* alternative offers no hope. The appeal to Shell's experience in such matters suggests more, but further details are not given. The audience deserves the evidence for why *this experience* suggested that quiet diplomacy was the best hope.

A number of other claims are left undefended, some of greater consequence than others. Among the more important we might observe the following: "The protesters understood the risk they were taking." Couching this assertion within a rhetorical question in Paragraph 3 does not absolve the arguers of the obligation to support it. In fact, the manner in which it is communicated suggests that this is indeed an instance of saying that for which they lack evidence.

The dialectical level of the analysis could be extended further, but enough has been said to demonstrate its utility as an integrated component of the assessment of the argumentation. The dialectical points of pertinence are drawn from the context, particularly the re-

lationship between the arguer(s) and audience(s), and their discussion feeds off the wider rhetorical base. As the "other party" to
the Shell arguers I have looked solely on the protester/boycotter
subgroup of the particular audience, because they represent the
clearest "antagonist" for much of the argumentative. But an alternative tact would be to trace the arguers' dialectical interaction
with the business/investor subgroup of the audience (one that has,
admittedly, been treated in my analysis as somewhat secondary in
importance).

A.5 The Logical Structure

When we turn to the "logic" here, understood in terms of the PPC
products, it is tempting to wonder about *the* argument of this text.
But, of course, from the rhetorical perspective we cannot assume
there is *an* argument here. In fact, the two principal groups comprising the immediate audience, already identified and discussed,
would each interact with the argumentation in a different way, recognizing a different thesis and, should they be persuaded to adhere
to it, being prompted to a different action.

The hostile subgroup of the audience, together with socially concerned people likely to consider joining a boycott, recognize the thesis as "do not boycott (stop boycotting) Shell products," and they
organize central claims in the discourse so as to form arguments supporting this thesis—principally:

1. Shell was not responsible for the death of Ken Siro-Wiwa
(with *its* supporting statements).

2. Shell is environmentally responsible (with *its* supporting
statements).

The sympathetic but concerned business and commercial subgroup of the audience recognize the thesis "continue investing in
Shell Oil," and they organize central claims in the discourse so as to
form arguments supporting this thesis—principally:

1. Shell will not pull out of the natural gas project in Nigeria.

2. Shell will not become involved in the politics of Nigeria.

Of course, the actual argumentative text is not organized into these
distinct patterns. It is the *audiences themselves,* from their specific
backgrounds and with their particular interests, who organize it
these ways. At the same time, the arguments are there, products of
the arguer(s). Similarly, evidence/premises/subarguments recognized as support for a thesis by one audience group may also count

in the arguments deemed important for the other. It will matter to investors that Shell will not pull out of Nigeria, but they may be convinced of this partly because they realize that the threat of a boycott has been successfully countered insofar as Shell has been shown to not be responsible for Saro-Wiwa's death.

So, identifying and evaluating the arguments can be a complex exercise, and one not to be entered hastily. We will consider some of the arguments these audiences would care about, starting with: "Boycotting Shell products should cease/not be undertaken because Shell was not responsible for Saro-Wiwa's death" (1).[3] The supporting claim is hidden and it is by virtue of our background knowledge of the criticisms that have sparked the production of this text that we are able to extract the claim. The discourse supports the claim in part by suggesting what *was* responsible. The reasoning begins with the claim that quiet diplomacy was the very best hope for Ken Saro-Wiwa (2). The support for this is the authority of Shell's own experience (3). However, quiet diplomacy was not given a chance to succeed (implied 4), *because* worldwide protests precipitated the executions (implied 5). This in turn is supported by the premise that indicates a correlation between an increase in worldwide threats and protests on the one hand, and the hardening of the Nigerian government's position on the other (6). Additional support is seen in the appeal to the authority of Wura Abiola (7).

Turning to the other subgroup's perspective on the argumentation, we can look at some of the reasoning they would consider. For example, "Investments in Shell Oil should continue because Shell will not pull out of the Natural gas project in Nigeria." The project and Nigeria are sufficiently related to be collapsed in this fashion and the principal reason for both is the harm that Shell's absence would cause.

If Shell pulls out from the project, then the project will collapse (8). And if the project collapses, considerable harm will result (9). Evidence of this harm is drawn from a number of considerations: the Nigerians who depend on the project and the local economy (10); the environment, through the continuation of gas flaring (11); and the future government and people, who will be deprived of the revenues (12). Likewise, if Shell pulls out of Nigeria, then things will stay the same except for the loss of the good Shell does (through sound business practice, investment, etc.) (13). Assuming as a general moral principle that it is wrong to do harm if it can be avoided (14), the case for Shell staying is completed.

The question of the strengths and weaknesses of these pieces of reasoning is part of the overall evaluation of the argumentation.

A.6 The Reasonableness of the Argumentation

Is the argumentation persuasive or convincing? It is obvious by now that this is a complex question. To fully answer it, we must consider how both principal subgroups of the particular audience provide the universal audience for this argumentation.

The universal audience reflects the elements of reasonableness in the particular audience. In this we are fortunate to have a composite audience of opposing interests that will balance out each other's more extreme reactions. The universal audience will consist of people knowledgeable about the oil industry and the business practices of multinational corporations, as well as those well versed in human rights and environmental issues. Such a universal audience would give Shell's arguers the space to make their points, to present "the facts" that have allegedly been excluded from the debate. But it would consider such facts with a critical eye, demanding their full support. It is, importantly, an educated audience, logical and reflective. Aware of the interests of the other subgroup within its membership, it would be alert to anything not acceptable to a middle-ground position, and anything that contradicts its own inherent sense of reasonableness.

In constructing the response of the universal audience for this argumentation, we can raise and answer a series of questions with respect to it, establishing in the process an idea of what would be reasonable here. For purposes of brevity, I will restrict this summation to four such questions that capture the salient features of the discussion.

1. Is the appeal to the ethos of the company appropriate?
2. Is the attack on the ethos of the (hostile) audience appropriate?
3. Have the Shell arguers met their dialectical obligations?
4. Is the logic sound?

1. In accordance with Aristotle's suggested procedure, the arguers here attempt to create the ethos of the company they represent through the discourse. Shell's "character" is presented as truthful, caring, philanthropic, socially aware, and environmentally responsible. The arguers' success in creating this character is important to both identified subgroups of the audience. As Alan Brinton (1986) noted, what makes such appeals strong is the presence of reasons to support the "claim" of trustworthiness, and this is what

the universal audience would require. Some aspects of the ethotic portrait are given support in the text. Paragraph 6 cites the money spent by the company on local projects that directly benefit the people, and Paragraphs 9 and 10 address the harm that would be done to Nigerian workers and the environment were Shell to withdraw from their country. These points represent evidence of philanthropy, social concern, and environmental responsibility. The last of these is the weakest, and the environmental survey that Shell is sponsoring (Par. 6) does not provide direct support for the question of its responsibility. On the important question of Shell's truthful character, whereby the discourse appeals to Shell's authority, no reasons are provided. Paragraphs 1 and 3 suggest much but demonstrate little. On balance, the universal audience would have to accept the fact that the text has some success in establishing a positive character. But not on the important issue of Shell's truthfulness, and not enough to counter other problems.

2. Beyond attempting to establish Shell's own credibility, the text also attacks the credibility of Shell's critics, many of whom would comprise the hostile subgroup of the particular audience. An attempt is made to portray the critics as inconsistent in their actions—as having harmed rather than helped Saro-Wiwa through their protests, and as not really caring about the Nigerian people. In a sense, this is the counterside of the development of Shell's own ethos, constructed in distinction to that of other players in the events. It is also a consequence of the attempt to shift responsibility from Shell. Since the strategy is unlikely to appeal to the group identified in it, its audience may be taken to be the other, sympathetic subgroup. Perhaps the intent is to strengthen that group's trust in Shell by showing that the company can be aggressive and is not afraid to attack its critics. But, again, without evidence to support the implicit charges of inconsistent and uncaring behavior, the universal audience will not be convinced of this. While it is in principle a reasonable strategy, without the elements of what good ethotic argument of this kind requires, it fails here.

3. This last point carries over into the question of dialectical obligations. As just shown, the discourse violates several important rules in this area, and a universal audience should note these. Reasonable argumentation will not attempt to discredit the holders of a position in the ways that are tried here. Nor will it be selective in its evidence, avoiding key objections, or overstate its case beyond what the evidence will support. A universal audience carefully scrutiniz-

ing what evidence is provided *and what is omitted,* will be alert to such problems.

4. Is the logic sound? Again, this is not an all-or-nothing judgment. There are strengths to be weighed against the flaws. For example, there is in general internal relevance between propositions in the PPC products and much of the discourse exhibits appropriate audience-relevance in addressing its information to the cognitive environments of its respective targets. The flaws that do appear are serious, however. Here I shall conclude my analysis with the most detrimental.

There is evidence of topic-irrelevance in both Paragraphs 5 and 6, which weakens the portion of the argumentation that concerns the environmental issues. While I was charitable in allowing the shift of topic in Paragraph 5, that in 6 would not be reasonable to the universal audience for this piece. While the shift to philanthropic matters has audience-relevance and strengthens the ethos of the company, it does not address the real issue of environmental devastation. Shifts of this nature cannot be allowed without doing general damage to the concept of topic-relevance. Thus, they contradict what is reasonable.

Looking at the two arguments that were just identified, neither would be acceptable to the universal audience in their current forms. The first of these, drawn from Paragraph 1, attempts to support the claim that Shell was not responsible for Saro-Wiwa's death and that, therefore, boycotts are not appropriate. The support for this is that Shell's own preference of quiet diplomacy was not followed. And, more importantly, that the international protests and threats were causally responsible for the executions. On the first point, Statement 3 is the primary evidence. This is the appeal to Shell's own authority, and its acceptance depends on Shell's trustworthiness. But as we saw in the examination of the ethotic elements, this trustworthiness is never established. The causal argument (Statements 5–7) is also weak. Statement 6, which claims a correlation between the increase in threats and the hardening of the government's position, is not adequately supported. How was the correlation determined? What sort of study was at stake? The appeal to the authority of Wura Abiola is appropriate as evidence, if we have no reason to doubt it. But such appeals are contributory proofs and not themselves sufficient to establish claims, particularly not one as controversial as seen here.

In the second argument the principal reasoning is again causal, this time forward-looking. It has the form of a Slippery Slope: if Shell pulls out of the project, the project will collapse (8). And from this will follow harm (9) to the local Nigerians (10), to the environment (11), and to the future government and peoples (12). A similar consequence is anticipated for the more general removal from Nigeria (13). What reasons do we have for believing these effects will follow, and that they would be as devastating as claimed if they were to transpire? The key statement is 8. Will the project collapse without Shell's involvement? Or will it be modified or reduced? While the likelihood of some harm is reasonable to believe, we cannot be sure the effects would be as devastating as claimed. Nor, more importantly, can we be sure that Shell's continued presence, given the implicit support it would give to the government, would be less harmful than its withdrawal. Statement 14, assumed as the principle at issue here, is important. The real weighing of harms is never addressed. Together with the selective character of this reasoning, just noted, omitting any reference to the harm that would ensue for Shell should it withdraw, the argument here is unacceptable for the universal audience of this argumentation. Such flaws and omissions, should we try to universalize them, are contradictory to what is reasonable.

As a consequence, we can conclude that the guilt has been shifted illegitimately and that Shell's importance to the region has been argued illegitimately, and not through reasonable argumentation. The audiences cannot complete the reasoning, and cannot legitimately construct understandings of the arguments, because of such factors as incomplete appeals to authority and inadequate causal reasoning. All three perspectives on argumentation have been combined to arrive at this assessment, but the fundamental role has been that of the rhetorical perspective, setting the terms for, and illuminating, the others.

5.2 Case B *Personality, Testimony, and Holocaust Denial*

This case study examines the use of personality and related matters (testimony and expertise) in argumentation. How is its use effective and when is it legitimate? If there is a text at the heart of this case, it is the somewhat infamous text of Holocaust denial *Did Six Million Really Die? The Truth at Last*[4] (hereafter *Six Million*), followed by the transcripts of the "Regina v. Zundel," case in the Ontario Court of Appeal (23 January 1987).[5] These two texts are connected by the 1985 trial (and subsequent retrial) of the Holocaust-denier Ernst Zundel, who was charged with publishing false news under section 177 of the *Criminal Code of Canada*. Ethotic argument, a significant aspect of rhetorical argumentation (see chap. 3), dominates the case, both in its deployment and with respect to decisions about its appropriateness.

B.1 The Initial Text

Six Million has none of the subtlety of "Clear Thinking in Troubled Times" in the way in which it engages its audience and presents its claims and evidence. If selectivity and falsehood impede an audience's involvement with the argumentation, then this text is guilty at every turn.

The author, Richard Harwood/Verral (I will refer to him by the pseudonym henceforth) presents his thesis in the opening sentence, namely that the Holocaust[6] did not occur:

> In the following chapters the author has, he believes, brought together irrefutable evidence that the allegation that 6 million Jews died during the Second World War, as a direct result of official German policy of extermination, is utterly unfounded. (1974:4)

The unqualified claim here is indicative of the tone throughout the text where "proofs" and "certainties" abound. But the argumentative strategies that are deployed are often suspect and occasionally risible. A lot of weight is placed on contradictory evidence drawn from various sources (and not always accurately depicted [see Lipstadt, 1993:104–21]), and documents of the International Committee of the Red Cross are selectively interpreted.

Harwood makes direct appeals to the logic of his own position. Why, he asks, would Hitler have allowed Jewish immigration from Reich territory if he intended to exterminate all Jews (1974:6); and surely "on grounds of logic alone," the Nazis would not contemplate genocide against the Jews when their labor was so essential to the success of a war being engaged on two fronts (ibid.). Aside from the fact that both pieces of reasoning are derived from questionable interpretations of events, they imply an underlying adherence to "reason" and "logic" that the principals' behavior on these matters appears to have contradicted. "Logic" might indeed have entailed the consequences that Harwood imagines, but on these occasions logic was in little evidence, and it is fruitless to appeal to the illogic of the plans as evidence against their having occurred.

The more significant argumentative strategy employed is the way in which testimonies attesting to the fact of the Holocaust (including those of many on trial at Nuremberg) are systematically derided, and those that challenge the Holocaust are elevated. It is to this strategy that I shall attend in the next section.

Understanding the audience for this text also helps with understanding its motivations and tone. The immediate audience of Harwood's text consists of Britons "as they have existed since the coming of the Saxons" (4). The point of contact the author wishes to make with these people is that he and they share a common threat from African and Asian immigrants who augur "the biological alteration and destruction of the British people. . . . In short, we are threatened with the irrecoverable loss of our European culture and racial heritage" (ibid.). But to raise such complaints, claims Harwood, is to invite charges of "racialist" and to be compared to the Nazis who murdered six million Jews because of racialism. Thus, by debunking the "myth" of the six million, Harwood would defend the interest of his principal audience.

While such an Anglo Saxon/European audience is not insignificant, many factions within it are unlikely to be in sympathy with Harwood's position. Hence, he appeals to "reasonableness" and logic. At one point, when challenging the number of Jewish deaths, he prompts: "These are the kinds of questions that the critical thinking person should ask" (23). Thus, he definitely sees himself appealing to a reasoning audience that should recognize the merits of his position. That he recognizes the hostile reaction with which any Jewish readers would respond to his remarks is evident in an early attempt to mollify them: "No one," he writes, "could have anything but admiration for the way in which the Jews have sought to preserve their race through so many centuries, and continue to do so today" (5). Such a sentiment is belied by the deeper anti-Semitism that emerges as the text develops.

Harwood, then, explicitly attempts to address a "reasonable" audience within his immediate audience. But the quality of the argumentation with which he addresses them, with its distortions and selectivity, is counterproductive to this move. The "critical thinking" component of his audience, if they in fact exhibit the characteristics of that activity, will not follow his logic to the conclusions he suggests. Nowhere is this more apparent than in the use of personality and testimony in Harwood's argumentation.

B.2 Harwood's Use of Ethotic Argument

As discussed in chapter 3, drawing principally from Brinton's (1986) development of the Aristotelian ideas, "ethotic argument" is argumentation that appeals to or represents character in some way as to lend credibility to (or detract it from) a claim. Appeals to authority (the *ad verecundiam*) and the attack upon the person (the *ad hominem*) are both types of ethotic argument, although the appeal to character exceeds the specifics of both of them.

Ethotic argument arises in Harwood's text in a number of these forms. I am not concerned with any attempt he might make to appeal through his discourse to his own ethos. Instead, I want to look at three uses of ethotic argument: (1) his dismissal of the credibility of witnesses and memoirs testifying to the extermination of Jews; (2) his appeal to the authority of an expert like Raul Hilberg; (3) and the direct appeal to the ethos of a major player in the denial movement—Paul Rassinier.

1. Harwood has two principal groups of witnesses with whom to contend: perpetrators of the crimes, and their victims. He disparages both groups, questioning their credibility by various means. The more difficult testimony for him to dismiss is undoubtedly that given in confessions by former Nazis and guards, often during trials, and often with the expectation that such confessions would result in their convictions.

He presents a series of *ad hominem* arguments against the Nuremberg confessors (1974:12–13). Their "spurious" testimony involving "extravagant" claims in support of the "myth of the Six Million" was "invariably given by the former German officers because of pressure, either severe torture . . . or the assurance of leniency for themselves if they supplied the required statements" (16). The wording here casts doubt on what was said because of the circumstances. In fact, "supplied the required statements" conveys the idea that the confessions did not originate with the confessors, but with their captors.

A major example in question concerns *Commandant of Auschwitz* by Rudolf Hoess (1960). Harwood approaches this incriminating memoir by questioning its authenticity and by attributing it to Hoess's Communist captors. Hoess's testimony at Nuremberg is deemed untrustworthy because he had been tortured and brainwashed (as evidenced by his monotone delivery). Conclusive evidence that the Hoess memoirs are a forgery is seen in the way in which they defame Jehovah's Witnesses: this "proves the document's Communist origins beyond any doubt" (1974:20).

The testimonies of victims are claimed to be unreliable in other ways. Concentration camp memoirs are discredited because they are "produced for commercial gain" (19). Accounts by people like Olga

Lenyi are said to be inconsistent (a general accusation Harwood makes against these documents) and therefore unreliable. In the face of an associated memoir like Anne Frank's *Diary,* Harwood repeats the often-made (and discredited) accusation that it is a forgery. All testimony that would authenticate the Holocaust, then, is dismissed by Harwood as discreditable in one way or another. As he often repeats: "no living, authentic eye-witness . . . has ever been produced and validated" (16). This is not surprising, given Harwood's position. There are many eyewitnesses, but none is "authentic"; none is "validated."

We should address the *ad hominem* arguments deployed here. While it is a legitimate argument form (Groarke and Tindale, 1986:307–10), particularly in rhetorical argumentation, these instances would fail to convince a reasonable (universal) audience because they are based on innuendo and speculation. Harwood fails to substantiate any of his charges of unreliability, and where he attempts to do so, as in the case of Hoess, the reasoning is tenuous at best.

The *ad hominem* itself may involve different argumentative moves, from abusiveness to the tu quoque, but essentially it involves an attack upon someone's *advocacy* of a position (Brinton, 1995) or an attack on the person (Walton 1995a:212). It offers only an indirect challenge to the position itself. But in cases like the one under consideration, where the testimony of witnesses is a principal piece of evidence for a particular position, then undermining that testimony weakens the position. A person's views may be legitimately questioned if the attack shows that the person is either not knowledgeable, untrustworthy, or biased. There is an element of each of these in Harwood's argumentation (contradictions that suggest a lack of knowledge and commercial bias), but his main strategy is to reveal the witnesses as untrustworthy. Yet no reasonable audience can be persuaded of this by only innuendo and speculation. There is a presumption in favor of a person's testimony, unless we have reason to believe otherwise. The extreme circumstances under which many of these testimonies were given strengthens that presumption. It is a feature of eyewitness accounts generally that inconsistencies between accounts can arise, invariably on matters of detail. Where Harwood has been able to locate some of these in the Holocaust literature, he is quick to exploit them. In these cases it is appropriate to question the trustworthiness of the witnesses with respect to the details. But the fact of the Holocaust itself stands behind these inconsistencies as a dominant, sobering presence.

2. As noted, the *ad verecundiam* is another type of ethotic argument. Here the argumentation involves an appeal to an expert, authority, or authoritative source in place of direct evidence. Given the diversity of areas in which knowledge is possible and our limitations with respect to such a range, the *ad verecundiam,* where appropriately deployed, is a necessary feature of argumentation. In fact, Charles Arthur Willard calls arguing from authority and accepting claims based on authority "the 20th Century's definitive epistemic methods" (1990:18).

It is not surprising, then, that Harwood should include the *ad verecundiam* in his argumentative repertoire. What *is* surprising is the twist of appealing to an historian of the Holocaust as an expert to establish the position that the Holocaust is a myth.

When experts are used, it is generally assumed that they are advocating the position for which their expertise is being sought. On a number of occasions Harwood visits the question of the actual number of Jewish deaths during the Second World War, always finding it substantially fewer than six million. To this end he enlists Raul Hilberg: "the Jewish statistician Raul Hilberg estimates an even lower figure of 896,892" (1974:30). Hilberg is an appropriate source to use: a noted historian, the author of the internationally acclaimed *Destruction of the European Jews,* and certainly not biased in favor of Harwood's position. But here Harwood has committed the most grievous of deceptions in appealing to an authority—Hilberg never said what was attributed to him. As Deborah Lipstadt notes: "Because of his extensive research on the German Bureaucracy during the Third Reich, specifically as it was used in the killing process, deniers have long felt obliged to destroy his [Hilberg's] credibility" (1993:58). Hilberg himself had an opportunity to set the record straight during the Zundel trial in Canada, where he denied ever giving the figure of 896,892 Jews killed ("Regina v. Zundel," 173). Hence, Harwood reveals the dark side of ethotic argument, attempting to discredit a man's work by making a false appeal to it.

Hilberg is not the only expert to whom an appeal is made; it is just that he is used in a strategy of a distinctive kind. Harwood also cites Thies Christopherson who was at Auschwitz during 1944, but who saw no evidence of any gas chambers (1974:17). (Christopherson's account did not come to light until 1973, following which the German lawyer who published the account was disciplined by his professional association.) But Harwood's strongest appeal, exhibiting all the characteristics of a wider appeal to ethos, is reserved for Paul Rassinier.

3. Rassinier was a formative influence on all subsequent deniers (Lipstadt, 1993:64). Harwood introduces him, thus:

> Without doubt the most important contribution to a truthful study of the extermination question has been the work of the French historian, Professor Paul Rassinier. The pre-eminent value of his work lies firstly in the fact that Rassinier actually experienced life in the German concentration camps, and also that, as a Socialist intellectual and anti-Nazi, nobody could be less inclined to defend Hitler and National Socialism. Yet, for the sake of justice and historical truth, Rassinier spent the remainder of his post-war years until his death in 1966 pursuing research which utterly refuted the Myth of the Six Million and the legend of Nazi diabolism. (1974:28)

Rassinier is portrayed here as a defender of justice and truth. A former inmate of concentration camps (Buchenwald and Dora), he was in a position to know of what he spoke and not to be biased in the Nazis' favor. He is presented as a French historian who "utterly refuted" the "Myth of the Six Million."

This "utter refutation" took the form of a series of strategies that are the precursors for those of the *Six Million* itself. Rassinier discredited former prisoners who, allegedly, reported only what they had heard, not what they had seen. In fact, "Rassinier also rejects any written or oral testimony to the Six Million given by the kind of "witnesses" just cited, since they are full of contradictions, exaggerations, and falsehoods" (29). It seems that Rassinier was also the source for the remark about Hilberg.

Harwood identifies the work of Rassinier as the "Truth at Last." He has no compunction about appealing to Rassinier's character and authority because he sees in Rassinier's work the definitive statement of his own position. At root *Six Million* is based on an extended appeal to the authority of Rassinier's work and of Rassinier himself. He provides the example, the statistics, and the strategies for Harwood's pamphlet.

Rassinier, however, is not without blemish. Called (contra Harwood) a defender of the SS (Lipstadt, 1993:51), and the author of "Fantastic Calculations" (Vidal-Naquet, 1992:31–38), Rassinier moved in his career from downplaying the numbers of those who died by gassing to denying the existence of gas chambers altogether.

Like Harwood and the other deniers who would follow him, Rassinier's principal task was to destroy the credibility of survivors, especially his fellow prisoners. He was fond of dismissing their testimony as *gossip* (Lipstadt, 1993:52), a derogatory term in the context and similar to the "hearsay" that will be discussed in the next section. Furthermore, his fellow prisoners were prone to exaggerate. This is, again, a problem since it has some basis in fact. As Lipstadt points out, some inmates did and do embellish their experiences. But she goes on to make an important methodological point relative to this and to the use of eyewitness testimonies:

> Historians of the Holocaust recognize this and do not build a historical case on the oral history of an individual survivor, engaging instead in what anthropologists call triangulation, matching a survivor's testimony with other forms of proof, including documents and additional historical data. But Rassinier blatantly dismissed all survivors' testimony. (53–54)

This corroborates my earlier point (in the preceding section and in chap. 3) that while types of ethotic arguments may contribute significantly to a thesis or position, they will rarely suffice. Lipstadt warns against reliance on any isolated testimony (e.g., perhaps, Harwood's use of Christopherson). Testimony is a "form of proof," to be combined with other, dissimilar forms of evidence to make a strong case. The pendulum may swing back the other way where the testimony is from an individual of outstanding character, that is, where a general appeal to ethos is appropriate. Then, the testimony would carry more weight as proof. Perhaps Harwood sees his culminating appeal to Rassinier in such terms. But given Lipstadt (and Vidal-Naquet's) counterportrayal, together with Rassinier's own texts (his first two books were reissued in 1977 as *Debunking the Genocide Myth* by Noontide Press), then we have enough reason to doubt Harwood's ethotic argument.

Six Million, with its background, is instructive for what it shows us about the use of personality, testimony, and authority in argumentation, or, rather, in their misuse. But studying this text does not give us as comprehensive an account of ethotic argumentation as we would like. In particular, questions remain about the appropriateness of some of these argumentative strategies. To pursue these questions further, I turn to the related "text" of the Zundel trial in Ontario and, in particular, to the appeal court's judgment about the appropriateness of various types of testimony.

B.3 Testimony in the Zundel Trial

Ernst Zundel's 1985 trial (the first of several) was a major test case for the denial movement, which strives to have its views expressed within the legitimate setting of a court of law and that may well have gained from the media exposure. Zundel is one of the leading deniers in North America, and is also well-known in Germany. He was charged with two counts of knowingly publishing false documents: *Six Million,* and "The West, War, and Islam." While he was acquitted with respect to the second of these, the jury found him guilty regarding *Six Million.*

An appeal was made on several grounds: principally on the unconstitutionality of the section of the *Criminal Code* that concerns "false news," and on the inadmissibility of "hearsay evidence." Two lesser grounds of appeal (which proved enough to justify a new trial) concerned the trial judge's instructions to the jury and materials that he had (or had not) allowed to be entered as evidence. On the constitutional challenge, the Court of Appeal rejected the argument. What concerns us, though, is the challenge over what was admissible and inadmissible as hearsay evidence.

It is the nature of the events in question that reliance must be placed on testimony of various sorts: experts, eyewitnesses, and historical documents. Accordingly, the Crown, in prosecuting Zundel, adduced the eyewitness evidence of several survivors of Nazi concentration camps concerning what had transpired in those camps. The Crown had also called Raul Hilberg as an expert witness on the Holocaust. Hilberg testified that in his research he relied primarily on documents and secondarily on witnesses with a direct knowledge of events.

As grounds for appeal, Zundel's lawyer challenged the admissibility of such evidence, claiming that it was based on hearsay ("Regina v. Zundel," 167). It is worth noting in passing, as the Appeal Court also noted, that the defense had been permitted to use its own expert witness, Robert Faurisson, on the same basis as Dr. Hilberg was allowed to testify. And Zundel had tried to get Richard Verral (a.k.a. Harwood) to testify, but he refused "as he had married a Jewish girl and given up political work" (140).

B.4 Ethos and the Law

To argue that an expert's evidence is based on hearsay is a substantial challenge, and were it to have been successful, the case against Zundel would have been significantly undermined, since so much reliance was placed on Dr. Hilberg's evidence. As the Court of Appeal noted, while an expert may take into account the statements of others while forming an opinion, where the facts that are relied upon are not proved, then the opinion is of no weight. This, effectively, is the hearsay rule (175).

There are, however, established qualifications to the hearsay rule, and in this case the court recognized two exceptions that were relevant and mutually supportive. In the first instance, events of general history may be proved by historical treatises on the ground that they represent "community opinion or reputation" about an historical event. Such an event would be one lacking living witnesses and of such general interest that there is a "high probability" that the matter underwent general scrutiny as the reputation was formed. The assumption is that what a community comes to believe has been scrutinized by that community, and where the belief is carried over into historical treatises, it can then be held as an historical fact (176).

Given this, the Court reasoned, it is logical to accept that "an expert historian may testify as to the existence of an historical event relying upon material to which any careful and competent historian would resort" (ibid.). And insofar as an expert can be cross-examined, her or his testimony is superior as evidence to an historical treatise.

The judgment here recognizes several features of bona fide appeals to authority in such cases: there must have been a general public interest in the original events (thus trusting in community knowledge), and the expert must proceed as any careful and competent expert of the sort (i.e., historian) would proceed. While not guaranteeing it, the latter is likely to encourage consensus among experts.

This second point becomes important in the case, because the expert, Hilberg, did not base his opinion on reputation or community opinion, but on documents. Thus his testimony did not fall exactly within the exception to the hearsay rule discussed. But while he based his opinion on documentary material "which was hearsay," the Court found it admissible to support the existence of the Holocaust (178). That is, they judged it was a legitimate exception to the hearsay rule because he acted as any careful, competent historian would act, and, furthermore, there was an unlikelihood of any living witnesses who had firsthand knowledge (i.e., victims) of the *implementation* of the policy that gave rise to the Holocaust.

The Court of Appeal further found that the Crown's case as to the existence of the Holocaust did not rest solely on the evidence of Dr. Hilberg. His expert testimony, we might say, was contributory, but not sufficient, evidence for the thesis. Also of note were the "several eyewitnesses . . . at least two of [whom] . . . gave evidence of direct observation of the destruction of prisoners on a large scale in gas chambers" (180–81). The combined effect of these accounts, together with eyewitness testimony to the effect that large numbers of people were taken to camps and did not emerge from them, made reasonable the inference that killings and the disposal of bodies were not isolated occurrences but a matter of Nazi government policy.

As we will see in the next section, it is important to the court that these testimonies included direct observations and that these were of different aspects of the process of destruction. The eyewitness accounts constitute a different kind of evidence to that of the expert witness. Together they strengthen the thesis.

The court's position on eyewitness testimony and expert evidence is clarified by its rejection of a further submission that had been allowed by the original trial judge. This was the film *Nazi Concentration Camps,* together with an accompanying narration. The film was made by the U.S. armed forces and was used as evidence in the International Military Tribunal at Nuremberg in Germany on 29 November 1945. The film and narrative were accompanied by several affidavits, including one by George C. Stevens, lieutenant colonel in the U.S. army, which stated that "[t]he accompanying narration is a true statement of the facts and circumstances under which these pictures were made" (196).

In spite of this, the Court of Appeal found that the narrative did not belong to the class of statements to which the public duty exception to the hearsay rule applies. While the narrative may have been admissible at Nuremberg, it was not deemed so in this trial and the trial judge was wrong in allowing it. In explaining this decision, the court stated: "The narrator is unknown; the author of the narrative is unknown; and the source of the information is frequently not revealed. The narrative is more than just a statement of fact as to what the film shows" (199).

In the terms of ethotic argument, the narrator is untrustworthy because unknown, as is the author of the narrative. This is *one* of the reasons why what they say is dismissed as credible evidence.

B.5 The Role of Ethotic Argument

The appeal trial gives us a practical view of when broadly ethotic considerations are appropriate as evidence in argumentation, when they are not, and something of the grounds for deciding in each case. The case study has revealed that the text *Did Six Million Re-*

ally Die? is primarily based on suspect authority, having taken its influence, example, and argumentative strategy from a source who, on reflection, lacks the full credibility attributed to him by Harwood. Despite other argumentative moves (involving other weaknesses), this is the argumentative form to which the text at last resorts and because of which a reasonable audience should be unpersuaded by the thesis promoted. It may be observed that, since the audience is likely to be unfamiliar with Rassinier and with many of the other witnesses and sources who are attacked or applauded, then the audience lacks the grounds to make such a judgment. But there are two things to note here:

1. As the text indicates with the reference to "The Truth at Last," the thesis propounded there counters the accepted view on the matter, which the weight of opinion of all sorts supports. Thus the burden of proof is on the author (Harwood) to present a compelling case. This he may feel he has done with his remarks on "proof" and "certainty." But insofar as his argumentation depends, in the final analysis, on the strength of his ethotic appeals, and particularly those made to Rassinier, then he has a particular burden to demonstrate Rassinier's good character and authority *in the face of* the counterview of so many other authorities.

2. In addition, as Lipstadt (1993:53–54) clarifies, historians of the events in question should build their case not on isolated oral histories (like Christopherson's), but by means of the method of triangulation that involves other kinds of proof. Harwood's proofs are largely restricted to speculation and to the distortion of documents. While an audience might initially be misled by these, any that went so far as to investigate the documents to which Harwood refers (or to consult other accounts), would quickly detect the inappropriateness of his conclusions.

Harwood's text, then, illustrates the improper use of ethotic types of argument like the *ad hominem* and the *ad verecundiam*. By contrast, the Ontario Court of Appeal's justifications of its decisions give considerable insight into what can count as appropriate ethotic argumentation. The Crown's argument further illustrates the merits of "triangulation" when building a case, thus corroborating Lipstadt's observation. This merit is recognized by the Court of Appeal, which sees in the combined weight of expert testimony and identified eyewitness accounts the mix of types of proof important toward establishing the Crown's claims. As I have noted before, personal testimony or expert testimony rarely suffices to convince an audience of a thesis, but each contributes a type of proof.

The identification of the eyewitnesses is important. The contrast here is the narrative to the film *Nazi Concentration Camps,* which is rejected in part because the narrator and author of the narrative are unknown. So many appeals to experts or witnesses are of the "many people hold, . . . " or "experts say, . . . " variety. They contribute little if any weight to a case because the audience has no way of verifying the statement, especially concerning experts. Legitimate argumentation of this kind must identify the sources as clearly as possible. This allows others to ascertain the grounds of their appropriateness to act as witnesses or experts, and for the possibility of any biases to be fully discussed. As we see here, in a court of law, where the defendant should not be disadvantaged, this kind of identification is essential.

One of the major consequences of this case study is that it emphasizes the importance of ethotic argumentation in certain contexts. While it may seem to be a peripheral strategy on many occasions, it was essential to the foundations of *Six Million* and to the argumentation used by the Crown in "Regina v. Zundel." The nature of the case and the events it concerned necessitated the primary deployment of types of ethotic argumentation.

This dependency on personality and authority also suggests an apparent downside. As Willard notes, authority dependence poses a dilemma: "it is presumptively rational in a consensualist world to argue from and acquiesce to authorities, but deference to authority has the effect of foreclosing debate" (1990:11). In effect, who do we trust, and where do we stop? In developing this case study I have also had to rely upon authority. While I can analyze Harwood's text as it stands and detect its flaws, I have depended largely on Lipstadt for an alternative portrait of Rassinier than the one provided in *Six Million.* In doing so, I look at the quality of her text and the reviews it has received. In my opinion she is the author of the most comprehensive study of the phenomenon of Holocaust denial and on that basis an authority. In recognizing her so, I provide support for my own analysis. As Willard recognizes, scholarship is authority-dependent, and without closing the circle too emphatically, I will accept his authority on this.[7] And he further notes (18) that fallacy theory has changed to accommodate the recognition that arguing from, or acquiescing to, authority is a sound argumentative strategy. I hope this case study has given some insight into the conditions that should govern such soundness.

Chapter 6

Fallacy

The existence of fallacies, particularly informal fallacies,[1] has been vigorously defended in recent literature (Govier, 1987; Adler, 1994). That they do indeed exist, at least in the minds of argumentation theorists, can be granted from the lists of varying lengths and overlap that populate textbooks on informal logic and argumentation (see, e.g., Johnson and Blair, 1993a), as well as more theoretically oriented works (see Woods and Walton, 1989). But this area of argumentation studies is characterized by, perhaps, more disagreement that any other: disagreement over the nature of fallacy, the composition of lists of fallacies, and the elaboration and analysis of individual fallacies within those lists. In short, fallacy theory, as I shall call it, is rife with problems, four of which stand out as particularly deserving of identification and clarification. Each of these problems bears on the disagreements just noted.

6.1 Problems with Fallacies

1. *The Problem of Theory:* Succinctly put, the nature of "fallacy" is considered so amorphous that coherent theory cannot be formulated. Reflecting on a rich history of fallacy treatments, C. L. Hamblin first blows the whistle when he notes: "We have no *theory* of fallacy at all in the sense that we have theories of correct reasoning or inference" (1970:11). There is little in common between, say, Locke's notion of an *ad hominem* argument and one of Aristotle's original thirteen like the Fallacy of Division.

Gerald Massey begins his complaint in a similar vein:

> [T]here is no theory to underpin or give structure to treatments of fallacy. Consequently, these treatments appear as a

hodgepodge or miscellany of "fallacies" individuated by historical accident and sometimes related only by possession of a common pejorative term. (1981:489)

But Massey takes the discussion further by noting an essential characteristic of fallacy in the so-called Standard Treatment definition: invalidity. Since fallacious arguments are invalid, any theory of fallacy must presuppose a theory of invalidity. But, claims Massey (494), no theory of invalidity has yet been developed.[2] Significantly, Massey's concern arises in part from the Standard Treatment definition, which itself is the source of a further problem.

2. *The Standard Treatment Problem:* Hamblin has also been acknowledged for capturing in a definition the sense of fallacy that is standard in historical treatments: "a fallacious argument, as almost every account from Aristotle onwards tells you, is one that *seems to be valid* but *is not* so"[3] (1970:12). This definition finds its own root in Aristotle's definition of "Sophistical Refutations": "what appear to be refutations but are really fallacies instead" (*Sophistical Refutations,* 164a20–21). The appearance of correctness is the common element shared by these two definitions.

As I noted when the topic of the Standard Treatment was first discussed in chapter 2, actual lists of fallacies themselves challenge the definition since they include fallacies like Many Questions, which is not an argument, and the *Petitio Principii,* which is not invalid (Grootendorst, 1985:161; Walton 1991a:216). Beyond this, a concern is raised about the role of "seeming" or "appearance." As John Woods (1995:183) puts it, a fallacy cannot be a transparently invalid argument. It must be one that at first appears valid, but is subsequently shown to be otherwise. As Woods further notes, Aristotle's examples are too transparent to fit his own definition.[4]

3. *The Problem of Relativity:* A remark by Stephen Toulmin, Richard Rieke, and Allan Janik has attracted both positive and negative attention. They write: "Arguments that are fallacious in one context may turn out to be quite solid in another context. So we shall not be able to identify any intrinsically fallacious forms of argument" (1984:131). Willard (1989:226; 1995:158) considers this an astounding confession that undermines the lists of fallacies proliferating in the textbooks. It leads to a belief that the fallaciousness of an argument is relative, depending on the context. Alternatively, if we are unable to categorize fallacious forms, we are moved one step closer to the position that there are no fallacies at all. Willard's position on all this, which I will consider in the next section, is that if the *form*

of an argument is not fallacious, then the origins of its fallaciousness must lie elsewhere.

Ralph H. Johnson and J. Anthony Blair's reaction is more negative. Understanding the claim to be that fallacies are not always fallacious, they suggest that it suffers from a fatal ambiguity. Much depends on how individual "fallacies" are defined. If the *Argumentum Ad Hominem* (AAH), for example, is understood to mean "an argument in which the person of the arguer is criticized," then some cases of AAH are legitimate; if, however, it is understood to mean "an irrelevant attack on the person of the arguer instead of criticism of the argument" (1993b:192) then no case of AAH is legitimate. Moreover, the Toulmin, Rieke, and Janik comment, as Willard adopts it, would have a number of undesirable consequences. It would permit us, in some contexts, to distort an arguer's position, to introduce irrelevancies, to use false premises, to be inconsistent, or to beg the question (ibid.). However, the problem may be the way in which the members of the Toulmin group have expressed their observation. They may have meant to say that fallacious forms of argument are countersides of good arguments. This interpretation can be derived from their comment, but it involves a slightly different problem.

4. *The Counterside Problem:* The concern here is best captured by Douglas N. Walton:

> The basic problem with fallacies [is] . . . that in each case the type of argument alleged to be "fallacious" can evidently, in some instances, be a correct—or at least not unreasonable— form of argument, or kind of move to make in argument. (1987a:3–4)

This does not mean that the *same* argument can be fallacious in one context but fine in another (such would be a far more extreme version of relativism), but that the argument *type* can have both fallacious and nonfallacious instances. The counterside proposal is also subject to Johnson and Blair's challenge. In fact, they could be interpreting the relativism problem widely enough to encompass the counterside problem as well. But what is at issue here is how exactly we define the fallacies. I would make two observations about this: (a) It matters whether fallacies are understood to include normative force. In this way irrelevance is part of any AAH such that any counterside argument to it would have to be something other than an AAH. (b) The counterside proposal pairs fallacies with legitimate moves in argumentation. Johnson and Blair are right to balk at the suggestion that it might sometimes be permissible to distort an arguer's position. The *legitimate* argumentative move should be the accurate depiction of the arguer's position. With respect to this, Straw Man reasoning becomes the counterside (or counterfeit). Likewise, as Aristotle notes (*Topics,* 111b31–112a11), it is legitimate to divert attention away from the main point in an argumentation, if that diversion is brought back to bear on the issue. The counterside to this is what we now call a Red Herring, where the diversion is not brought back to the issue.

If the counterside proposal is granted, the problem becomes one of identifying the boundary between legitimate and illegitimate cases. This calls for careful, sensitive analyses on a case-by-case basis and eschews fixed definitions of fallacies when those definitions are only approximated in ordinary experience. This has obvious repercussions for a fallacy approach to the teaching of reasoning. As Hans V. Hansen and Robert C. Pinto note: "Because of this difficulty [identifying legitimate instances] which inheres in most informal fallacies, our time is better spent teaching the canons of good reasoning than the characteristics of some kinds of bad reasoning" (1995:316).

Each of these problems has a noticeable impact on how argumentation theorists approach the fallacies and accounts for some of the disagreement over the nature of fallaciousness and categorization of fallacies. In what follows, I will explore some of the current senses of "fallacy" and trace them through the three perspectives of argumentation discussed in earlier chapters. The goal is to explore ways in which the rhetorical account of argumentation sheds light on the problems of fallacy.

6.2 Senses of "Fallacy"

Studies of fallacy that trace their roots to Aristotle are hampered by problems of translation. As Hamblin warns us: "Greek has no precise synonym for 'fallacy'," and the word rendered such is usually *sophisma* (1970:50). The young Aristotle of the *Sophistical Refutations* shares Plato's low opinion of the Sophists, who exercise apparent but not real wisdom (165a21–22). The important dichotomy throughout the work pitches what appears or seems to be real against what is real. The *Sophistical Refutations* introduces its notion of fallacy with the word *paralogismos,* a recognized Aristotelian usage. But translators have also been moved to render *pseudos* as "fallacy." When Aristotle lists the five aims of argument in competitions (165b12), the second (*pseudos*—"deception" or "falsehood") is often given as "fallacy."[5] Hamblin follows this, although he (like Aristotle) discusses the point as the attempt to convict the answerer of "*some* falsehood, relevant or irrelevant" (1970:51). But when Hamblin returns to this a few pages later he identifies the second aim of the questioner as "To show that the opponent has committed a fallacy" (63). This reveals in Hamblin's usage a wider sense of fallacy beyond *sophisma,* to include *pseudos.* It likewise places "fallacy" within a wider range of "falsehoods," of things that are not.

In chapter 2, I discussed how Walton traces his own conception of fallacy to two senses dominant in Aristotle's work: a sophistical sense, and an error-of-reasoning sense. They are distinguished by the first relying on context in argumentative dialogue, while the second, involving a breakdown in the inference from premises to conclusion, is context free. Walton's work is notable both for its revival of the sophistic sense of fallacy and for his attempt to develop a sense of fallacy that accommodates both of the Aristotelian varieties. In the latter case, I found some difficulty with the result. That earlier misgiving will be further developed in section 6.4.

Textbook accounts of *fallacy* often seem to be defining the term by extension: reeling off a list of labels and, maybe, offering some vague and general intension like "errors of reasoning" in a bid to corral the disparate herd.

In fact, the error of reasoning, as Walton explained it, is a popular starting point for many of the more concerted efforts at defining "fallacy." Trudy Govier considers "fallacy" "a mistake in reasoning" requiring, therefore, that the culprit be reasoning and, thus, excluding "false beliefs" (1987:177). Similarly, stress may be placed on the presence of inference or argument. Michael Wreen (1994a:96) opts for a bad or mistaken inference; Maurice A. Finocchiaro (1995:125) cites the failure of one proposition to follow from others as the essential aspect of a fallacy; and Ralph H. Johnson (1987b:246), in an important essay, insists that it is an *argument* that violates conditions of good argument.

A slight shift in emphasis can be seen in a definition provided by Jonathan E. Adler, who returns to the "seeming" and "appearance" (1994:272) of goodness masking a defect in the underlying form or structure. Sally Jackson (1995:257) also begins with a definition that highlights fallacy's effects when she identifies it as a form of argument that gains assent without justification. Such a concern with effects forms the core of James Crosswhite's (1993:391) Perelmanian definition, wherein a fallacious argument is one that seems to persuade a universal audience when it persuades only a particular one. This brings to mind the importance of rhetorical features in the treatments of "fallacy" offered by theorists like Willard (1989, 1995) or Alan Brinton (1985, 1995).

Finally, in this incomplete and unsystematic survey, we should not neglect the sense of fallacy offered by the pragma-dialecticians, as discussed in chapter 2: that a "fallacy" is a hindrance or impediment to the resolution of a dispute (van Eemeren and Grootendorst, 1984, 1992a); that is, it is a violation of a rule of dialogue. In addition there is the elaboration of this idea proposed by Walton: that a "fallacy" is an "argumentation technique" that can be used correctly in one context of dialogue but that has been used incorrectly to hinder "the real and legitimate" goals of the dialogue (1992a:267; 1995a:15).

What conclusions can we draw from this varied compilation of definitions? All the definitions imply some remnant of Aristotelian sensibilities. But if this suggests the prospect of a coherent theory emerging from such diverse definitions, further reflection indicates that it would be difficult to accommodate all the threads unraveled here. In fact, the more one looks at the range of definitions and considers the motivations animating them, the more one sees at work the inclinations I have associated with the distinct perspectives on argumentation: the logical and the dialectical and the rhetorical. If this is the case, then what is being presented to us are three different models of fallacy plausibly identified as *bad product, bad procedure,* and *bad process.* A broad definition, but one of very limited usefulness, would encompass all three. For example: A "fallacy" is an instance of unreasonable argumentation resulting from bad product, bad procedure, or bad process, or any combination thereof.

The usefulness of such a definition would be limited since what may emerge as an instance of bad process may have no relation to any instance of bad product also present. However, I will explore each of these further to illustrate the divergences, and will pay particular attention to developing the notions involved in "bad process."

The emphasis in the tradition has been to talk about a fallacy as a bad (invalid) argument. But this is a tradition that has likewise emphasized the logical sense of argument or argumentation at the expense of the dialectical and rhetorical senses. Consequently, as attempts are made to rehabilitate the dialectical and rhetorical perspectives on argumentation, we should expect a commensurate interest in associated concepts of fallacy, whether or not people are clear that this is what they are doing.

6.3 Fallacy as *Bad Product*

At the forefront of fallacy treatments has been the attention given to bad arguments as the products of argumentation. This is clearly spelled out in Finocchiaro's definition: "fallaciousness is essentially the failure of one proposition to follow from others: that is, an argument is fallacious if and only if the conclusion does not follow from the premises" (1995:125). From this definition, Finocchiaro is able to identify six types of fallaciousness corresponding to six ways in which a conclusion may fail to follow from its premises. One of these is "simply invalidity": that familiar standby, well skewered on Massey's lance but still apparently kicking with life. In addition to this, the premises may just as likely yield a different conclusion, or a presupposition may be false, or the premises may actually support a proposition inconsistent with the conclusion. Beyond this, the conclusion may not follow because the premises contain an ambiguous term, or because it is the same as one of the premises, thus begging the question.

These senses of fallaciousness do take us beyond a mere interest in invalidity, but they are quite restricted to the internal relations between the product's components. It is difficult to see, for example, how Straw Man reasoning (as this was discussed in chap. 1) would fit into Finocchiaro's scheme.[6]

By contrast, Johnson's product-oriented definition of fallacy does permit a wider sense of fallaciousness. Investigating the standard definitions, he detects a common pattern wherein a fallacy is "an X which appears to be Y but is not in fact Y" (1987b:241). After subjecting this to extensive criticism, he concludes the need to retain the idea of "fallacy as a logically bad *argument*"; delete all references to "matters of appearance", and "introduce the notion of frequency" (245). From this he derives the following definition:

> A fallacy is an *argument* which violates one of the criteria/standards of good argument and which occurs with sufficient frequency in discourse to warrant being baptized. (246)

The criteria/standards of good argument are identified as relevance, sufficiency, and acceptability, and the corresponding "basic" fallacies are irrelevant reason, hasty conclusion, and problematic premise, with other fallacies subsumed under these three (247). This does allow Johnson to treat a much wider range of fallacies (including Straw Man [Person]), as is illustrated in the textbook he coauthors with J. Anthony Blair (1993a).

In spite of the achievement here, and the general importance of Johnson's (1987b) paper, there are several things to lament in the account. If the restriction to argument-as-product does not exclude, or at least limit, the importance of audiences, then the purging of all "subjective and psychological nuances," with all reference to matters of appearance, does.

Johnson, in statements that evoke the problem of relativism, considers the "subjective" view of fallacy "as a matter of *appearance*" to mean that an argument can appear fallacious to one person but not to another. It is such a definition, Johnson believes, which provides the material for disagreements about whether or not there are fallacies and whether fallacies are context-dependent. To avoid this the term *fallacy* must "do serious logical duty" and, hence, "it cannot be defined that way" (242). This effectively places "fallacy" with the "logical elements of argumentation" (if any nonlogical elements are even granted). Not only does this undermine the importance that Johnson elsewhere places on contextual features (see chap. 1), but it shifts attention away from how people reason, how they consume arguments, and how they interpret them. Arguably, such things are the "nuts-and-bolts" of everyday argumentation.

Another noteworthy feature of Johnson's definition is the inclusion of frequency, "because a fallacy is not just any mistake in argument, but one that occurs with some frequency" (245). Govier (1987:177) shares this penchant for repeatability as a feature of "fallacy"; and Hansen and Pinto (1995:13) remind us that Locke held a similar view about the "ad" arguments. There may be something odd in requiring frequency of occurrence to be essential to the definition of things that critics complain occur so rarely (outside of textbooks) as to be virtually nonexistent, but it is a useful way to curtail the proliferation of lists. However, it raises the question of what would count as an error of reasoning that was not a fallacy, that is, an argument that violated one of the criteria/standards but in a (so far) unclassified way. Johnson (and Blair's) three "basic" fallacies would seem to accommodate all errors, frequent or otherwise. Supplemental to this is the more obvious question of how frequently in discourse an error must occur before it is elevated (and by whom?) to the class of "fallacy." This is an important consideration, because the list changes: Johnson and Blair's list is not that of Aristotle. Fallacies come— consider Johnson and Blair's Fallacy of the Freeloading Term

(1993a:155); and fallacies go—consider Aristotle's Fallacy of Accent (*Sophistical Refutations* 166b1–9). And, as I shall suggest in the next section, we should expect this process of evolution to continue. Moreover, the reference to "frequency in discourse" in Johnson's definition leads one to wonder whether fallacies are language- or culture-specific. Again, Aristotle's Fallacy of Accent is brought to mind with respect to this.

Finally, and perhaps of greater concern. Johnson defines "fallacy" in relation to a violation of the (principally three) criteria of good argument. If we look closely at one of these—relevance—we should see that he is more literal in this than he might intend since he focuses exactly on the violation (irrelevance) rather than on the standard (relevance). Johnson writes: "First the premises must be *relevant* to the conclusion. If it can be shown that one of the premises is irrelevant to the conclusion, then it has been shown that the argument is not a good one" (1987b:246). Attention to the textbook that elaborates upon the approach reveals the same imbalance: the focus is on irrelevance, not relevance (Johnson and Blair, 1993a:52–56). Where the question of relevance itself is addressed it is done indirectly through a test for irrelevance:

> if P were true (just supposing), would that give some basis for judging that C is true? Or try it the other way: "If P were false, would that give some basis for supposing that C is false?" If, in both cases, the answer is "No," then you have some reason to assert that P is irrelevant to C. (55)

Willard (1995:145) suggests that fallacy theory is groping its way toward a theory of relevance. This is a challenging observation, important for the process-oriented approach, and I will explore it in the next section 6.5. But if fallacy theory is doing any such thing, product-oriented definitions like those just noted will not be in the vanguard. The effect, if not the intent, is to emphasize the negative, not the positive. In light of this, one feels some appreciation for why the fallacy-approach is not the choice of many logicians when it comes to teaching reasoning (Hitchcock, 1995b).

6.4 Fallacy as *Bad Procedure*

Hamblin proposed that if we wanted to understand Aristotle's account of fallacies, we needed to "give up our tendency to see them as purely logical" (1970:66). He recommends the study of Dialectic as a promising avenue to which the modern student can turn. Chapter 2 explored the merits (and drawbacks) in making such a turn, and paid particular attention to the account of fallacies offered by one dialectical school—that of the pragma-dialecticians. Thus, I intend to say less about them here, other than to locate their efforts within the present discussion and to offer a few further comments on Walton's model made possible by the direction that this study of fallacy is pursuing.

To identify a fallacy as "bad procedure" in argumentation is to say that it violates or impedes some legitimate move in dialectical argumentation. Alternatively, it is to say that it violates a rule for the resolution of a dispute that dialectical argumentation encompasses. This, as has been seen, is a limitation. "[T]he norms provided by the rules for critical discussion apply only where and insofar as the discourse concerned is indeed aimed at resolving a difference of opinion" (van Eemeren and Grootendorst, 1995b:136–37). Since not all argumentation is argumentation aimed at resolving disputes, and since the pragma-dialectical definition of fallacy is "every violation which may result in the resolving of the dispute being made more difficult or even impossible" (1984:182), then it is possible to have argumentation outside of the influence of fallacies, *in the pragma-dialectical sense.* In effect, Walton (1989, 1990, 1991a, 1995a) accommodates this by expanding the range of dialogues within the account so that it includes more than the critical discussion. Thus, he opens up the possibility of extending fallacies to other dialogues like quarrels or negotiation. In all cases though, we are looking at two or more parties cooperating in the resolution of some disagreement over a viewpoint, with *both* parties promoting a thesis (Walton, 1995a:19).[7]

Furthermore, I mentioned the misgivings I had over Walton's concept of fallacy as discussed in chapter 2. He presents a unified model that falls somewhere between the sophism and the error of reasoning (272). Yet it was never clear that these two distinct features could be wed happily or easily. In light of the present discussion, the ground for the distinctness between the two poles of Walton's definition is clearer. The error-of-reasoning type fallacy belongs to the argument-as-product model's sense of *bad product,* whereas the sophistical tactic type of fallacy (as Walton defines this) belongs to the argument-as-procedure model's sense of *bad procedure.* Walton's "unified" model would straddle the two, and this is the source of its difficulties. The labels *bad product* and *bad procedure* denote quite distinct flaws, different in nature and in focus.

The Dutch members of the pragma-dialectical school have indeed achieved a comprehensive theory of fallacy. The problem does not arise of deciding when the *ad hominem* is legitimate and when not: "The pragma-dialectical approach offers a systematic solution to the problem of the many exceptions to the rule that an *argumentum ad hominem* is a fallacy. The solution is very simple: there are no exceptions" (van Eemeren and Grootendorst, 1995c:226).

It always violates the first rule for critical discussions and so is always a fallacy. But this all-or-nothing stance, while theoretically tidy, may be too simple a solution, because reasonableness and unreasonableness are painted here in black and white. The careful weighing of an argument's merits is not required, and of this we might be concerned. Fallacy as bad procedure is a useful tool within its sphere of influence, but that sphere may exclude too many of argumentation's important aspects (like judging the degrees of reasonableness). This, together with the difficulties involved in establishing the grounds for (intersubjective) agreement between protagonist and antagonist (discussed in chap. 2) continues to limit the reach of this model of argumentation.

6.5 Fallacy as *Bad Process*

Willard believes that the informal logicians have been moving for sometime toward a rhetorical turn. He analyzes the treatments given to a number of informal fallacies in order to show that, at root, they involve pragmatic questions of relevant fits between "discourse and context and between intention and utterance" (1995:146). He considers the ethical and procedural ways logicians treat suppressing evidence, guilt by association, and name-calling (1989:223), as well as how they proceed with the "ad" arguments, particularly the *ad populum*. As a general observation, he concludes:

> The pattern discerned in the [aforementioned]fallacies is a narrowing movement: broad labels are introduced with clear-cut, extreme examples. Because these are often caricatures, the fallacy rule gets studded with caveats and exceptions. In accounting for exceptions, the fallacy rule gets winnowed down, narrowed or softened—typically to the relevancy rule. (232).

In the case of the *ad populum,* for example, this winnowing down reduces the rule for what counts as a fallacy to something that asks an audience to trust a product or idea simply because other people supposedly do (1995:157). This, he notes, is "the rhetorical end of the road," where the rhetorical view of the *ad populum* as "the use of emotional appeals or aesthetic images that distract the persuadee from reflective thinking about the arguments being made" (148) has been adopted by fallacy theorists.[8]

While Willard suggests that the informal fallacies are gradually being turned toward their natural home, others argue that some of these fallacies always were primarily rhetorical. Thus Alan Brinton calls the *ad hominem* "primarily a rhetorical phenomenon rather than a logical one" (1985:50). Elsewhere, in a full account that takes note of the rich variety in *ad hominem* reasoning, he understands it as "an assault on the rhetorical *ethos* of a speaker or writer whose *ethos* would otherwise be regarded as more of a persuasive factor than the adhominist believes reasonable" (1995:222). And this, as he notes with respect to Aristotle's endorsement of the move in the *Rhetoric* (2.1.1378a), "is not in itself either rhetorically or logically inappropriate." The adhominist wishes to influence the hearers' attitudes about a person's advocacy of a claim (and not about the claim itself). Then it is a question of whether the facts about the advocate are relevant to her or his advocacy of the claim. The appropriateness of an *ad hominem* hinges on this point.

The ethos of an arguer, the attitudes of an audience, and the relevance of a charge all combine to define the *ad hominem* as an essentially rhetorical tool for argumentation. Individually, informal fallacies like the *ad hominem* and the *ad populum* can have their rhetorical roots revealed in this way. Yet in spite of Willard's suggestion, not all informal logicians can be interpreted as taking this path. Johnson and Blair with their pointed objections and logical definitions are a case (or cases) in point.[9] But just as dialecticians are able to accommodate the informal fallacies as flaws of bad procedure, it may be possible for those adopting a rhetorical perspective to recast them as flaws of process where the communication between arguer and audience is at stake. A good place to begin considering this is where one of Brinton's remarks would point us—Aristotle's *Rhetoric.*

With so much attention given to the list of fallacies in the *Sophistical Refutations,* the list in the *Rhetoric* (2.24) is often overlooked. Hamblin notes that Aristotle believed he could "sort out a set of peculiarly rhetorical argument-types which are purveyors at once of persuasive force and logical validity" (1970:73). Much of the

Rhetoric is a later work than the *Sophistical Refutations,*[10] and its list would appear to be a later list. Within the list, reference is made to Demades and to "the war" (2.24.1041b). The war would have been that between Athens and Macedon, culminating in the Greeks' defeat in 338 B.C. when Aristotle would have been around forty-six years of age. We can imagine the list to date from sometime after that, probably within Aristotle's last decade. Fallacies are at issue here no longer with respect to arguing in dialogue games (Hintikka, 1987) but with respect to arguing so as to persuade an audience.

As we saw earlier (introduction, sec. 6), central to rhetorical argument is the enthymeme, one of Aristotle's "greatest and most original achievements" (Burnyeat, 1996:91). Contrary to the logical tradition, having a premise suppressed is not essential to the enthymeme, although Aristotle allows that such may occur when the audience already knows what is being assumed: "if one of these [premises] is known, it does not have to be stated, since the hearer supplies it" (1.2.1357a).[11] This does however, capture one possibility of what is essential to the enthymeme—an active role for the audience. Enthymemes are short, probable, noncomplex arguments intended for popular consumption. The audience is actively involved in their understanding, assessment, and perhaps completion in cases where they supply the assumptions. In light of this, we might expect any corresponding sense of fallacy to involve cases of improper omissions or, alternatively, cases where such "completion" is impeded. Following this cue, we find that Aristotle's neglected list does corroborate such a suggestion. It provides nine fallacies, some of which overlap those in the *Sophistical Refutations.* Paraphrased, these spurious enthymemes, which are enthymemes only in appearance, comprise the following:

> 1. Apparent enthymemes that are verbal:(a) *Compact wording gives the appearance of an enthymeme, but is the mere collation of facts.* Insofar as the enthymeme is the rhetorical correlate of the logical syllogism, due to its brevity and compactness, then just as something can appear to be a syllogism when it is not, so there may be an appearance of an enthymeme. Here the compactness simulates the form of the enthymeme, but the hearer, on reflection, would be able to supply nothing, since it is not a real enthymeme. (b) *Homonyms are employed to suggest that the same thing is involved when in fact different things are at issue.* Again, there is no enthymeme due to the equivocation—as the

hearer should discover when trying to supply something that has been assumed.

2. *The speaker combines what is divided or divides what is combined.* Were someone to claim that they knew a word because they knew each of the letters that comprise it, or that a single portion of something was harmful because a double portion of it was, then they would have committed this infraction. We cannot always assume that what is true of the parts is true of the whole, and vice versa, which is the assumption on which these arguments depend. The distinctions here seem to be unrelated to Combination and Division in the *Sophistical Refutations* (166a23–36) because in the latter the error depended on meaning changing when one combined or divided words. In the *Rhetoric,* the error lies rather with the assumption the hearer is meant to supply.

3. *The speaker constructs or demolishes an argument by exaggerating.* The hearer assumes the guilt or innocence of a defendant due to the way in which the accuser or defendant exaggerates the change so as to give an appearance of guilt or innocence. But the proof for this is omitted and the hearer's assumption is ungrounded. As Aristotle puts it: "the hearer falsely reckons" (1401b).

4. *The speaker supports a point with one (nonnecessary) example or sign.* There is something of the unrepresentative or insufficient sample in the examples of this fallacy that Aristotle provides: "Lovers benefit cities; for the love of Harmodius and Aristogeiton destroyed the tyrant Hipparchus" and "Dionysus [of Syracuse, who is known to be wicked] is a thief (II.24.1401G12)." In the first case, the example does little to make the claim probable. In the second case, being wicked does not make one a thief. The two examples, being quite dissimilar (one general, the other particular), must be variants of the problem Aristotle has in mind. In both cases the audience would be familiar with the example, but no assumption will get them to the claim, *from that assumption alone.*

5. *The speaker treats as important (essential) what is only an accident.* I interpret the fallacy this way in order to fit the accompanying examples. The Rhys Roberts translation (McKeon edition, 1941), which Hamblin adopts, renders this

fallacy as to "represent the accidental as essential" (1401b14). Such a definition appears to help it correspond to the Fallacy of Accident in the *Sophistical Refutations*. There, the mistake is one of confusing what is accidental with what is essential. Thus Coriscus is different from a man because he is different from Socrates, and Socrates is a man. But being a man is deemed accidental to Socrates and not essential. In the *Rhetoric*, however, the thrust is different: an intention is attributed where the action has in fact been accidental. The examples bear this out: Polycrates claims that mice aided the Egyptians by gnawing the bowstrings of the invading Assyrians. But the mice had no such intent. That this behavior happened to aid the Egyptians was quite accidental. It is, though, difficult to see the concern here. The mice aided the Egyptians (claim); for they gnawed through the bowstrings (premise). Presumably, since the result (in the claim) was an accident (premise), Aristotle sees a breakdown between the premise and the claim that the audience should not fill.

The other example is slightly different: To be invited to dinner is the greatest form of honor (claim); for Achilles' wrath against the Achaens at Tenedos resulted from not being invited (premise). Here, the support is not what it appears to be because, says Aristotle, Achilles was angered by the insult involved; that he was not invited to dinner just happened to be the form of the insult.

6. *The speaker draws a conclusion from a false assumption (para to hepomenon).* This is most intelligible if examples are cast in syllogistic form, where their invalidity is apparent. Three examples are cited, each with the same form. As a case in point: "Paris was high-minded" because "Paris looked down on a crowd" and "the high-minded have this quality (of looking down on a crowd)." Again, "beggars and exiles might seem to be happy" because "beggars sing and dance and exiles can live wherever they want" and "these predicates are true of people who seem to be happy." Aristotle points out that the confusion lies in the different circumstances, of those people mentioned and those who are really happy. "Thus, he says, "it, too, falls under [the fallacy of] omission (1401G)." What omission? Presumably, of that which, were it

present, would make this a real enthymeme rather than only appearing to be one. The audience cannot complete the reasoning in an appropriate way because a reasonable assumption has not been provided.

7. *The speaker takes a noncause as a cause.* Here we have a first glimpse of what comes to be called the *post hoc ergo propter hoc* fallacy. People, especially those involved in politics, "take what happens later as though it happened because of what preceded" (1401b). The mistake is to attribute a causal relationship where none exists. The erroneous assumption required of the audience is simply that of the causal relationship. Sometimes there *is* a causal relationship between events, of course; but Aristotle does not distinguish the legitimate from the illegitimate here.

8. *The speaker omits to consider the bearing of time and / or circumstance.* For example, an exception may be made in excusing a person from an exam, but it would be wrong to think that they were thereby excused from all future exams; and, there are circumstances that may allow physical aggression toward another (self-defense and preventing a person from harming another), but it is not permissible in every case. With the relevant consideration omitted, the audience cannot complete the reasoning in a legitimate way; the exception does not make the rule.

9. *The speaker confuses what is a general probability with what is not a general probability.* This is compared to what occurs in sophistic argument. Since some improbable things happen, then the improbable will be probable. But this is not generally so. The deception lies in omitting the particular reference and circumstances.

Without too much difficulty, we can see the role played by the audience in bringing to light the fallacies of the *Rhetoric*. The audience does not commit the fallacies, but the fallaciousness of the reasoning is revealed once viewed from the perspective of the audience and from the assumptions they are expected to supply in each case. Hence, the fallacies are often fallacies of omission. While this may also have been the case with many of the fallacies in the *Sophistical Refutations,* with its stress on "appearing," it becomes a defining feature of fallaciousness in the *Rhetoric,* where audience considerations are core to the process of argumentation. What impedes that process of legitimate communication between arguer and audience is fallacious.

In many ways, this is similar to some of the pragma-dialectical formulations with the difference that there there the talk is about dialogues where both parties promote a thesis, while the rhetorical model does not observe this restriction. For example, Walton's general sense of a fallacy hindering the argumentation or preventing its development (and violating the maxims of "polite collaboration" [1995a:272]), reaches beyond the logical account in just the right sense.

If we now go back to the "Standard Treatment" or to its root in Aristotle, what should attract our attention in the language is an aspect that Johnson's "logical" definition looked to exclude: the *semblance* of validity that a fallacious argument *seems* to have but does not; the *appearance* of refutation in what is not a refutation at all. These definitions themselves accord importance to the audience. For if an argument *seems* to be valid (or acceptable, or cogent), we must ask to *whom* it seems so? It would be plausible, following from this, to only count as fallacious arguments those that actually do/did deceive an audience. This would eliminate many of the textbook examples. It would also suggest a way of demarcating the line between fallacious argument and nonfallacious argument. Woods (1995) puts his finger on what is at issue here when he notes that the examples that Aristotle provides in the *Sophistical Refutations* do not fit his definition because they do not *seem* to be correct when they are not—they seem, right from first perusal, to be incorrect. But of course, they seem this way to the practiced, astute eye of an experienced argumentation theorist like Woods, and likely most other members of the audience of argumentation theorists react the same way. Less competent audiences may well be deceived, particularly in the kinds of argumentative contexts envisioned by Aristotle, and particularly those in the *Rhetoric*.

The problem with making context and audience the determinants of fallaciousness is that it appears to throw us back into the mire of the problem of relativism where the same argument may be fallacious in one context but not in another. But there are two things that should dissuade us from closing the door on the suggestion in this way.

1. In the first case, it overlooks the fact that argumentation itself is context dependent. Strictly speaking, there is no one context in which an argument may be fallacious and another in which it may not. There is only *the* context in which the argument arises, in which it is considered against the background of all the elements comprising that context (see chap. 3), and within which the question of fallaciousness will arise and be determined.

2. We should also pay attention to the other part of the "seeming" definition in the "Standard Treatment": it seems valid *"but it is not."* Again, we should ask, to *whom* is it not? Here is indicated an objective judge, a principle of reasonableness overseeing the argumentation. This is how I have been employing the principle of the "universal audience." Now, for an argument to be fallacious, it must seem not to be so to the particular audience, but be found to be so by the universal audience for that argument.

Once this is recognized, much of standard fallacy theory that seemed on the verge of being dismissed is suddenly reclaimed. But again, this reclamation takes place from within a rhetorical perspective of argumentation. For it is quite reasonable to talk about argument forms (like the *argumentum ad hominem*) which have the *potential* to be fallacious and that when deceptive in a context become *actually* fallacious. But if they fail to deceive, if they are delivered to an audience of John Woodses, for example, then their potential is not actualized, they do not succeed in seeming valid. But, as we know, they do succeed in many cases, because the audiences of arguments are diverse, and only when the universal element of reasonableness is alert in audiences is the flaw detected.

6.6 Crosswhite's Perelmanian Account

Tying fallacy to the reactions of particular and universal audiences brings me close to the similar treatment of the concept proposed by James Crosswhite. But there are several differences between what I am suggesting and what Crosswhite has explored.

At first glance, Crosswhite seems to do away with the "so-called fallacies." In fact, working from a close reading of Perelman's ideas, he argues that they are "part of a larger account of what it means to argue reasonably or unreasonably" (1993:390).

> A fallacious argument, considered from this perspective, is: one that seems to persuade a universal audience, but does not. Instead, it persuades only a particular audience. Thus, in the case of a fallacy, we have an instance of a particular audience's mistaking itself for a universal audience. The general feature of unreasonable argumentation is just this fact that a person or group which reasons in a way it assumes to be universal actually reasons in a way that is particular either to an individual or some group of people. To commit a

fallacy is to mistake the scope of the effectiveness of an argument. (391)

I would note two things at this juncture: (a) Crosswhite's treatment retains the "seeming" of traditional accounts. To seem to persuade a universal audience is in effect to seem reasonable, but to *be* otherwise. (b) There is some ambivalence about the source of fallaciousness. As the passage begins, the problem lies in the fallacious argument, which seems to persuade. But as the passage closes, we learn that to commit a fallacy is to mistake the argument's effectiveness—a flaw in the arguer or audience. As Crosswhite continues, it is the second sense that is stressed. For a fallacy to arise: "a particular audience must seem to itself capable of judging as a universal audience, and yet be unable to do so" (ibid.). Thus the fallaciousness lies not with the arguer or in the argument, but with the audience's misconception of itself; the deception is a self-deception. Hence, what appeared to be well rooted in the history of the concept reveals itself to be quite new, or, at least, have an element that is quite new, because Crosswhite's discussion never completely escapes the initial ambivalence in talking about two roots of fallaciousness.

"A traditional "fallacy" may be invalid," he tells us. "but still be effective and so not unreasonable, when it persuades a particular audience but cannot convince a universal one" (ibid). By consequence from this, invalid arguments may be reasonable, so their fallaciousness cannot reside in their formal features. But this is to equate reasonableness with effectiveness, something I have been loath to do. Since the same argument "cannot convince" the universal audience for that context, it would be preferable to speak of the argument as actually fallacious: it seemed reasonable to the particular audience, but not to the universal audience constructed from it.

Crosswhite follows this by detailing three general "ways in which arguments can go wrong" for audiences, which Chaim Perelman offers in place of traditional fallacy theory.

First, the framework of argumentation may not be in place. Second, the starting point of an argument may not be reached. Third, the particular techniques of argumentation may not be effective. An exhaustive analysis of these three ways in which reasoning goes wrong would require a commentary on the whole of *The New Rhetoric* (392).

Earlier, Crosswhite had criticized fallacy theorists' penchant for treating fallacies as violations of rules, logical or dialectical. Yet this turn in his discussion serves to undermine the force of that critique. The shift from talking about fallaciousness as a feature of arguments to talking about it as a feature of audiences has not been complete after all. Rather than audiences misconceiving their role or nature, we are alerted to ways in which *arguments* can go wrong for them. It is a short step to suggesting that for each of these three ways there is a way the argument can "go right" and a rule for ensuring such correctness, the violation of which constitutes a fallacy.

Crosswhite does provide examples of the three ways of going wrong (which he calls "argument-criticism," and that he collects under "headings taken from traditional theory" [ibid.]),[12] and in the course of these he illustrates the other dimension to his account, with its interesting definition of a fallacy being an instance of argumentation that seems to convince a universal audience but really does not.

Take the *argumentum ad baculum,* now conceived as an instance of the framework of argumentation not being in place. This informal fallacy qualifies here because, if argumentation eschews all use of force, then where it is used the conflict is not an argument. Technically, this means that in not being an argument, the *ad baculum* is not a fallacy. But the merit of Crosswhite's (and, by extension, Perelman's) proposal is that it can show what is unreasonable in the *ad baculum.* Of two main examples used to illustrate this, the most instructive is the following:

> A husband and wife are trying to reason together about how to educate their children. The husband announces the conclusions he has reached, and gives his reasons. He also remarks that he cannot leave the matter up in the air any longer because he is losing his peace of mind. He takes the remark to be a sincere expression of his devotion to his children's education. His wife takes it to be a threat that if his plans are not accepted he will become angry. She opposes his plans but is too afraid of his anger to state her own arguments. (394)

Crosswhite asks the identity of the universal audience to which an appeal is being made in this case. It is not the ideal citizen or rational person because the issue is not the education of children per se, but how this particular couple should educate its children. Nor can it be only one or other of the partners, since they are "trying to reason together." Thus, the universal audience in the case must be the concrete universality of both partners.

From that perspective, the husband undermines the framework for argumentation by mistaking the view of a particular audience (his own) for that of the universal audience. He misconceives himself as the universal audience and thus his reasoning is fallacious. The actual universal audience—both partners reasoning together— would not accept his threat as legitimate argumentation.

Set out this way, the case fits Crosswhite's definition—almost. We do have a person reasoning in a way he assumes to be universal when it is only particular. And we do have a particular audience seeming to itself capable of judging as a universal audience, and yet being unable to do so.

The difficulty arises in that the guilty party is both arguer and audience, so that the relationship between them is not clarified. Fallaciousness lies in the arguer who thinks he provides acceptable argumentation. Yet he does so because he is part of the audience for that argument, but is confused about what role he plays in that audience. And, of course, in the end the *definiendum* of the definition ("fallacious argument") is not present, because the flaw is that there is no argument at all.

This highlights the key difficulty in Crosswhite's Perelmanian account: a fallacious argument is one that seems to persuade a universal audience. But how does one *seem* to persuade a universal audience? The answer, it appears, is that the universal audience is *never* deceived. The mistake is always in substituting another audience for it.

On one level, this seems right. But in other respects it does not take us far enough. There is a vagueness, particularly surrounding the root of fallaciousness, that the account still needs to clarify. Beyond this, as a rhetorical theory of fallacy, it does not tell us enough about the breakdown of the communicative process between arguer and audience.

In many respects Crosswhite is attuned to the incompleteness of his account and notes as much. Its many merits recommend its further development. It recognizes fallaciousness, like argumentation itself, as a social phenomenon, and draws attention to its impact on the human psyche. In fact, Crosswhite observes: "The most interesting and intractable dilemmas that fallacy theory faces are conflicts about what it means to be human" (401).

6.7 The "Act" of Fallacy

Indeed, the study of the "seeming correctness" of fallacious reasoning promises general insights into both human receptivity of
ideas and the nature of informal fallacies. Such a path would take
me beyond the stated focus of this chapter, but I would note here the
important steps in this direction taken by Sally Jackson. She attends
to the actual persuasiveness defective patterns of argument have.
Key to the analysis is the idea of presumption. Hearers, following
general rules governing communication (like the Cooperative Principle), presumptively accept what they hear unless it is contradicted
by other evidence or presumptions. Jackson observes: "informal fallacies may describe not the material presented by a speaker but the
interpretive and reconstructive choices of the hearer" (1995:260).
And she concludes with the suggestion that "fallacies are not incorrect argument schemes or correct argument schemes applied incorrectly, but failed diagnostic strategies" (266).

Again, attributing the root of fallacies to the audience rather
than to the argument (or arguer) is suggestive. Of course, the frequency of certain defective patterns of argument, noted by Johnson
and Govier, would imply some correlation between potentially deceptive argument patterns and the actual deceiving, on some occasions in some contexts, of audiences.

The existence of a fallacy, at least in its *bad process* variant, appears to require this relationship between a potentially defective argument and its actual (successful) effect on an audience as noted
earlier, because we should want to distinguish between those arguments with only "seeming correctness" that fool or mislead an audience and those arguments with only "seeming correctness" that are
recognized for what they are and do not fool or mislead the audience.
The fallaciousness, when it arises, takes place in the transmission,
in the activity of arguing, between arguer and audience. It is the bad
process. This would explain, with a twist, why some arguments with
defective patterns are accepted in some contexts and not in others.
The mistake is to accept them; then the fallacy occurs. Where they
are not accepted, where they are recognized and rejected, no "act" of
fallacy has taken place. Hence, the universal audience, as an instan-
tiation of reasonableness, would never be convinced by a potentially
fallacious argument.

This proposal concretizes the relationship between argument
and audience required for fallacy to occur. There are argument-pat-
terns that seem to be correct, but they require an audience in order

to seem so (and a further—universal—audience to judge that they are not so). This accommodates the findings of the *Rhetoric,* where *bad process* appeared as a flaw/omission in the argument pattern that prevented the audience from properly playing its role in the act of argumentation. It also acknowledges the efforts of scholars like Willard and Crosswhite in turning "fallacy" toward a more contemporary rhetorical base.

Like the idea of reasonableness that judges that argument patterns are not what they seem, the idea of unreasonableness (with its subspecies of fallaciousness) is also a developing notion. As reason evolves it develops new ways to construct effective reasoning and to misconstruct it. Hansen captures the propensity for change in the fallacies when he observes the following:

> [A]n account of fallacies is always an account from some point of view or other of good reasoning, or correct logic. As the account of what makes arguments right grows and changes it is to be expected that the attempted accounts of fallacies will also change. (1996:11)

Interestingly, no one seems to suggest that as good reasoning develops, as the idea of reasonableness unfolds in history, then bad reasoning will diminish. Fallaciousness, like argumentation, is a fact of everyday life.

If the suggestions of this chapter are plausible, then a further step would be to try and classify or allocate the traditional fallacies according to whether they are seen as an instance of bad products, bad procedures, or bad processes.

Problems of premise irrelevance (detailed in chap. 4) would fall under "bad product," as would so-called formal fallacies ("Denying the Antecedent," "Undistributed Middle," etc.), along with fallacies like those of Division and Combination and Begging the Question. Fallacies of bad procedure will include those of topic irrelevance, like the Red Herring and Straw Man/Person, as well as cases involving selective evidence, statistical fallacies (involving biased and nonrepresentative samples), and special pleading. Bad process fallacies would embrace those of audience irrelevance, like unwarranted emotional appeals and the other "ad" arguments, as well as those with premises deemed unacceptable within the cognitive environment of an audience (see chap. 4).

There would likely be much debate about even such a preliminary attempt at categorizing and the proposals of the last paragraph are obviously not intended to be exhaustive. It is also apparent that some of the fallacies can be recast under more than one category (as we have seen in Aristotle), depending on the distinct way they arise in the different perspectives on argumentation. Theorists of all three inclinations, for example, want to lay claim to giving the key account of the *argumentum ad hominem,* but in doing so each casts it in a manner appropriate to a concern in logical, dialectical, or rhetorical argumentation.

What I have been most intent on doing in this chapter, however, is exploring the sense of fallacy as "bad process." As we have seen, this concerns the breakdown of the communication process between arguer/argument and audience in rhetorical argumentation. It involves the key feature of exploring fallaciousness from the audience's perspective, considering ways that prevent the audience from fulfilling its role in argumentation, where it is unable to appropriately supply assumptions required to complete the argumentation.

Headway has also been made in addressing the problems associated with fallacy theory, although my proposals are unlikely to satisfy everyone. The failure to develop a unified fallacy theory is now understood not as a limitation on the study of fallacies but as a recognition of the way in which fallacies, traditional and contemporary, are distributed across the three primary senses explored here, with particular analyses of a fallacy often drawing insights from more than one sense. Where attempts at a unified theory have appeared successful, as in the pragma-dialecticians' project, the fallacies have been coordinated *within* a coherent picture of one of the three senses.

The problem of the Standard Treatment also deserves a revised appreciation. That some of the traditional fallacies "are not arguments" must be seen as a comment as much on the idea of "argument" as on that of "fallacy." It is, clearly, a criticism sustained by the product-oriented conception of the logical perspective on argumentation. The other perspectives, particularly the rhetorical, in conceiving of "argument" in different senses, should be less concerned by that particular criticism. Again, the "seeming correct" criticism of Standard Treatment fallacies deserves reconsideration. Far from being uniformly rejected by fallacy theorists, seeming correctness finds its way, under modified guises, into several of the treatments. It is particularly important to the analysis of bad process because it provides the necessary focus on the audiences of argumentation to whom things seem correct or not.

The final problems first encountered in this chapter—of relativism and counterside—are the most affected by a focus on bad process. The problem of relativism as a serious problem should be rejected. It is, simply, a result of misunderstanding the contextual nature of argumentation. That the *same* argument may seem correct in one context but not in another is a concern that only arises if we make the mistake of lifting arguments out of their natural environments and cutting the lifelines that make them what they are. The context is an essential component of the argument itself, not just an occasion for its occurrence. There is no *same* argument in another context.

Revising the complaint under the counterside problem provides important clarification. Both potential and actual fallacies are flawed in some way. The difference lies in the latter fooling the audience. Some argument patterns, it would seem, are always flawed. They may be so obviously flawed as to never fool an audience, and so never be actually fallacious in the audience-deceiving and -impeding senses, hence, the criticism that textbook fallacies are artificial and not "real." But this can only be decided from case-by-case investigations. The identification of a flawed pattern, which may be *the* analysis of an argument for some, is only a step in the full process of evaluating argumentation. Fallacies, as bad products, procedures, or processes, are tools in deciding the question of what merits and demerits argumentation exhibits; they are not themselves the answer.

Chapter 7

Argumentation and the Critiques of Reason

7.1 Common Concerns

Fallacy, as we saw in the last chapter, has an often overlooked richness and can be approached with quite different results depending on whether that approach is made from the perspective of a logical, dialectical, or rhetorical model of argumentation. In a similar vein, recent discussions of various "modes" of rationality (feminine, masculine, cultural, ethnic, etc.) suggest that fallaciousness could be construed according to the different ways in which it is determined within each mode of rationality. Andrea Nye, for instance, enlivens her detailed critique of the history of logic with the insight that, according to the dictates of that logic, she has "committed fallacy after fallacy" (1990:174), particularly the genetic and *ad hominem* fallacies. Her point is not to undermine her own critique, but to illustrate how a concept of fallaciousness is the product of a certain conception of logic, and that, standing beyond the constraints of such a conception, her apparently fallacious reasoning is not so at all.

While this could take us further in our treatment of the relativity of fallaciousness, instead I want to shift attention to the other problem announced here, which is how reason or logic, with associated terms like *argument,* has been reevaluated in the light of recent critiques, particularly but not exclusively those wrought from the pens of postmodernists and feminists. Much of the critical analysis has been mercilessly thorough and dismissive in its tone. This has brought equally forceful discussions aimed at defending or rehabilitating reason and argument. Where such reconstructions have been successful, I will argue, the results bear a marked similarity to the model of rhetorical argumentation I have been discussing in this book. In fact, I would go further by suggesting that rhetorical argumentation is a prime candidate for a post-postmodernist theory of argument that promises, with development, to meet the concerns of feminists and other critics alike. To do this is particularly important in light of Agnes Verbiest's observation that "[n]o special attention is paid to gender issues in prominent studies of argumentation as is shown in the work of Toulmin, Perelman, Willard, Blair and Johnson, Paul, Woods and Walton, Grize, Barth and Krabbe, Van Eemeren and Grootendorst" (1995:823).

The critics themselves by no means speak with a common voice. "Second-wave" feminists disagree over the nature of reason and "first-wave" critiques (Anthony and Witt, 1993; Code, 1995:217–23), and similar occasions for debate arise between feminism and postmodernism when, for example, it is asked whether "postmodernism [is] singularly the theory of white men whose universalistic project is (rightly) seriously under question" (Rose, 1993:216). Even defenders of reason and argument disagree as to whether those ideas must be redrawn from the ashes of critique, since postmodernism and argument are antithetical in all respects (Russman, 1995); or as to whether they can be envisaged as parts of a common project, since postmodernism and argument enrich and inform each other (Billig, 1991; Cherwitz and Darwin, 1995). Depending on which path is taken, the prospects for the future of argument and the model involved in that future can vary enormously.

It is necessary, then, while not avoiding all discussion of these disagreements, to collect the common components of the critiques of reason, rationality, and argument, weigh their import, and consider how historical argumentation stands in relation to them.

Initially, there are problems of definition, not least of which concern the terms *rationality* and *postmodernism*. The meaning lent to *rationality* can vary from critic to critic (or defender) depending on the focus and motivations of the writer involved (Meyerson, 1994:51). We might consider defining "rationality" through the example of the "rational person" who, minimally, uses good reasons, and supplement this with notions of impartiality and critical judgment. I will return to such ideas later in the chapter. As it happens, these are not the ideas at the center of concern. Thomas A. Russman identifies the common concern with the model of rationality at work in modern philosophy:

> The model of modern rationality was geometry, with what were taken to be its self-evident axioms used as premises for

formal demonstration. The modern rationalist project in its purest form can be put simply: to reorganize and refound knowledge in every domain whatsoever on this geometrical model. (1995:127)

This is the model, together with its conception of logic, that Nye scrutinizes that transforms language into the propositions of the logician (1990:181) and which, in her opinion is taken to its insane extreme in the dichotomized thinking of the Nazis that measures existence itself (170).

Critiques of this rationalism are not new to recent decades. In many respects a quite decisive critique of traditional rationalism was served up by Clarence Irving Lewis in his reevaluation of the a priori. Lewis challenged the conception of "an absolute human reason, universal to all men and to all time" (1929:233), calling it a superstition, comparable to the belief of primitive peoples that the general features of their life and culture were universal. Ultimately, for Lewis, the a priori element in knowledge is pragmatic, "the most fundamental ground . . . for a truth of any sort"[1] (266).

Paul Feyerabend, when he holds "argument" up for scrutiny , develops a similar line of criticism. The concept was established long before the Greeks, he tells us. But they invented it as a special and standardized form of arguing, "independent of the situation in which it occurred and whose results had universal authority" (1987:8). From this developed, objectivity, or tradition-independent ways of finding truths "and using reason now meant using these ways and accepting their results" (ibid.). The Greeks' standardized form of argumentation "explicitly rejected personal elements" (87). By contrast, "argument" should take into account the beliefs and attitudes of the participants.

In the traditional model of rationality we also discover the specter of the "rational agent," that singular Rodinian figure, embodying calculation and predictability. The predictability of such instrumental rationality pervades areas of Western thought like contemporary economic theory. As George Meyerson notes, "Economics is scientific only if people are predictable, and the rational agent is more predictable than many other human characters" (1994:36). He then offers this observation from Christina Bicchieri: "In order to be able to arrive at generalisations, economists have to assume that individual behaviour follows some regular pattern, that all actions possess a common structure. . . . Generality is attained by modelling individuals as rational decision-makers"

(1987:502 cited in Meyerson, 36). Such generalizing of the "rational agent" is a poignant illustration of what Nye laments in the course of Western logic.

Rationality, on the terms under discussion, can also be considered masculine, and not gender-neutral; as excluding the "irrationality" of the feminine, understood by the tradition to include the emotional and the physical and to be the province of women (Verbiest, 1995:827–28; Atherton, 1993:19). In fact, such thinking associates with the model a considerable set of hierarchical pairings, notably including valid/invalid, logical/emotional, reason/unreason, where the valued first category both rules and excludes the second (Warren, 1988:32). As a result of its detachment from life, continues the criticism, of the gulf between the objective and the subjective, Reason is seen to be in crisis. Variously depicted, this crisis is described most potently as an *"inability to rationally know itself"* (Grosz, 1993:189).

This marks a connection with the concerns exhibited through postmodernism, which aims to displace the hierarchical system of authority and truth upon which the modern world was founded. We see an example of this in Jean-François Lyotard's (1984:44) identification of "proof" as something that needs to be proved, and his tracing of the idea to the discourse of power (46).

Postmodernism's own illusive definition is not helped by the tendency of many associated with it to deny that the term applies to them (Appignanesi, 1989). But the avoidance of such classifications is in keeping with the skeptical mien of the postmodernist perspective, which not only challenges inclinations to categorize and classify, but also to decide and settle issues, and to resolve disputes and arguments. I will understand postmodernism in these terms, and also as resistant to conclusions, convictions, and even adherence (Russman, 1995:126). For our purposes, it is seen at work in the dual moves of deconstructive analysis: first, inverting the opposing terms in a hierarchical pairing, so that unreason becomes the condition by which reason is possible, or the nonserious that by which the serious is possible; and secondly, observing that if such a reversal is possible, then neither of the pair can have priority over the other and the pairing itself should be displaced, lose its identity, in an underlying generality of "marks" or contexts.[2] Associated with this is the loss of many staples of Western metaphysics, including the subject, the arguer, and even *the* argument. In fact, I came close to this position myself in chapter 3 when observing the ubiquity of context. It becomes difficult to detach *the* argument from *the* context, especially when we take the viewpoint(s) of a composite audience. But I did not go so far as to suggest that it is impossible to derive arguments-as-products from the argumentative context and to analyze these as part of the argumentation. Many postmodernist thinkers would feel no reticence about suggesting just such an impossibility.

7.2 Argument, Persuasion, and Critique

Robert Rowland raises a common objection to the critiques of reason and argument: that in order to make their points, to convince, the critics must use the tools (e.g., argument) belonging to the very institution they wish to challenge. Thus, the critics seem to be inconsistent. "[F]eminist theorists," for example, "rely on argument to attack argument" (1995:361).[3] But while this raises interesting questions, such as how the history of Reason can contain the conditions that give rise to its own critique, it fails to engage the debate in a useful manner, it fails to meet the critics where they stand. Besides, there may be no inconsistency in using argument to show that it does not have the value that has been attributed to it. Problems may lie in the claims made for argument (certainty, resolution, or adherence) rather than with argument itself.

On the other hand, Russman insists that the postmodernist *cannot* argue. Invoking concepts reminiscent of Perelman, he observes that the purpose of argument is to bring about or strengthen adherence in the audience. "But for postmodernism such adherence is a sort of mistake, or rather an object for parody. Strong adherence to any one position is a failure to appreciate the alternatives. The response of the postmodernist is to parody any such adherence as a species of 'ethnocentrism'" (1995:126). Again, to judge an argument by appeal to its success with even a hypothetical "wise" audience presupposes one of the dichotomies that haunt modernist thinking, this time between "wise" and "unwise." It assumes that one group's perspective is better than another, and this the postmodernist would again parody (127). In such ways Russman shows real dichotomies between "the activity of argument" and "the postmodernist temper." He concludes that "[t]he postmodernist claim that he/she does not argue is not only defensible, the claim that the postmodernist *cannot* argue is more than plausible. To argue is to step outside postmodernism" (ibid.).

Notwithstanding the question of what then *does* the postmodernist do, or the objection that parody cannot serve the human community as more than an intermediate measure, forcing a reevaluation of sacrosanct methods, it may still benefit us to wonder what lies beyond postmodernism, seen as a stage in intellectual development. That is, might not argument emerge from the period of postmodern debate, informed by the critiques, and better equipped to serve the future?

If such is to be the case, no doubt we will need to rethink some of its tendencies and terminology. The tradition of argument supported by (and supporting) this model of rationality disambiguates language, for example, whereas feminist theorizing (and postmodernism) extols the virtues of ambiguity (Rose, 1993:218). Perhaps more significantly, there is the widely condemned terminology of aggressiveness that founds the metaphor Argument Is War. Kenneth J. Gergen illustrates this in the pragma-dialectical model of arguments promoted by Frans H. van Eemeren and Rob Grootendorst (1984,1992), although it can be just as evident in other models (see Berrill 1996; Cohen 1995).

> Consider the position of argumentation theorists van Eemeren and Grootendorst, "a language user who has advanced a point of view in respect of an expressed opinion must be prepared to *defend* that standpoint and . . . a language user who has cast doubt upon the tenability of that standpoint must be prepared to *attack* it" . . . Given this formalization of a broadly shared conception of argumentation, the posture of one who is targeted for criticism can scarcely be other than defensive. (Gergen, 1994:63)

Of course, we might quickly object that a mistake made here by Gergen, and by others who invoke the Argument Is War metaphor, is that it is not the *person* who is "targeted" for criticism, it is the *standpoint*. The concern indicates a failure to disassociate people from their ideas common to many accounts of the *ad hominem*. But on reflection, it is unwise to issue too hurried a gloss on this. Although it is the argument that is criticized, the rhetorical perspective on argumentation shows us that argument *is* an extension of the arguer, and that the beliefs challenged may be central to the self-conception of an audience. Accordingly, we should stress the language of cooperation and community that is currently suppressed in works on argumentation and analyses of arguments, where the language of aggression is too often unnecessarily adopted. The Argument Is War metaphor promotes a one-sided and misleading picture of the nature of argumentation, overlooking the sense of consensus that pervades informed argumentative communities, who interact in cooperative ways on an equal basis.

Nowhere is the understanding (or misunderstanding) of argumentation as aggression more graphically denounced than in Sally Miller Gearhart's frequently cited paper on the womanization of rhetoric. She directs her comments at rhetoric, but insofar as her concern is to detail feminism's rejection of "the conquest/conversion model of interaction" (1979:202), then the adversarial model of argumentation is clearly caught in her nets. Identifying aggression at the heart of this model of interaction, Gearhart begins her discussion with the announcement that "any intent to persuade is an act of violence" (195). The actual violence is in the *intention* to change another, which she compares to the general male propensity for conquest throughout history. While extreme in its expression, her point merits consideration: the traditional sense of rhetorical persuasion can be read as treating the audience as an object, something malleable, to be beaten with discourse and converted to the speaker's point of view. Little concern for the sensibilities of the audience is seen in such a model. Gearhart presents the contrast between what she is rejecting and what she is advocating by means of a metaphor that Mao Tse Tung uses in an essay "On Contradiction." The metaphor is that of the chicken and the stone. Her reliance on this warrants close attention:

> No one can change an egg into a chicken. If, however, there is the potential in the egg to be a chicken—what Mao calls the "internal basis for change"—then there is the likelihood that in the right environment (moisture, temperature, the "external conditions for change") the egg will hatch. A stone, on the other hand, has no internal basis for hatching into a chicken and an eternity of sitting in the proper conditions of moisture and temperature will not make possible its transformation into a chicken.

> If we think of communicative acts not as attempts to change others or even as attempts to inform them or to help them, then perhaps we can understand Mao's metaphor. Communication can be deliberate creation or cocreation of an atmosphere in which people or things, if and only if they have the internal basis for change, may change themselves; it can be a milieu in which those who are ready to be persuaded may persuade themselves, may choose to hear or choose to learn. (198)

People, if they have the appropriate internal basis for change, may persuade *themselves*. They take control of the situation. Although Gearhart does not mention it, her discussion of Mao Tse Tung's metaphor bears a striking similarity to Aristotle's key distinction between potentiality and actuality and his associated discussions. It is surprising, since Gearhart insists that "[w]e have all diligently studied our Aristotle" (201), that she has not recovered the same ideas from that (admittedly less revolutionary) source. Aristotle's *Physics* is noted for advocating a concept of "change" that improves considerably on that of his predecessors, particularly Parmenides and Plato. Change is an internal process, the transformation of what is potential into what is actual or fulfilled (*Physics*, 3.1). But it requires the right environment to occur: the acorn will not become the oak except under appropriate external conditions of moisture, temperature, and so forth. Something will change, "starting from some principle within itself" (2.8.199b17) and move toward some end. The Aristotle to whom Gearhart alludes appears to be the Aristotle of the *Rhetoric*, the manual of persuasion. But that same nonviolent process of internal change that informs Aristotle's scientific and ethical writings can be read behind the ideas of the *Rhetoric* if we understand that text to advocate the audience's involvement in the process of argumentation. The conquest/conversion model, which she is right to condemn, may have dominated the tradition. But, as we did with argumentation itself, we would be wise to look for other models at the source of this tradition.

Similar Aristotelian echoes can be heard in the development of Gearhart's critique that comprises the work of Sonja K. Foss and Cindy L. Griffin. Like Gearhart, they challenge the patriarchal bias in the definition of rhetoric as persuasion (1995:2). In its place they advocate, wherever possible, an *invitational rhetoric* (5). When it is the understanding of an issue that is the rhetor's (arguer's) goal, rather than changing or controlling others, then an invitation may be extended to the audience to enter the rhetor's world and to see it as he or she does. The audience listens and then presents its own position. Thus the examination of an issue is a cooperative venture. Such a view of rhetoric, suggest Foss and Griffin, promotes equality, immanent value, and self-determination.

There is something of the pragmatic dialogue at the heart of this proposal, which might serve the pragma-dialecticians in responding to Gergen's criticism. Rather than treat the parties in the dialogue as protagonist and antagonist, it recognizes them as equals, mutually respectful of each other. Beyond this, the stress on invitation is reminiscent of a similar sensibility in Aristotle's *Rhetoric,* where, as we have see, the audience is invited to complete the argumentation. Thus, the all-important element of audience self-determination pervades both the Aristotelian model of rhetoric and the Foss and Griffin proposal. The audience, when persuaded, is persuaded by its own deliberations, after reflection on reasoning that it has understood in its own terms and may even have had an hand in completing.

7.3 Femininity, Emotion, and the Body

Gearhart's indictment of the conquest/conversion model of persuasion represents only a small part of the feminist reproach of reason, albeit a quite relevant one for our purposes. Also of pertinence for the argumentation theorist are debates over feminine and masculine modes of reasoning, over the logical and emotional aspects of argumentation, and over the way in which the tradition values a detached reason over the involvements of the body. At one level or another, these three debates are connected. But I will attempt to separate them for the purposes of discussion since salient points are made in each debate.

Michael A. Gilbert identifies the Critical-Logical Model of reasoning (C-L)[4] as a repository for male attitudes and values. Following Karen Warren (1988), Gilbert finds C-L's assumptions oppressive since they "are essentially male and preclude female concerns and modes of reasoning" (1994:103). In particular, the C-L approach fails to incorporate notions of "context and inclusiveness that are arguably significant components of female reasoning" (104).

Such arguments announce a debate that divides many of those sharing a feminist perspective. For Nye, logic is a male domain: "an invention of men"; and "something that men do or say" (1990:5). Thus it might be expected to assume a male image and concern male interests. Deborah Orr contrasts the "narrow and too often inappropriate conception of rationality" born from this to the "feminine mode of rationality," features of which she elaborates. But interestingly, when calling for the feminine mode to be incorporated into models of rationality and argumentation, Orr insists that the latter must be understood as "human, not masculine, practice" (1989:9). This points in the direction of those who seek to get beneath the feminine/masculine dichotomy and to talk about *human* reason and reasoning, although they pursue this in different ways and with different motivations.[5]

Sandra Menssen, for example, challenges the conclusions of Orr and of the seminal studies of Carol Gilligan (1982). Gilligan's work stresses essential differences between the genders. Women, for example, emphasize relationship and attachment, while men stress independence. This is illustrated through a study of the way in which boys and girls play, with the boys adhering closely to the rules of games while girls would promote the value of playing the game over the rules.

Menssen contests the claim that there are masculine and feminine modes of rationality, arguing that neither Gilligan nor Orr provides sufficient support for the thesis. Looking closely at Gilligan's work, particularly at the interviews with boys and girls, Menssen provides her own interpretation of the responses to propose that the interviewees are not adopting different patterns of reasoning but variants of the same model. She concludes that "Gilligan's work does *not* show that women are less frequent or less skilled users than men of traditional logical tools, or that women are, even given a traditional understanding of rationality, less rational than men" (123). This, however, casts male logicians in a harsher light than might be expected. As long as a distinction between male and female patterns of reasoning could be maintained, there was an explanation for excluding women from male thought. If, however, men and women reason in the same way, sharing the same model of rationality, the failure to include women's voices cannot be so easily explained (136).

Genevieve Lloyd shares the concern about a gendered reason, whether male or female. The claim that Reason is male should not suggest that "principles of logical thought valid for men do not hold also for female reasoners" (1993:109). The danger she sees is not that envisaged by Menssen, with whose position Lloyd is unlikely to agree. What she shares with Menssen is a desire for a common concept of reason that is the domain of neither men nor women. In the preface to the second edition of *The Man of Reason: "Male" and "Female" in Western Philosophy,* Lloyd reviews the state of the dialectic on the subject since the first edition of 1984, and worries that some feminist deconstructions of the male/female opposition are advocating the rise of a new feminine. Lloyd is skeptical about such a move:

> It may well be appropriate in some contexts to affirm the value of human activities and traits traditionally conceptualized as feminine. And the hierarchical relations between reason and its opposites—or between higher and lower forms of reason—have undoubtedly contributed to the devaluing of

things associated with the feminine. But should those neglected traits now be affirmed *as* feminine? (1993:x)

This is to suggest that just as a male conception of reason has
been challenged, so might a female conception. In the evolution of
any critique of an idea, it is understandable that the pendulum
should swing from that which is scrutinized to its opposite pole. The
concern is that it might stay there. A deconstructive critique requires
a return of the pendulum to the center, where it points beneath the
opposites and to their erasure. This is not Menssen's view that the
traditional logic/rationality *is* the common mode that both men and
women share. It is rather to argue that reason should never have be-
longed to sex or gender. That in usurping it men diminished it or developed only part of its potential. It calls for a recovery of those lost
elements that have always been present in the lives and reasoning
of women (and men), but that have been marginalized by the tradition of reason and argument.

A similar approach should be taken to the debate over the relative values of the logical and the emotional. The concern in question
here is well articulated by Marcia L. Homiak:

> Thus the basis of the feminist critique of rational ideals is
> that such ideals, in their application to moral questions, ig-
> nore the role of emotion and of the nonuniversalizable par-
> ticularity of human life. But these domains, of emotion and
> of specific and particular relationships, are the domains his-
> torically associated with women. Hence, the rational ideal
> suggests that the concerns most typical of women's lives are
> irrelevant to the best human life and to reasoning about
> what to do. (1993:2)

Homiak's response is to return to the root of the problematic conception of the rational ideal in Aristotle. She then provides a reading
of Aristotle's ethics, which argues that the development of the nonrational side of the person is essential to the development of Aristotle's virtuous person.

One problem in this is that while it may rehabilitate Aristotle
and challenge the logical/emotional opposition usually seen there
(and, after all, the rhetorical argumentation gleaned from Aristotle
is concerned with integrating reason and emotion[6]), it trades on the
stereotypical assumption that the emotional *is* the domain of women.
While this is a perspective we might associate with the feminist critiques, it too is questioned. Lorraine Code finds Homiak to be tacitly

confirming "the very stereotypes . . . which construct the passions and feelings as women's domain, while leaving men in charge of the more serious business of reasoning, rationality" (1995:219). Again, "[t]he passions and feelings do not gain in prestige if they are simply "included" in reason with their long-standing feminine and irrational associations intact" (ibid.). However this is resolved (and Code points in the direction of "naturalized epistemology" and "the interpretive turn" [223–33] in the philosophy of the social sciences), the problem lies in the acceptance of gender-associated traits. If, as Lloyd suggests, we avoid classifying traits as masculine or feminine, then the prospects for a more inclusive model of reason (and of argument) are heightened.

Connected to both the masculine/feminine and logical/emotional pairings is that which opposes reason to the body. A tradition that finds its roots in the body-as-prison metaphor of the *Phaedo* elevates Reason as "universal, perspectiveless, and free of desire" (Alcoff and Potter, 1993:9). Consequently, feminists have been concerned with examining the *body,* since it is considered the negative and excluded term in the pairing (Grosz, 1993:195), and since it is associated with woman as the "other" of masculine reason (Rose, 1993:208).[7] Descartes is a primary source for this hierarchical pairing (Lloyd, 1993:38–50; Atherton,1993[8]). The thinking ego, detached from the body, is the foundation for any knowledge that matters, for certainty. Other "knowledges," where recognized, are relegated in the Cartesian tradition.

There is a general call to reach beyond Cartesianism, or to go back to a conception of rationality that existed before it (Toulmin, 1990). But with respect to the mind/body debate, Lloyd looks to Descartes' contemporary Spinoza for an alternative account. And she finds there a fitting response to all three of the oppositions I have discussed in this section:

> Spinoza rejects Descartes's ideal of a relation of dominance between reason, belonging to mind, and the passions, conceived as alien intruders from the realm of the body. He offers instead a picture of passion transformed into rational emotion through the replacement of inadequate ideas by more adequate ones. The polarities which made male-female symbolism appropriate to express the relations between reason and its opposite are thus undermined. (1993:xiii)

Lloyd sees this pointing in the direction of fruitful future research. As she notes, "Spinoza opens up the possibility of taking seriously differences—grounded in body—in the context, style, motivation or interest of reasoning, without denying the commonalities that arise from the shared humanity of our differently sexed bodies" (xiv–xv). The concern here is to accommodate differences, not to exclude them. These differences, some of cultural origin, distinguish male and female "thought styles" without losing the essential commonality of reason shared by humans.

The foregoing discussion suggests that the prospect for a widely endorsed, unified conception of reason (and argument) does exist behind critiques of the unbalanced account handed down to us in the tradition. But any reconceptualization must reclaim what was lost at the start of that tradition, assimilate the cultural, sexual, and other differences of reasoners, and be presented as an involved (as opposed to detached), coordinating feature of epistemic communities. Before proceeding to these possibilities, I want to consider the details of Nye's critique, because it culminates in a proposal to get "beneath the logic" that shares strategies with the rhetorical approach to argumentation.

7.4 Nye's Logics

Maryann Ayim poses the question: "Is Nye's logician a straw man?" While Ayim does not directly answer her own question, the tenor of her analysis of *Words of Power* (1990) leaves no doubts about her position. She finds Nye's treatment of logic problematic, imbalanced, dependent on that which it eschews (argument), and proposing an alternative that is inadequately worked out (reading). Notwithstanding such critical feminist readings of Nye, which assail her eagerness to speak for all feminists, *Words of Power* stands as a vivid account of the thesis that logic is masculine and of the historical and social consequences of such an understanding. It is a text that demands to be read and that deserves to be taken seriously.

Nye traces the course of logic from Parmenides, Plato, Aristotle, and the Stoics, through Abelard and Ockham, to its culmination in the work of Frege. Along the way there are paths not taken—some acknowledged by Nye, like the Sophists or John of Salisbury; others passed over in silence, like Mill or Russell.[9] It is also the case, as Gilbert (1994:107) points out, that logic changes after Frege, particularly through the innovations of Gödel, Wittgenstein, and Lorenzen. At the same time, Frege's influence has been pervasive and ongoing (Johnson, 1987a), as we saw in chapter 1. Still, Nye makes no claims to having produced an exhaustive account; such would be foolish given the obvious omissions. But her story gives the origins and culmination of logic as a male idea, along with some of its medieval links. She illustrates her claim that there is no Logic, only men and logics (1990:5), by juxtaposing the details of each "logic" with the life of the logician involved. Those who claimed to have carried their thought beyond the fray, dealing with truth and objectivity, are represented as investing their work with their own image, thereby using logic to promote their view of society and, accordingly, their interests. She shows, for example, how "logic," as the debating skill described by Aristotle, moves from having relevance only for professional disputants (42), to its elevation as science and the blueprint for social policy (57).

What strikes one about this is the retention of the term *logic* for the many variants embraced by Nye's history. At first it is abstract, concerning only the logical form of arguments (9). But later she associates it with the many techniques of dialogue games (42) and of the dialectic of Abelard (87). She ends with a view of logic "*as* Critical Thinking" (181, italics mine) as it is recommended for all courses of study. Ostensibly, these are quite different creatures and I have detailed their particular characteristics in earlier chapters. Perhaps what links each of these is a masculine propensity for thinking in a certain way. Or maybe she sees formal abstractness common to all the variants, just as she presents Aristotle's dialectical argumentation as if it was no more than a vehicle for the syllogism. But it would be difficult to see formal reasoning, detached from the exigencies of language, at the heart of modern notions of Critical Thinking.

In the same vein, what Nye advocates as an alternative to masculine logic bears a distinct resemblance to a number of accounts of Critical Thinking, which themselves are attempts to redress the imbalance of formal treatments of reasoning (Siegel, 1988; Missimer, 1986). Nye wants to do more than merely reclaiming language from the logicians' propositions. Her notion of reading teaches that the circumstances in which something is said and the person who says it are relevant considerations, not to be ignored in the manner of the logician. Reading, as a context-dependent activity, is opposed to logical analysis. As Gilbert understands this: "When we *read* the emphasis is on understanding; when we *analyse* the emphasis is on judging" (1994:107).

Nye's text is itself a compelling illustration of this "reading": each of her studies of a stage in the development of "logic" involves the telling of a story that weaves the logic expressed with the life or lives that expressed it. The readings are critical in the sense that they challenge received views, introduce elements that might elsewhere be viewed irrelevant, and make claims about motives and meanings. She *shows* a history wherein logic has been an extension of the lives of men, but then separated from them; the whole process has turned around so that lives have been lived according to the logic.

Nye's reading as a contemporary tool for working with texts is later illustrated through two instances drawn from the Bush/Dukakis presidential campaign of 1988. Dukakis, when governor of Massachusetts, had vetoed a bill that would have required students to recite the Pledge of Allegiance to the American flag in public schools. Bush interpreted this as a knock against patriotism. More tellingly, Bush's campaign exploited images of a large black man, held by police, who had raped a white woman and killed her husband. The man was on furlough from a Massachusetts jail. Bush used messages associated with these instances to tap into Americans' fears about crime and about a lack of patriotic conviction. And, as Nye sees it, the people bought the "logic" of Bush's messages. This, of course, is a logic that isolates statements from circumstances and from the people involved. "A reader," Nye insists, "would have been harder to fool."

> She would have heard the tone, strident, military, rigid, that demands that there can be no discussion of the rightness of anything American, no discussion of the rights of black murderers or the social reasons for crime. She would have taken account of the public to which Bush spoke, worried, shaken by the stock market crash of the year before, afraid to rock the boat of an economy floundering in debt, but eager to believe in the American values that all around them have disappeared. She would have understood the reference to the color of the prisoner and his size, the black rapist who is the symbol of a sexual prowess that threatens white men in their possession of women, black like most criminals, prisoners who deserve what they get, because it must be them, these aliens, barbarians, not like us, who are causing things to go wrong. . . . She would have read beneath the logic, she would have read the desires, the concerns, the hopes of these men, twisted as they might have become. And once having read, she might have had an answer. (1990:184)

Nye's account of reading clearly involves *a reasoned account* of
events, carefully weighed, according to relevant features of context.
It does not involve thoughtless conformity to logical structures (181)
nor, surprisingly, does it entail "a language spoken between women
for women" (179). She rejects this latter alternative to male logic because it is outside of logic, other than logic, and thus cannot challenge
the authority of logic.[10] "Reading," on these terms, must have some
association with "logic"; it must serve as an alternative to the role
that logic performs on the occasions that it performs it. What Nye advocates is an alternative model of argumentation grounded in context. What she may have missed is the fact that this model was
always there in the background to her history, marginalized by the
tradition, unrecognized by Nye because not expected by her.

Ayim's reaction, as noted already, is less sympathetic. In her
judgment, the problem is not so much with logic but with (a) its treatment as the exclusive avenue of truth and reason, rather than *an* avenue (1995:810), and (b) the way it has been taught. Consequently,
beyond endorsing women's talk (see the above endnote), she encourages teaching logic rather than Nye's notion of reading. The
Bush/Dukakis example, claims Ayim, shows "serious problems in
Nye's analysis of logic" (808). These are seen mainly in Nye's pro-
clivity for rhetorical questions—constantly assuming what she
needs to demonstrate. More significantly, Ayim challenges Nye's notion of reading itself: It "has no monopoly on 'attention, listening, understanding, responding' . . . indeed, these are the central goals of
many critical thinking classes" (809). Ayim illustrates this with an
account of a feminist teaching logic. It is an account composed from
autobiography, conversation, student comment, and imagination.
The class is localized in the lives of its teacher and students, drawing on their backgrounds of domestic strain, resentments, confusions, and apprehensions. They discuss Michael Scriven's seven-step
analysis of an argument. Participation is encouraged, as is the use of
first-person experience and cooperative discussion of the students'
own examples. All in all, Ayim conveys a picture of an exciting, challenging, and rewarding environment. But what must strike us is how
different this description of the logic classroom is from Nye's autobi-
ographical account at the start of *Words of Power* (1990:1–3). The approach is different, the subject matter is different, and the *logic* is
different. Nye's was a class in abstract logic, centered on Quine;
Ayim's is a class in engaged argumentation, centered on Scriven. The
model of logic involved in the latter facilitates the integration of
things like attention, listening, and understanding. The model Nye

was taught did not. If Ayim's class illustrates a feminist teaching logic, then it must be said that this is never what Nye means by "logic." The problem lies not so much, then, in how logic is taught but with what is taught as logic. At root, the agreements between Nye and Ayim are stronger than Ayim allows. They both reject dealing with isolated statements that have no connection with the circumstances and lives that delivered them. They both accommodate different styles of approach along with the differences of those involved. Ayim's is a method of analysis; Nye's, while not adopting that label, demonstrates all the features of the same. Both would reject the vestiges of any masculinity that might still cling to "Logic." While not avoiding the obvious differences between them, then, we should note the shared refusal to ignore logic altogether, and in the details of their separate accounts see elements important to the future of argumentation as well as the recognition of the need for that future.

7.5 Postcritique Faces of Argument

As feminist writers appeal to context or to the involvement of audiences (Orr, 1989:8), there is a genuine sense that argument itself is not dead or denied but being challenged to change or, as I have suggested, recover its early possibilities. Without committing ourselves to some uncontrolled exercise in eclecticism, we can see in the proposals of a Lloyd, a Nye, an Ayim, or Foss and Griffin a range of suggestions that match characteristics in the rhetorical model of argumentation discussed in earlier chapters. The desires to expand the concept of "reason" to include emotions, to stress circumstance and character, to endorse a wider model of relevance and of acceptability, and to avoid defining argument in exclusionary ways, are all motivating desires in rhetorical argumentation. Of course, the various proposals discussed here must be built around a coherent core that gives direction and justification to the model. And this is what argument's defenders have tried to do.

The more ambitious defenders offer models of argument informed by postmodern and feminist critiques. Meyerson's concept of "double arguability," for example, involves the internal formation of an argument through the interaction of the people involved. Emotional components are included, and "[i]t becomes relevant what their motives may be for arguing: in short, what kind of people they are, and *how* they live, what place the argument has in their lives" (1994:16).

Robert C. Rowland (1995:360) responds to the postmodern critique with a model of argumentation derived from Jamesian pragmatism. The pragmatic method is used to justify principles of argument that themselves can check the excesses of instrumental reason. Rejecting the confrontational sense of argument in favor of rational discussion, Rowland observes "[v]iewed from a pragmatic perspective, rational argument is quite consistent with consciousness raising and feminism" (361).

A more detailed proposal takes the form of Gilbert's (1995b) coalescent argumentation. A direct challenge to traditional logic, coalescent argumentation is a broadly based dialectical account that explicitly tries to accommodate the values and practices of women (1994:104). Gilbert follows Walton (Walton, 1992c) by including emotion as a nonlogical component. In particular, the central role of empathy allows for the depth of listening, observation, and understanding desired by Nye (Gilbert, 1995b:846).[11]

Present in many of these projects that rethink the role of arguments in the wake of critique, implicitly or explicitly, is an appeal to rhetoric. Interestingly, observers of the "rhetorical turn" in the human sciences are prone to comparing it to the movement of postmodernism (Billig, 1991; Roberts and Good, 1993). Both, argues Billig, have an element of pastiche. The postmodernist borrows from here and there: old styles, bits and pieces of traditional design. Likewise, the rhetorical theorist intermingles past and present: a bit from Protagoras, a bit from social psychology (Billig, 1991:195). And in a similar way, we have seen rhetorical argumentation mixing early understandings of audience and ethos with modern innovations from relevance theory and cognitive psychology.

Russman counters the postmodernist nihilation of argument by going "beyond the modern rationalist's notion of argument which sets up that nihilation" (1995:132). What he uncovers is a model of argument as process, with a stress on adherence in an audience, and that uses a "whole range of rhetorical procedures (most if not all of those mentioned by Perelman, for example)" (133).

Similarly, James W. Hikins insists that argument must be understood against "the backdrop of a much larger rhetorical context" (1995:139), which will view argument as social practice directed at a public good. Richard A. Cherwitz and Thomas J. Darwin also see a shared perspective between argumentation and postmodernism. But this is because they interpret argumentation in the manner of Chaim Perelman's reaction to formal demonstration and scientific method. Such methods "assume not only that there is *one* outcome or answer to a problem, but that the answer can be *demonstrated*" (1995:198). In contrast, argumentation promotes differences where "understanding and respecting the multiplicity of selves is precisely the project and raison d'etre of argument" (200).

7.6 Differences, Gestures, and the Good

It is not surprising that this particular inquiry into reason and rationality has found its way back to Perelman's work. Perelman offers a panoply of answers to postmodernist and feminist concerns over argument and reason. While his model may not meet every concern in the critiques, it indicates the general direction that should be pursued by any model of argumentation interested in the issues raised by the critiques. Perelman's own critique of the "rational" (discussed in chap. 1) anticipates much of what we discover in the later critiques. As long as "rational" is restricted to the separation of reason from the other human faculties, it will reflect a being "deprived of humanity and insensible to the reactions of the milieu" (1979b:118). In place of this, Perelman proposes a community-oriented "reasonable" person. This gives reasonableness/rationality over to the diversities and differences that exist among people, arguers, and audiences. It was this that made a fixed definition of "argumentation," and its cognate "argument," so illusive for the rhetorically directed Perelman. Arguers address the whole person, not the isolated intellect or emotion, and they consider as a natural course the circumstances and differences involved (1982:13). This is a fitting source for the "logic" that Ayim's feminist strives to teach.

The concept of a "whole person" should involve, by necessity, the union of mind and body. The arguments of the "body" that "which, in dialogue, flings toward another body" (Barthes, 1985:5) seeking to *hook*, to persuade, are welcomed here; the argumentative "gestures" that were noted in chapter 3 (Willard, 1989). Lloyd (1993) evokes Spinoza, for whom the mind and body is a single unity, dual expression of one reality. The rhetorical model of argumentation accommodates this.

An argumentation theory based on the concept of rationality contained in logocentric discourses reflects the dominant gender relations and thus cannot question them, claims Verbiest. She suggests two possible solutions to this: Either a theory of argumentation must assume two rationalities, masculine and feminine, not derived from a basic concept; or it understands "one universal human rationality that takes on different forms depending on many factors, one of which is sex/gender" (1995:828).

The rhetorical model of argumentation elaborated upon throughout this book endorses the second of these options: a universal human rationality that takes different forms depending on the circumstances: according to culture, religion, race, class, education, and sex/gender. As Verbiest (ibid) rightly observes, the second option means an expansion of the domain covered by argumentation theory.

This universal human rationality, which becomes concrete in ideas like Perelman's universal audience, is not Menssen's traditional notion of rationality, hidden beneath the feminine/masculine divide but common to both. It is the full notion of which the traditional concept is only a divorced limb. It requires a return to what the tradition failed to include as it started down the path of masculine expression. Rehabilitated by Perelman and others, developed from its Aristotelian moorings, it is a concept that animates rhetorical argumentation, calling forth its multiple faces and differences.

Hilary Putnam (1981) connects rationality with human flourishing, judging by standards of betterment and improvement rather than on its own exclusive terms (Meyerson, 1994:92). The crisis of reason as Putnam suggested it was a failure to see "how the goodness of an end can make it rational to choose that end" (1981:173). On such terms, "being rational involves having criteria of *relevance* as well as criteria of rational acceptability" (201). This was just the sentiment endorsed in the discussion of these ideas in chapter 4 and expressed throughout my development of the rhetorical model. As such it is true to Perelman's motivations: a theory of argumentation and its associated notion of reasonableness should contribute to the development of the idea of the human, facilitate an environment in which it can flourish, and promote ends that connect the threads of that project. This, and more, rhetorical argumentation promises.

Conclusion
Summation and Prolepsis

Beyond the goal of adherence, the rhetorical argumentation theorist is motivated by the further goals of human development and understanding. He or she recognizes and pays constant attention to the wider contexts that define argumentative communities. Understood in this way, argument is not just a tool for resolving local disputes, but is instrumental in the improvement of human communities. And in connection with this, as Aristotle observed (*Rhetoric* 1.5), the arguer needs to understand the objectives and values of human life, "which may provide additional premises for argument" (Kennedy, 1991:56).

Thus it is not surprising that Chaim Perelman, as a noted popularizer of rhetorical argument, should espouse views so in concert with the rethought notions of reason and argument called for in the previous chapter. Perelman's own interest in argument, as we have seen, grew out of concerns over the notion of justice and in particular over the need to clarify the relation between justice and reason (1967:17). As has been documented by writers such as Mieczyslaw Maneli (1994) and James Crosswhite, the new rhetoric, as a model of argumentation for a contemporary world, arose as a "response to a postmodern Europe shaped by systemic (and systematic) violence" (Crosswhite, 1995:137). Consequently, Perelman's concept of the reasonable "is inherently pluralistic; it is incompatible with all pretensions of monism or totalitarianism" (Maneli, 1994:19).

This pluralism, which is at the heart of argumentation itself, escapes the "constricted view of reason" (Perelman and Olbrechts-Tyteca, 1969:510), born of the narrow conception of proof and logic. A broader concept of proof and an enriched logic emerges that alters the way in which we conceive our reasoning faculty.

203

But at the same time, this pluralism and broadening tendency invites criticism, both from within the camps of argumentation theorists and from without. I have addressed several concerns associated with rhetorical argumentation earlier in the book, but one must anticipate two significant, related objections. (a) The first response, likely to be felt by argumentation theorists of a logical and/or dialectical bent could be stated in the form of an "anything goes" complaint, that is, the conception of "argument" inherent in rhetorical argumentation may be simply too broad and undefined for some tastes. (b) A second anticipated complaint is suggested in a remark from Michel Meyer:

> It is this ambiguity, inherent in natural language, which lies at the basis of the bad reputation of argumentation. For if the terms of a message are ambiguous, nothing keeps us from playing on this plurality of meanings, and manipulating the agreement of the audience by means of vagueness. (1986:92)

1. The open-endedness of the concept of "argument" in rhetorical argumentation might indeed concern the theorist loath to leave the relative comfort of forms and structures, but at the same time it should appeal to those, like some informal logicians and pragmadialecticians, who also acknowledge the recourse to contexts in deciding when an argument is present.

Besides, it is not the case that anything goes in a sense that would allow all discourses to be construed as arguments. Rhetorical argumentation requires the attempt to address an audience with a view to adherence to some claim on the basis of understanding, and it requires a speech or "text" (broadly conceived) which can be identified as the product of an arguer or arguers, even though the identity of such an arguer may be lost or otherwise unknown. But rhetorical argumentation cannot, by its nature, decide in advance what will count as an argumentative speech or text. An advertiser's image, or a homeless person's gesture both have argumentative force within appropriate contexts. Likewise, rhetorical figures that are deemed argumentative, like allusion, or even prolepsis, can belong to the extension of "argument." Here again, though, we are reminded that "it is impossible to tell in advance if a given structure is or is not to be regarded as a figure, or if it will be an argumentation or a stylistic figure" (Perelman and Olbrechts-Tyteca, 1969: 169–70).

Discomfort with such suggestions may really stem from the fact that such images, gestures, or figures are not easily (if at all) "translated" into propositions, to be cast as premises or conclusions. But, as we have seen, premise-conclusion complexes, which are characteristic of much argumentation, are not the paradigms against which all arguments should be measured; nor do they express the totality of all argumentative "events"; nor, even, are they necessary for argumentation to occur. Perhaps the gesture or the image may be said to "represent" the propositions of an argument. But this, while being not especially objectionable, still suggests a retreat to a traditional way of restricting "arguments" to premise-conclusion complexes. Rhetorical argumentation, for its sins, does not restrict or exclude in this way. It allows the possibility for adherence to be sought in unexpected or uncharacteric ways. These ways in which the *process* of argumentation is enacted between arguer and audience then become one of the components recovered by the theorist in reconstructing the total "argument."

2. The first complaint is also reflected in the concern over the ambiguity in argumentation, but there is much more to the latter. Ambiguity, in an important sense, is an essential feature of rhetorical argumentation. Like the postmodernist or feminist who criticizes the logician's need to reduce meanings to one "correct" sense, the rhetorical arguer eschews univocity and welcomes multiplicity. Perelman, again, exemplifies just this feature. One of the key distinctions that separates demonstration from argumentation is the way in which demonstration must conform to rules in formalized systems, while argumentation flows out of natural language (1982:9). And natural language, as Meyer just noted, is essentially ambiguous. Argumentation must adapt itself to the nature of language, not vice versa. Demonstrations require an essential univocity (Perelman, 1982:45), and the grounds from which they start must be completely free from ambiguity. As Perelman and L. Olbrechts-Tyteca crisply put it: "Things are different in argumentation" (1969:120).

Perelman and Olbrechts-Tyteca do not deny the possibility of arriving at one interpretation of an argument; there may well be provisional or conventional agreements to decide meanings. But even in such cases the interpretations are understood against a range of alternatives, and incompatible interpretations should always make us wary. In arriving at an interpretation, "[r]hetorical or pragmatic considerations inevitably play a part" (Perelman, 1979a:89). Here he has in mind a deeply personal, or subjective, element. Interpretation of meaning cannot be treated impersonally. To do so perverts the hermeneutical reality in so many facets of experience, including "in the social sciences and in everyday communication" (ibid.).

In general, "it is rare in a nonformalized language that a text appears absolutely clear to everybody. In most cases the impression of clarity, linked with univocity, is the product of ignorance or lack of imagination" (Perelman and Olbrechts-Tyteca, 1969:125). The necessity of interpretation, of working with meanings, becomes the rule; eliminating all interpretation is part of an artificial situation (126).

Meyer's concern is not fully addressed by what I have said here, however. What does keep us from playing on the plurality of meanings, and thereby manipulating the agreement of the audience? I have dealt repeatedly with the specter of manipulation, so often associated with rhetorical accounts. The model of rhetorical argumentation espoused here does not relate effectiveness with manipulation, and does not countenance manipulative treatments of audiences. Adherence is sought through understanding, and this is pursued through the creation of an argumentative environment in which the arguer and audience complete the argument as equal partners. On this model, an audience is not aggressively persuaded by the arguer, but is persuaded by its own understanding of the reasoning.

The suggestion of manipulation thus conflicts with the notion of reasonableness that has been advocated throughout, beginning in the first chapter. Again, what polices an audience's susceptibility to vagueness is the underlying reasonableness captured in the universal audience for that particular audience. If argumentation as an activity is to have credence, then there must be a sense of reasonableness at work. All audiences have such a sense. The exercise of audience construction is important as an exercise even if it is not always successful. We attempt to uncover that working notion of reasonableness alive in any audience and to speak to *it*. As such, the primary attitude with which audiences are approached is one of respect.

The concern that Meyer invokes is essentially an arguer's equivocating on the sense of a term in her or his discourse, and as such this brings to mind traditional concerns about a fallacy of equivocation. In the sense of fallacy introduced in chapter 6, we can see how an audience could be impeded from performing its contributory role in the argumentative process by having multiple meanings suggested as if only one were at stake, or having multiple meanings combined to create vagueness. Thus a valuable feature of rhetorical argumentation—the recognition of ambiguity—could be distorted for unreasonable ends.

The fallacy of equivocation is one of the three that Crosswhite discusses in his treatment of Perelman on fallacy. He also recognizes the legitimacy of ambiguity and equivocation as they are employed by Perelman. Equivocation "is the argumentative use of the plasticity of notions for reasoning about issues which do not permit demonstration" (1993:398). In keeping with his view of what constitutes a fallacy in the Perelmanian account, equivocation is considered unreasonable when a particular audience mistakes a specific meaning for a universally acceptable one (ibid.).

So the retention of ambiguous meanings does have its dangers, as Meyer recognizes, and can be misused by the unscrupulous arguer. But this does not justify a "bad reputation of argumentation," and particularly not rhetorical argumentation. The traditional logician may prefer the simplicity of univocal meaning in a clear proposition but, as the history of fallacy indicates, this approach is also susceptible to misuse by unscrupulous arguers. It seems that any tool used to promote communication and effective reasoning can be misused for ulterior ends. Argumentation, since its domain is the everyday circumstances of ordinary reasoning and ordinary language, has more room for abuse to occur. But that is why it has been so important to take seriously the nature of rhetorical argumentation and to develop an account that contains checks against such abuse.

Given how useful it is for addressing the myriad contexts in which arguers and audiences interact, and given the goals to which it aspires and the respect with which it treats audiences, rhetorical argumentation is far too important to be dismissed because of its negative aspects, since many are necessary features of the sphere in which it operates.

The singular attention given to rhetorical argumentation throughout this book may have given the impression that I am advocating it as *the* sole model of argumentation worth considering. But I have argued that rhetorical argumentation is not a replacement for logical or dialectical argumentation, nor simply a supplement to them. It is the branch of argumentation that has been most overlooked in a tradition that has stressed the logical, and it has still been undervalued in the recent welcome rehabilitation of dialectical argumentation. At the least, it stands together with logical and dialectical perspectives as an equal partner providing a complete and comprehensive picture of argumentation.

What would be most welcome would be the kind of synthesis whereby practitioners and theorists of argument would acknowledge the features of all three and employ them as required. I have shown how the logical and dialectical accounts can be interwoven in this way, particularly in the work of Douglas N. Walton. And I have argued that features of the rhetorical perspective are often implied in the work of informal logicians and pragma-dialecticians, and that where they are not implied, those accounts lack something important.

Because of the imbeddedness of rhetorical features in the argumentative contexts, in the backgrounds of audiences, or in the goals of arguers, rhetorical argumentation is not something that should be added on to other accounts as a final or further consideration. It represents the underlying features of the context, an understanding of which affects how the argument-as-product or -procedure is to be interpreted. Thus, it is most fundamental. Recognition of this will not only complete the picture and right the balance, but it will enrich the accounts of argumentation already enjoying so much renewed success.

Notes

Introduction

1. Unless otherwise noted, references to the *Rhetoric* are to the Kennedy translation (1991), and references to other Aristotelian works are from Barnes's edition (1984).

2. Detailed discussions of the various perspectives that characterize current argumentation theory can be found in Frans H. van Eemeren, Rob Grootendorst, and Francisca Snoeck Henkemans (1996).

3. Following Solmsen (1929) and Jonathan Barnes (1981), M. F. Burnyeat (1994:31) argues that the *Rhetoric* belongs among those works of Aristotle (and here we must include the *Topics* and the *Sophistical Refutations*) which were written before he had conceived of the syllogism, references to the *Prior Analytics* being later additions.

4. Here I follow the general view that understands the *Sophistical Refutations* to be the final book of the *Topics*.

5. For a detailed discussion and illustration of dialectical debates in Aristotle as it relates to argumentation studies see van Eemeren, Grootendorst and Tjark Kruiger (1984), updated in van Eemeren, Grootendorst, and Henkemans (1996).

6. As Joseph W. Wenzel puts it: "From a rhetorical perspective, argument is an open-ended construct. There is no way to specify *a priori* what counts as an argument" (1987b:106).

7. Jurgen Habermas (1984:20) frames his criticisms within the context of proposing what a theory of argumentation *should* involve. It must serve moral ends and settle practical questions. But above this, essentially, it must relate to what it means to be rational and be grounded in a sense of universal validity that is not context-dependent.

8. The explosion of rhetoric, or the "rhetorical turn," which has emerged since Paul Ricoeur's study does not restrict rhetoric to this third part, but

recognizes all of its elements in a wider context. See, for example, Herbert W. Simons (1990) and Stephen Mailloux (1995).

9. Heidegger (*Being and Time,* 1962:178) hailed the *Rhetoric* for heralding the "first systematic hermeneutic of the everydayness of being with one another" (cited in Kennedy, 1991:124). This "Publicness" has a "mood" and creates "moods," which in turn the orator must understand in order to arouse and guide them.

10. When speaking of maxims, Aristotle attributes ethos to the speech itself (2.21.1395b). But his point here is that the maxim contains a moral evaluation that will reflect on the character of the speaker.

11. In a related way, Douglas N. Walton (1995a) argues that the determination of formal fallacies like "affirming the consequent" involves essential linguistic and contextual elements.

Chapter 1

1. Stephen Toulmin (1958) discusses the Aristotelian origin of the geometrical approach to logic in his fourth essay. By contrast to the general reaction, Jaakko Hintikka (1989:14) sees the study of formal deductive logic arising out of Aristotle's study of interrogative argumentation. Given the development of Aristotle's logical concepts discussed in the introduction, this is highly plausible, and further indicts a tradition that has played down the nonformal elements.

2. As the term first arose in the *Topics,* it referred to any kind of verbal proof (see the introduction). Here, in the *Prior Analytics,* it has acquired the meaning still attached to it, referring to a three-term, three-proposition argument.

3. The translation is by J. Barnes (Clarendon Aristotle Series, 1975; Revised Oxford Aristotle, 1984).

4. Ironically, one of Frans H. van Eemeren and Rob Grootendorst's complaints is that it is difficult to apply Toulmin's model to real-life argumentative discourse.

5. It is fair here to note Hintikka's somewhat contrasting comment, to the effect that "There is no such thing as a completely informal logic of argumentation or reasoning. The very term "informal logic" is a solecism" (1989:13).

6. Ralph H. Johnson himself adopts a less formalistic view. He sees the practice of argumentation as "a complex socio-cultural activity constituted by three components: the process of arguing; the arguers; and the product— the argument itself" (1995:242). This is quite similar, as he admits, to the view of van Eemeren and Grootendorst, as well as to that of Douglas N. Walton. It is also similar in that it too omits any explicit role for the audience.

7. I have avoided any discussion of the relationship between informal logic and critical thinking. They seem to have shared a common origin, and some people still consider them synonymous. Generally, though, while informal logic is a branch of logic, critical thinking is a more general approach to reasoning skills, involving an educational ideal and the development of a particular type of person (see Siegel, 1988).

8. John Woods raises the reasonable objection that using the term *translation* is unfortunate: "It is not intended that such [translation] rules preserve meaning. It is required only that they reconstruct English arguments on the hoof in ways that ensure that they have the backward reflection property with respect to target properties such as validity and invalidity" (1995:185). While clarifying the intent behind such maneuvers, the proposal serves to strengthen the criticism that formal arguments are not capturing the nuances of everyday argumentation.

9. This background, however, refers to "beliefs shared, or debated, by the community of informed people for whom the key propositions of the argument arouse interest and attention" (Blair and Johnson 1987:45). The community that J. Anthony Blair and Ralph H. Johnson have in mind here, it transpires, is a *model* community and not the audience of the argument. This model of ideal interlocutors is discussed in chapter 4.

10. At the same time, Michael A. Gilbert seems to include informal logicians in his idea of a conservative approach to argumentation, which concentrates upon the language of an argument, thereby missing crucial features like "the context, tonality, history and personalities of the arguers" (1995a:71).

11. For a more detailed discussion of this problem and a more extensive account of relevance see Christopher W. Tindale (1994).

12. At least one exception is to be found in Leo A. Groarke, Tindale, and Linda Fisher (1997/1989), where a wider account of relevance is given.

13. Other texts in the field choose to approach the question in terms of an account of irrelevance, offering tests for this (cf. Johnson and Blair, 1993a:55).

14. In this chapter, I have barely touched on the role played by fallacy theory in informal logic. For many it is an integral part. For example, Johnson's three principal criteria for evaluation (relevance, sufficiency, and acceptability) are shadowed by three basic fallacies: irrelevant reason, hasty conclusion, and problematic premise (1987b:247). For a detailed discussion of the relationship see Charles Arthur Willard (1989:220–38). I devote a later chapter to an extensive treatment of fallacy in the light of ideas developed in this book.

15. One is reminded here of Henry W. Johnstone Jr.'s remark that "To render a system of logic explicit is to formalize it; but behind the formalization

there is always an informal and intuitive logic that is presupposed by our very grasp of the formalization" (1978:40).

Chapter 2

1. In my judgment, excellent synopses of the approach may be obtained from the papers "Argumentation Analysis: A Dutch Counter-balance" (van Eemeren, 1988), and "Rationale for a Pragma-dialectical Perspective" (van Eemeren and Grootendorst, 1988). See also the description in van Eemeren, Grootendorst, and Snoeck Henkemans (1996).

2. So there is an underlying notion of "Reasonableness" associated with this account. See my article "Reasonableness and the Limits to Persuasion" (1993) for a critical discussion of this idea.

3. The argument from analogy is an example of an argumentation scheme. Generally, the introduction of this concept seems to be an innovation of the post-1984 work, although it is influenced by other authors. An argumentation scheme is defined as "a more or less conventionalized way of representing the relation between what is stated in the argument and what is stated in the standpoint" (van Eemeren and Grootendorst, 1992a:96).

4. A summary of the rules can be found in (209).

5. Hence, fulfilling the promise seen in him by Frans H. van Eemeren and Rob Grootendorst: "What is needed for the development of the study of argumentation and fallacies is, in our view, a radical pragma-dialectical approach. Walton is on his way. He only needs a small push" (1989b:105).

6. In 1990 Walton adds three more: the planning committee dialogue, the pedagogical dialogue, and the dialogue of expert consultation; and in 1991a (43) we find a further two: the deliberation dialogue and the interview.

7. More recently, the very existence of such a tradition of a "Standard Treatment" has been challenged by Ralph H. Johnson who, while recognizing the significance of Hamblin's work in stimulating subsequent study of fallacies, argues that Hamblin's list of texts is selective and even then offers no "uniform and homogeneous treatment of fallacies" (1990:153–67).

8. Certain "critical questions" for assessing analogies had been suggested earlier (van Eemeren and Grootendorst, 1992: 99, 102).

9. Of course, given the context-dependency assumed by the account, there would be no *same* argument.

10. Elsewhere (1993:49), van Eemeren, Grootendorst, Jackson, and Jacobs, speak of a rational judge who evaluates the discussants and their discourse. This seems to refer, however, to the same idea in van Eemeren and Grootendorst, where "argumentation" is defined as a speech act which is

"calculated in a regimented discussion to convince a rational judge of a particular standpoint" (1984:18). In the context of that discussion, a "rational judge" is identified with one of the participants of the dialogue who adopts the required rational attitude.

11. As Michael A. Gilbert (1995a:73) points out, a maxim like this tends to be culturally specific, and even in the Anglo-Saxon society of its origin it is still wise not to insult one's host by being unduly honest about the quality of food that is served. Thus, Grice's maxims may not have the broad applicability previously thought, and they need to be employed with discretion.

Chapter 3

1. The *ad misericordiam,* for example, is a form of legitimate pathotic argument characterized by pity (Brinton, 1988a:79).

2. Alan Brinton (1985:245) distinguishes between ἔθος (ethos) with an epsilon, and the lengthened form ἦθος (ethos) with an eta. The first carries the sense of "custom" or "habit"; the second, which is the one that interests us here, means "character."

3. In fact, Douglas N. Walton seems to have Brinton's Aristotelian idea in mind when he refers to the *argument from* ethos in an entry for *The Oxford Companion to Philosophy:* "[it] puts forward a proposition as being more plausible on the ground that it was asserted by a person with good character" (1995c:49).

4. I should qualify this by noting how John Locke understands the *ad verecundiam* in his *Essay Concerning Human Understanding,* 1690. There it is introduced as follows: "to allege the opinions of men, whose parts, learning, eminency, power, or some other cause has gained a name, and settled their reputation in the common esteem with some kind of authority" (Book 4, chap. 17, secs. 19–22). This broad definition, with references to "eminency" and "the common esteem" has obvious links to ethos, as it was employed by Aristotle. Subsequent accounts, however, have tended to narrow the *ad verecundiam,* to cases of specific expertise.

5. Brinton's discussion is to be recommended for the way in which he develops the features of ethotic argument out of the pages of the *Nicomachean Ethics.*

6. However, in a 1993 joint project with Frans H. van Eemeren, Rob Grootendorst, and Sally Jackson, Scott Jacobs does adopt a speech-act based account with which to approach argumentation. This project follows the van Eemeren and Grootendorst assumptions (1984): "Having an argument is a kind of speech activity composed of speech acts, while making an argument is the performance of a particular kind of speech act. The making of an argument is a complex speech act made up of simple speech acts (of asserting)"

(van Eemeren, Grootendorst, Jackson, and Jacobs, 1993:4). Interestingly, a footnote alerts us to Jacobs (1989) "For a quite different understanding of the relation between speech acts and arguments" (17).

7. Hence, his obvious attraction for the pragma-dialecticians.

8. Certainly, there is also an element in J. L. Austin's work of the exclusion of what does not fit the serious, central case of a speech act, as is brought out in Jacques Derrida's critique of the Austinian text (1982). This, however, is only one of the "openings" to the study of speech acts that Austin's text allows. It happens to be the one that John Searle followed. But there is ample indication in Austin's writings (including *How To Do Things with Words*) that it is not necessarily the path he would have taken had he lived to pursue this work. For a more detailed discussion of these indications in Austin and the differences between the concrete and abstract speech act, see Christopher W. Tindale (1986).

9. As we will see in future chapters, the internal logical support of an argument *is* a consideration in evaluation insofar as this is to be recognized by the universal audience for that argument.

10. I leave aside here the question of whether this traditional objection is an accurate description of the sophists' activity.

11. In fact, it is *more* appropriate, since the details of the comment do not seem to conform to the idea of two parties *both* promoting a thesis to each other.

Chapter 4

1. This, of course, indicates a relativism. But it is overlooked in the adherence to a *Truth* and the assumption that both sides of the debate have in mind the same thing when they use this term.

2. In chapter 1, I noted Douglas N. Walton's (1982) work on propositional relevance. Later he moves beyond this to consider what he calls "pragmatic relevance" or "pragma-dialectical relevance" (1995:194). This indicates a wider appreciation for contextual relevance in that it refers to speech acts in the larger context of dialogue (rather than propositions in a PPC set). As a kind of dialectical relevance, Walton's new conception relates to what fits or does not fit the type of dialogue involved in a particular context. If a move in a dialogue does not fit the appropriate dialogue type, it is irrelevant (163). My discussion of contextual relevance, drawn from a rhetorical perspective, is not restricted to moves in dialogues.

3. Their account differs quite significantly from Paul Grice's, however: Grice assumes a greater degree of cooperation in communication. Also, his

principle and maxims are norms; Dan Sperber and Deidre Wilson's principle of relevance is a generalization about ostensive-inferential communication (1986:161–62).

4. I am grateful to David Hitchcock for first posing the example of the physics professor as a problem to be accommodated by this account.

5. I am grateful to Tony Blair for pointing out to me in a private communication the ideas discussed in this section.

6. There's also a presumption in favor of self-evident or necessary truth, and so forth. But the more relevant case for argumentation is common knowledge.

7. In saying this I would add that as argumentation theorists we often have to deal with arguments for which the intended audience is unclear. Arguments from periods of history removed from our own are a case in point. However, even here the task is to recover as much as possible of the intended audience from the context that is known, if we are to say we have fully grasped the argumentation.

8. Of course, a particular audience can and will be persuaded by unreasonable argumentation. But the issue becomes whether they *should* be so persuaded and the conditions for judging that they should not.

9. James Crosswhite (1989:163) includes the further technique of adding together particular audiences until one eventually comes to the whole of humanity. But it is difficult to see when this would be useful or desirable, and Crosswhite himself notes the difficulties that are involved.

10. Walton (1995a:42, 224) makes reference to this case, and he also devotes a whole article to it (1995b). In both instances, he examines it in terms of its emotional appeal. While I approach it from a somewhat different perspective, I am indebted to Walton's analysis for some of the details of the case.

11. This has been only a cursory treatment of the case. I have not looked at the mode of expression used to convey the argument, for example, nor fully investigated the complex goals of the arguers (Hill and Knowlton, the Citizens for a Free Kuwait).

Chapter 5

1. We can imagine other interested subgroups. Shell's competitors read it with a view to possibly exploiting the situation. They can be addressed by the points that are intended to cut off any thoughts of instability. Nigerian expatriates, angered by Shell's association with the military regime, would be most interested in attempts made throughout the argumentation to distance Shell from events and responsibility.

2. See *The Economist* (2–8 December 1995) "Multinationals and Their Morals," 337:18–20.

3. The statements are numbered to facilitate the discussion of the arguments in the next section.

4. I will refer to the 1974 British edition: *Did Six Million Really Die? The Truth at Last,* by Richard Harwood (London). It has been reprinted in many places, notably in Canada in 1983 by Ernst Zundel, who added to the title "The Truth at Last Exposed," and provided a foreword and postscript. This publication became the occasion for Zundel's court case, discussed in the next section. It was later reproduced as an afterward to *Did Six Million Really Die? Report of Evidence in the Canadian "False News" Trial of Ernst Zundel,* edited by Barbara Kulaszka, 505–33.

Apparently, the work was largely based on an earlier American version, *The Myth of the Six Million,* published in 1969 by Noontide Press (see Lipstadt, 1993:105). Richard Harwood is a pseudonym of Richard Verral.

5. Zundel was convicted in March 1985 for knowingly publishing "false news" under sec. 177 of the *Criminal Code of Canada.* The text in question was *Six Million* (a second charge, for which he was acquitted, concerned the article "The West, War, and Islam"). Zundel appealed the conviction on several grounds. The one that interests this case study, is the claim that certain evidence should have been inadmissible, since it was based on hearsay.

6. During Zundel's 1988 trial, the Jewish scholar Dr. Raul Hilberg defined the *Holocaust* as "the annihilation by physical means of the Jews in Europe during the Nazi regime, 1943–1945" ("Regina v. Zundel":170). This is the understanding that I shall attach to the term in this case study.

7. Nonetheless, his remark is confirmed by the experience of those of us working in the academic fields we do. It is also, like any appeal to authority, open to revision in light of subsequent considerations. Appealing to authority may close a local dispute, but it does not foreclose global debates.

Chapter 6

1. Hans V. Hansen and Robert C. Pinto define these informal fallacies negatively, where "what is at issue in them is not a violation of the "rules" of formal logic" (1995:199).

2. For a detailed discussion of, and response to, Gerald Massey's argument see Trudy Govier (1987:184–89).

3. The existence and nature of this Standard Treatment has at least one forceful critic: see Ralph H. Johnson (1990).

4. Although, in Aristotle's defense, since he sees the need to explain the examples to his audience, he presumably does not see them as all that transparent.

5. Forster's translation in the Loeb edition (1955) provides a "fallacy" here. Hansen and Pinto include the Pickard-Cambridge translation from W. D. Ross's (1928) edition, which also renders it as a "fallacy." The Pickard-Cambridge translation is also the source for the Barnes edition of *The Complete Works of Aristotle: The Revised Oxford Translation* (1984). But in this edition the passage in question has been emended to read "falsity," which is surely the preferred translation.

6. A similar concern could be raised about Michael Wreen's account with its restriction to bad arguments. For Wreen "[t]here are, then, only two ways in which an argument can go wrong, or be a bad argument. The premises, one or more of them, could fail to be epistemically worthy . . . or the inference could be a bad one, one that shouldn't have been made" (1994a:97). This would seem to accommodate all of Maurice A. Finocchiaro's senses, but few besides.

7. One confusion that could arise with Douglas N. Walton's model of fallacy, defined within the contexts of dialogues, is that the cases he explores in illustrating the model do not always involve dialogues. See, for example, Case 104 (1995a:212).

8. As noted, Charles Arthur Willard's views on this have been criticized by Ralph H. Johnson and J. Anthony Blair (1993b). They observe (192) that he builds his case around the so-called ad fallacies and not with reference to other fallacies. As we have seen, he does refer to more than the "ad" fallacies, although he does not include these among those he analyzes in any detail.

9. In fact, we could now interpret Johnson and Blair's reaction as coming close to a recognition that features of *bad process* are being confused with features of *bad product.*

10. C. L. Hamblin (1970:53) dates the *Rhetoric* to 335 on the rather sparse evidence that the text contains the observation that the mind is at its prime at the age of forty-nine, the year of Aristotle's return to Athens. George Kennedy cites "historical allusions" (1991:301) to the period as the most compelling evidence that Aristotle worked on the text between 340 and 335.

11. Kennedy notes the following about the enthymeme: "The Aristotelian distinction between a syllogism and an enthymeme thus seems largely one of context—tightly reasoned philosophical discourse in the case of the syllogism versus popular speech or writing with resulting informality in the expression of the argument in an enthymeme" (1991:33).

12. The first way is illustrated by means of the *ad baculum,* the second way by means of Equivocation, and the third through Composition and Division.

Chapter 7

1. Clarence Irving Lewis (1929:267–73) is concerned with pointing out the fact that, while his pragmatic theory allows for the alteration over time of concepts and principles thus giving rise to a "new truth," this does not contradict an old truth in any sense other than the verbal. Categories and concepts are simply given up and replaced by better ones. I am grateful to Bernard Hodgson for stressing to me the importance of Lewis's work.

2. The deconstructive strategy can be gleaned from the texts of any of its practitioners, but noteworthy is Jacques Derrida (1981). The method (as such I believe it to be—agreeing with Norris) is well detailed in Christopher Norris (1982) and Jonathan Culler (1982).

3. Maryann Ayim (1995:808) makes a similar point with respect to Andrea Nye (1990).

4. The C-L Model is illustrated by linear and careful examples of reasoning. All extraneous materials—emotion, social consequences, and so forth— are separated from the text so as to get at the argument (Gilbert, 1994:96).

5. We should also distinguish here between sex and gender, because many of the claims lend themselves to a different interpretation depending on which they are understood to mean. For the most part, these issues involve focusing on masculinity and femininity as a gendered difference, not a biologic or anatomic one. Following T. de De Lauretis (1987), we will understand by "gender": "the representation of each individual in terms of a particular social relation which preexists the individual and is predicated on the conceptual and rigid (structural) opposition of the two biological sexes" (cited in Verbiest, 1995:825).

6. See also George Meyerson (1994:45) who makes a similar point.

7. This is not to deny the interest in the body that women have, particularly as the site for reproduction and disease (cf. Murphy, 1995). The concern is with the sense of an exclusive dichotomy that restricts women to the body, and with the commensurate assumption of oppression or conquest of the body/Nature discussed by Sally Miller Gearhart (1979).

8. For a critique of Margaret Atherton see Lorraine Code (1995:220–21).

9. Ayim (1995:805) wonders whether the fact that Mill and Russell supported the women's movement of their time accounts for their exclusion from Andrea Nye's list of prominent male logicians.

10. Ayim (1995:811) is critical of Nye's rejection of women's language. She traces the rejection to a failure on Nye's part to read the current literature on gender and language, which reveals a different perspective on women's talk.

11. See Michael A. Gilbert (1997) for a detailed elaboration of coalescent argumentation, especially the importance of goals and the incorporation of commonly neglected elements like physicality, insights, and hunches. This work, which incorporates the papers of Gilbert discussed in this chapter, did not appear until after my project was complete.

References

Adler, Jonathan E. 1994. Fallacies and alternative interpretations. *Australasian Journal of Philosophy*. 72:271–82.

Alcoff, Linda and Elizabeth Potter. 1993. Introduction: When feminisms intersect epistemology. In *Feminist Epistemologies*. L. Alcoff and E. Potter. eds., 1–14. New York: Routledge.

Anderson, Alan Ross and Belnap, Noel D. 1975. *Entailment: The logic of relevance and necessity*. Princeton, N.J.: Princeton University Press.

———. 1968. Entailment. *Logic and philosophy*. Gary Iseminger. ed. New York: Appleton-Century-Crofts.

Andrews, Richard. 1995. *Teaching and learning argument*. London: Cassell.

Anthony, Louise M. and Charlotte Witt. eds. 1993. *A mind of one's own: Feminist essays on reason & objectivity*. Boulder, Colo.: Westview Press.

Appignanesi, Lisa. ed. 1989. *Postmodernism: ICA documents*. London: Free Association Books.

———and Sara Maitland. eds. 1989. *The Rushdie file*. London: Fourth Estate.

Aristotle. 1984. *Prior analytics*. P. T. Geach. trans. Oxford: Clarendon Aristotle Series.

———. 1975/1984. *Posterior analytics*. Jonathan Barnes. trans. Oxford: Clarendon Aristotle Series/Revised Oxford Aristotle.

———. 1983. *Physics*. E. Hussey. trans. Oxford: Clarendon Aristotle Series.

———. 1991. *Aristotle 'On rhetoric': A theory of civic discourse*. George A. Kennedy. trans. with Introduction, Notes, and Appendixes. Oxford: Oxford University Press.

———. 1984. *The complete works of Aristotle: The revised Oxford translation*. Jonathan Barnes. ed. Princeton, N. J.: Princeton University Press.

———. 1941. *The Basic Works of Aristotle.* Richard McKeon. ed. New York: Random House.

———. 1955. *On sophistical refutations.* E. S. Forster. trans. Cambridge: Harvard University Press.

———. 1928. *On sophistical refutations.* W. A. Pickard-Cambridge. trans. *The works of Aristotle translated into English.* W. D. Ross. ed. London: Oxford University Press. (Excerpted in Hansen and Pinto, *Fallacies:*19–38.)

Arnold, Carroll C. 1982. Introduction: In Chaim Perelman. *The realm of rhetoric.* William Kluback. trans. Notre Dame: University of Notre Dame Press.

Atherton, Margaret. 1993. Cartesian reason and gendered reason. In *A mind of one's own: Feminist essays on reason & objectivity.* Louise Anthony and Charlotte Witt. eds., 19–34. Boulder, Colo.: Westview Press.

Austin, J. L. 1962. *How to do things with words.* Cambridge: Harvard University Press.

Ayim, Maryann. 1995. Passing through the needle's eye: Can a feminist teach logic? *Argumentation.* 9:801–20.

———. 1991. Dominance and affiliation. *Informal Logic.* 13:79–88.

Barnes, Jonathan. 1981. Proof and syllogism. In *Aristotle on science: The posterior analytics.* E. Berti. ed. Padua, Italy: Padova.

Barth, E. M. and E. C. W. Krabbe. 1982. *From axiom to dialogue.* Berlin: Walter de Gruyer.

Barthes, Roland. 1985. *The grain of the voice: Interviews 1962–1980.* Linda Coverdale. trans. New York: Hill and Wang.

Battersby, Mark. 1989. Critical thinking as applied epistemology. *Informal Logic.* 11:91–99.

Berrill, Deborah P. 1996. Reframing argument from the metaphor of war. In *Perspectives on written argument.* Deborah P. Berrill. ed., 171–87. Cresskill, N.J.: Hampton Press.

Berg, Jonathan. 1992. Validity and rationality. In *Argumentation illuminated.* Frans H. van Eemeren, et al. eds., 104–12. Amsterdam: Sic Sat.

———. 1991. The relevant relevance. *The Journal of Pragmatics.* 16:411–25.

Billig, Michael. 1993. Psychology, rhetoric and cognition. In *The recovery of rhetoric: Persuasive discourse and disciplinarity in the human sciences.* R. H. Roberts and J. M. M. Good. eds., 119–36. Charlottesville: University Press of Virginia.

———. 1991. *Ideology and opinions: Studies in rhetorical psychology.* London: Sage Publications.

———. 1987. *Arguing and thinking: A rhetorical approach to social psychology.* Cambridge: Cambridge University Press.

Biro, John and Harvey Siegel. 1992. Normativity, argumentation and an epistemic theory of fallacies." In *Argumentation illuminated.* Frans H. van Eemeren, et al. eds., 85–103. Amsterdam: Sic Sat.

Blair, J. Anthony. 1989. Premise relevance. *Norms in argumentation.* R. Maier. ed., 67–83. Dordrecht-Holland: Foris Publications.

———and Ralph H. Johnson. 1993. Dissent in fallacyland, part 1: Problems with van Eemeren and Grootendorst. In *Argument and the postmodern challenge: Proceedings of the eighth SCA/AFA conference on argumentation.* Raymie E. Mckerrow. ed., 188–90. Annandale, Va.: Speech Communication Association.

———. 1987. Argumentation as dialectical. *Argumentation.* 1:41–56.

———. 1980. Introduction: *Informal logic: The first international symposium.* J. Anthony Blair and Ralph Johnson. eds. Pt. Reyes, Calif.: Edgepress.

Blakemore, Diane. 1992. *Understanding utterances: An introduction to pragmatics.* Oxford: Blackwell.

Brinton, Alan. 1995. The *ad hominem.* In *Fallacies: Classical and contemporary readings.* Hans V. Hansen and Robert C. Pinto. eds., 213–22. University Park: Pennsylvania State University Press.

———. 1988a. Appeal to angry emotions. *Informal Logic.* 10:77–87.

———. 1988b. Pathos and the "appeal to emotion": An Aristotelian analysis. *History of Philosophy Quarterly.* 5:207–19.

———. 1986. Ethotic argument. *History of Philosophy Quarterly.* 3:245–58.

———. 1985. "A rhetorical view of *ad hominem. Australasian Journal of Philosophy.* 63:50–63.

Brockriede, W. 1978. Argument as epistemological method. In *Argumentation as a way of knowing.* D. Thomas. ed. Speech Communication Association.

Burnyeat, M. F. 1996. Enthymeme: Aristotle on the rationality of rhetoric. In *Essays on Aristotle's rhetoric.* Amelie Oksenberg Rorty. ed., 88–115. Los Angeles: University of California Press.

———. 1994. Enthymeme: Aristotle on the logic of persuasion. In *Aristotle's rhetoric: Philosophical essays.* David J. Furley and Alexander Nehamas. eds., 3–55. Princeton, N. J.: Princeton University Press.

Carey, Christopher. 1996. Rhetorical means of persuasion. In *Essays on Aristotle's rhetoric.* Amelie Oksenberg Rorty. ed., 399–415. Los Angeles: University of California Press.

Cherwitz, Richard A. and Thomas J. Darwin. 1995. On the continuing utility of argument in a postmodern world. *Argumentation.* 9:181–202.

Clear thinking in troubled times. *The Globe and Mail,* Toronto 21. Nov. 1995: A17.

Code, Lorraine. 1995. *Rhetorical spaces: Essays on gendered locations.* New York: Routledge.

Cohen, Daniel H. 1995. Argument is war . . . and war is hell: Philosophy, education, and metaphors for argumentation. *Informal Logic.* 17:177–88.

Copeland, B. J. 1980. The trouble Anderson and Belnap have with relevance. *Philosophical Studies.* 37:325–34.

Copi, I. 1986. *Informal Logic.* New York: Macmillan.

Crosswhite, James. 1995. Is there an audience for this argument? Fallacies, theories, and relativisms. *Philosophy and Rhetoric.* 28:134–45.

———. 1993. Being unreasonable: Perelman and the problem of fallacies. *Argumentation.* 7:385–402.

———. 1989. Universality in rhetoric: Perelman's universal audience. *Philosophy and Rhetoric.* 22:157–73.

Culler, Jonathan. 1982. *On deconstruction: Theory and criticism after structuralism.* Ithaca, N. Y.: Cornell University Press.

Damasio, Antonio R. 1994. *Descartes' error: Emotion, reason, and the human brain.* New York: Grosset/Putnam.

Davidson, Donald. 1984. *Inquiries into truth and interpretation.* Oxford: Clarendon Press.

Derrida, Jacques. 1982. *Margins of philosophy.* Alan Bass. trans. Chicago: Chicago University Press.

———. 1981. *Positions.* Alan Bass. trans. Chicago: University of Chicago Press.

Easterman, Daniel. 1992. *New Jerusalems: Reflections on Islam, fundamentalism and the Rushdie affair.* London: Grafton.

The Economist. 2–8, December 1995. Multinationals and their morals. 337:18–20.

Ede, Lisa S. 1989. Rhetoric versus philosophy: The role of the universal audience in Chaim Perelman's *the new rhetoric.* In *The new rhetoric of*

Chaim Perelman: Statement & response. Ray. D. Dearin. ed., 141–51. New York: University Press of America.

Edwards, Derek, Malcolm Ashmore, and Jonathan Potter. 1995. Death and furniture: The rhetoric, politics and theology of bottom line arguments against relativism. *History of the Human Sciences*. 8:25–49.

Eemeren, Frans H. van. 1988. Argumentation analysis: A Dutch counterbalance. In *Critical thinking: Proceedings of the first British conference on informal logic and critical thinking*. Alec Fisher. ed., 39–53. Norwich: University of East Anglia.

———. 1987. For reason's sake: Maximal argumentative analysis of discourse. In *Argumentation: Across the lines of discipline*. Frans H. van Eemeren, et al. eds., 201–15. Dordrecht, Holland: Foris Publications.

———. 1986. Dialectical analysis as a normative reconstruction of argumentative discourse. *Text*. 6:1–16.

———. 1985. Response. In *Argument and social practice: Proceedings of the fourth SCA/AFA conference on argumentation*. J. Robert Cox, Malcom O. Sillars, and Greg B. Walker. eds., 154–59. Annandale, Va.: Speech Communication Association.

———and Rob Grootendorst. 1995a. Perelman and the fallacies. *Philosophy and Rhetoric*. 28:122–33.

———. 1995b. The pragma-dialectical approach to fallacies. In *Fallacies: Classical and contemporary readings*. Hans V. Hansen and Robert C. Pinto. eds., 130–44. University Park: Pennsylvania State University Press.

———. 1995c *Argumentum ad hominem:* A pragma-dialectical case in point." In *Fallacies: Classical and contemporary readings*. Hans V. Hansen and Robert C. Pinto. eds., 223–38. University Park: Pennsylvania State University Press.

———. 1994. eds. *Studies in pragma-dialectics*. Amsterdam: Sic Sat.

———. 1992a. *Argumentation, communication, and fallacies: A pragma-dialectical perspective*. Hillsdale, N.J.: Lawrence Erlbaum Associates Publishers.

———. 1992b. Relevance reviewed: The case of argumentum ad hominem. *Argumentation*. 6:141–59.

———. 1991. The relevance problem in the analysis of argumentative texts: A pragma-dialectical reconstruction. Unpublished. McMaster University, Hamilton, Ontario.

———. 1989a. A pragma-dialectical perspective on norms. In *Norms in argumentation*. Robert Maier. ed., 97–112. Dordrecht-Holland: Foris Publications.

———. 1989b. "A transition stage in the theory of fallacies. *Journal of Pragmatics.* 13:99–109.

———. 1989c. "Writing argumentative texts from analysis to presentation: A pragma-dialectical approach. In *Spheres of argument: Proceedings of the sixth SCA/AFA conference on argumentation.* Bruce E. Gronbeck. ed., 324–30. Annandale, Va.: Speech Communication Association.

———. 1988. Rationale for a pragma-dialectical perspective. *Argumentation.* 2:271–91.

———. 1987. Fallacies in a pragma-dialectical perspective. *Argumentation.* 1:283–301.

———. 1984. *Speech acts in argumentative discussions.* Dordrecht, Holland: Foris Publications.

———. 1983. Unexpressed premises, part 2. *Journal of the American Forensic Association.* 19:215–25.

———. 1982a. The speech acts of arguing and convincing in externalized discussions. *Journal of Pragmatics.* 6:1–24.

———. 1982b. Unexpressed premises, part 1. *Journal of the American Forensic Association.* 19:97–106.

———, Sally Jackson, and Scott Jacobs. 1993. *Reconstructing argumentative discourse.* Tuscaloosa: University of Alabama Press.

Eemeren, Frans H. van, Rob Grootendorst, and Tjark Kruiger. 1984. *The study of argumentation.* New York: Irvington Publishers. (Reprinted in 1987 as *Handbook of argumentation theory: A critical survey of classical backgrounds and modern studies.* Dordrecht, Holland: Foris Publications.)

Eemeren, Frans H. van, Rob Grootendorst, and Bert Meuffels. 1989. The skill of identifying argumentation. *Journal of the American Forensic Association.* 25:239–45.

Eemeren, Frans H. van, Rob Grootendorst, and Francisca Snoeck Henkemans. 1996. *Fundamentals of argumentation theory: A handbook of historical backgrounds and contemporary developments.* Mahwah, N. J.: Lawrence Erlbaum Associates.

Evra, J. van. 1985. Logic, the liberal science. *Teaching Philosophy.* 8:285–94.

Farrell, Thomas. 1993. *Norms of rhetorical culture.* New Haven: Yale University Press.

———. 1977. Validity and rationality: The rhetorical constituents of argumentative form. *Journal of the American Forensic Association.* 13:142–49.

Feyerabend, Paul. 1987. *A farewell to reason.* London: Verso.

Finocchiaro, Maurice A. 1995. The dialectical approach to interpretation and evaluation. In *Perspectives and approaches: Proceedings of the third international conference on argumentation,* vol 1. Frans H. van Eemeren, et al. eds., 183–95. Amsterdam, Holland: Sic Sat.

———. 1987. Six types of fallaciousness: Toward a realistic theory of logical criticism. *Argumentation.* 1:263–82. (Excerpted in Hansen and Pinto, *Fallacies:*120–29.)

———. 1980. *Galileo and the art of reasoning: Rhetorical foundations of logic and scientific method.* Dordrecht, Holland: D. Reidel Publishing.

Fisher, Walter R. 1986. Judging the quality of audiences and narrative rationality. In *Practical reasoning in human affairs: Studies in honor of Chaim Perelman.* James L. Golden and Joseph J. Pilotta. eds. Dordrecht, Holland: D. Reidel Publishing.

Foss, Sonja K. and Cindy L. Griffin. 1995. Beyond persuasion: A proposal for an invitational rhetoric. *Communication Monographs.* 62:2–18.

Frede, Dorothea. 1996. Mixed feelings in Aristotle's *rhetoric.* In *Essays on Aristotle's rhetoric.* Amelie Oksenberg Rorty. ed., 258–85. Los Angeles: University of California Press.

Freeman, James B. 1994. The place of informal logic in logic. In *New essays in informal logic.* Ralph H. Johnson and J. Anthony Blair. eds., 36–49. Windsor, Ontario: Informal Logic.

———. 1993. *Thinking logically: Basic concepts for reasoning.* 2d edition. New Jersey: Prentice-Hall.

———. 1991. *Dialectics and the macrostructure of arguments: A theory of argument structure.* New York: Foris Publications.

Gearhart, Sally Miller. 1979. The womanization of rhetoric. *Women's Studies International Quarterly.* 2:195–201.

Gergen, Kenneth J. 1994. The limits of pure critique. In *After postmodernism: Reconstructing ideology critique.* Herbert W. Simons and Michael Billig. eds., 58–78. London: Sage Publications.

Gilbert, Michael A. 1997. *Coalescent argumentation.* Mahwah, N.J.: Lawrence Erlbaum Associates.

———. 1995a. The delimitation of 'argument'. *Inquiry: Critical thinking across the disciplines.* 15:63–75.

———. 1995b. Coalescent argumentation. *Argumentation.* 9:837–52.

———. 1994. Feminism, argumentation and coalescence. *Informal Logic.* 16:95–113.

Gilligan, Carol. 1982. *In a different voice.* Cambridge: Harvard University Press.

Golden, James L. 1986. The universal audience revisited. In *Practical reasoning in human affairs: Studies in honor of Chaim Perelman.* James L. Golden and Joseph J. Pilotta. eds., 287–304. Dordrecht, Holland: D. Reidel Publishing.

Goodwin, David. 1992. The dialectic of second-order distinctions: The structure of arguments about fallacies. *Informal Logic.* 14:11–22.

———. 1991. Distinction, argumentation, and the rhetorical construction of the real. *Argument and Advocacy.* 27:141–58.

Gough, James and C. Tindale. 1985. 'Hidden' or 'missing' premises. *Informal Logic.* 7:99–106.

Govier, Trudy. 1995. Non-adversarial conceptions of argument. In *Perspectives and approaches: Proceedings of the third ISSA conference on argumentation,* vol. 1. Frans H. van Eemeren, et al. eds., 196–206. Amsterdam: Sic Sat.

———. 1992. *A practical study of argument.* 3rd edition. Belmont, Calif.: Wadsworth. (2d edition, 1988.)

———. 1987. *Problems in argument analysis and evaluation.* Dordrecht-Holland: Foris Publications.

Grice, Paul. 1989. *Studies in the way of words.* Cambridge: Harvard University Press.

Groarke, Leo A. 1992. In defense of deductivism: Replying to Govier. In *Argumentation illuminated.* Frans H. van Eemeren, et al. eds., 113–21. Amsterdam: Sic Sat.

———and Christopher W. Tindale. 1986. Critical thinking: How to teach *good* reasoning. *Teaching Philosophy.* 9:301–18.

———, and Linda Fisher. 1997. *Good reasoning matters!: A constructive approach to critical thinking.* 2d edition. Toronto: Oxford University Press. (1st edition, with J. F. Little [1989] Toronto: McClelland & Stewart.)

Grootendorst, Rob. 1992. Everyday argumentation from a speech act perspective. In *Readings in argumentation.* William L. Benoit, Dale Hample, and Pamela J. Benoit. eds. Berlin/New York: Foris.

———. 1987. Some fallacies about fallacies. In *Argumentation: Across the lines of discipline.* Frans H. van Eemeren, et al. eds., 331–41. Dordrecht-Holland: Foris Publications.

———. 1985. Response. In *Argument and social practice: Proceedings of the fourth SCA/AFA conference on argumentation.* J. Robert Cox, Malcom

O. Sillars, and Gregg B. Walker. eds., 159–61. Annandale, Va.: Speech Communication Association.

Grosz, Elizabeth. 1993. Bodies and knowledges: Feminism and the crisis of reason. *Feminist epistemologies.* Linda Alcoff and Elizabeth Potter. eds., 187–215. New York: Routledge.

Habermas, Jurgen. 1984. *The theory of communicative action: Reason and the rationalization of society,* vol. 1. Thomas McCarthy. trans. Boston: Beacon.

Hajek, Alan. 1992. Trick-arguing. *The Times literary supplement.* 23.

Hamblin, C. L. 1970. *Fallacies.* London: Methuen.

Hansen, Hans V. 1996. Aristotle and the senses of fallacy. Manuscript.

—— and Robert C. Pinto. 1995. eds. *Fallacies: Classical and contemporary readings.* University Park, Pennsylvania State University Press.

Harpine, William D. 1985. Can rhetoric and dialectic serve the purposes of logic? *Philosophy & Rhetoric.* 18:96–112.

Harwood, Richard. 1974. *Did six million really die? The truth at last,* London (pamphlet). Reprinted 1983 by Ernst Zundel. Toronto: Samisdat Publishers.

Heidegger, Martin. 1962. *Being and time.* John Macquarrie and Edward Robinson. trans. New York: Harper & Row.

Hikins, James W. 1995. The given of achievement and the reluctance to assent: Argument and inquiry in the post-postmodern world. *Argumentation.* 9:137–62.

Hintikka, Jaakko. 1989. The role of logic in argumentation. *The Monist.* 72:3–24.

——. 1987. The fallacy of fallacies. *Argumentation.* 1:217–38.

Hitchcock, David. 1995a. Does the traditional treatment of enthymemes rest on a mistake? In *Analysis and evaluation: Proceedings of the third ISSA conference on argumentation,* vol. 2. Frans H. van Eemeren, et al. eds., 113–29. Amsterdam: Sic Sat.

——. 1995b. Do the fallacies have a place in the teaching of reasoning skills or critical thinking? In *Fallacies: Classical and contemporary readings.* Hans V. Hansen and Robert C. Pinto. eds., 319–28. University Park: Pennsylvania State University Press.

——. 1985. Enthymematic arguments. *Informal Logic.* 7:83–97.

Homiak, Marcia L. 1993. Feminism and Aristotle's rational ideal. In *A mind of one's own: Feminist essays on reason & objectivity.* Louise M. Anthony and Charlotte Witt. eds., 1–17. Boulder, Colo.: Westview Press.

Honderich, Ted. 1995. ed. *The Oxford companion to philosophy.* Oxford: Oxford University Press.

Irwin, T. H. 1996. Ethics in the *rhetoric* and the ethics. *Essays on Aristotle's rhetoric.* Amelie Oksenberg Rorty. ed., 142–74. Los Angeles: University of California Press.

Iseminger, G. I. 1980. Is relevance necessary for validity? *Mind.* 89:196–213.

Jackson, Sally. 1995. Fallacies and heuristics. In *Analysis and evaluation: Proceedings of the third ISSA conference on argumentation,* vol. 2. Frans H. van Eemeren, et al. eds., 257–69. Amsterdam: Sic Sat.

————. 1985. What can speech acts do for argumentation theory? In *Argumentation and social practice: Proceedings of the fourth SCA/AFA conference on argumentation.* J. Robert Cox, et. al. eds., 127–38. Annandale, Va.: Speech Communication Association.

Jacobs, Scott. 1989. Speech acts and arguments. *Argumentation.* 3:345–65.

Jeffrey, Richard. 1981. *Formal logic: Its scope and limits.* 2d edition. New York: McGraw-Hill.

Johnson, Ralph H. 1995. Informal logic and pragma-dialectics: Some differences. In *Perspectives and approaches: Proceedings of the third ISSA conference on argumentation,* vol. 1. Frans H. van Eemeren, et al. eds., 237–45. Amsterdam: Sic Sat.

————. 1990. Hamblin on the standard treatment. *Philosophy and Rhetoric.* 23: 153–67.

————. 1987a. Logic naturalized: Recovering a tradition. In *Argumentation: Across the lines of discipline.* Frans H. van Eemeren, et al. Dordrecht, Holland: Foris Publications.

————. 1987b. The blaze of her splendors: Suggestions about revitalizing fallacy theory. *Argumentation.* 1:239–53. (Excerpted in *Fallacies: Classical and contemporary readings.* 1995. Hans V. Hansen and Robert C. Pinto. eds., 107–19. University Park: Pennsylvnia State University Press.)

————. 1981. "Toulmin's Bold Experiment." *Informal Logic Newsletter.* 3:2–3.

———— and J. Anthony Blair. 1994. Informal logic: Past and present. *New essays in informal logic.* Ralph H. Johnson and J. Anthony Blair. eds., 1–19. Windsor, Ontario: Informal Logic.

————. 1993a. *Logical self-defense.* 3rd edition. Toronto: McGraw-Hill Ryerson.

————. 1993b. Dissent in fallacyland, part 2: Problems with Willard. In *Argument and the postmodern challenge: Proceedings of the eighth*

SCA/AFA conference on argumentation. Raymie E. Mckerrow. ed., 191–93. Annandale, Va.: Speech Communication Association.

Johnstone, Henry W. Jr. 1978. *Validity and rhetoric in philosophical argument: An outlook in transition.* University Park, Pa.: Dialogue Press of Man & World.

Keith, William. 1995. Argument practices. *Argumentation.* 9:163–79.

Kelley, David. 1994. *The art of reasoning.* 2d expanded edition. New York: Norton.

Kennedy, George. 1991. Introduction, notes and appendixes. *Aristotle 'On Rhetoric':A theory of civic discourse.* Oxford: Oxford University Press.

Kulaszka, Barbara. 1992. ed. *Did six million really die? Report of evidence in the Canadian "false news" trial of Ernst Zundel—1988.* Toronto: Samisdat Publishers.

Laughlin, Stanley K. and Daniel T. Hughes. 1986. The rational and the reasonable: Dialectic or parallel systems? In *Practical reasoning in human affairs: Studies in honor of Chaim Perelman.* James L. Golden and Joseph J. Pilotta. eds., 187–205. Dordrecht, Holland: D. Reidel Publishing.

Laurentis, T. de. 1987. The technology of gender. In *Technologies of gender: Essays on theory, film and fiction.* Bloomington: Indiana University Press.

Lear, Jonathan. 1988. *Aristotle: The desire to understand.* Cambridge: Cambridge University Press.

Levi, Don. S. 1995. In defense of rhetoric. *Philosophy & Rhetoric.* 28:253–75.

Lewis, Clarence Irving. 1929. *Mind and the world-order: Outline of a theory of knowledge.* New York: Dover.

Lewis, D. K. 1969. *Convention.* Cambridge: Harvard University Press.

Lipstadt, Deborah. 1993. *Denying the Holocaust: The growing assault on truth and memory.* Toronto: Penguin/Plume.

Lloyd, Genevieve. 1993. *The man of reason: "male" and "female" in Western philosophy.* 2d edition. Minneapolis: University of Minnesota Press. (1st edition, 1984.)

Locke, John. 1959/1690. *An essay concerning human understanding.* A. C. Fraser. ed. New York: Dover.

Lyotard, Jean-François. 1984/1979. *The postmodern condition: A report on knowledge.* Geoff Bennington and Brian Massumi. trans. Minneapolis: University of Minnesota Press.

Mailloux, Stephen. 1995. ed. *Rhetoric, sophistry, pragmatism.* Cambridge: Cambridge University Press.

Makau, Josina M. 1987. Perspectives on argumentation instruction. In *Argumentation: analysis and practices.* Frans H. van Eemeren, et al. eds., 376–85. Dordrecht, Holland: Foris Publications.

Maneli, Mieczyslaw. 1994. *Perelman's new rhetoric as philosophy and methodology for the next century.* Dordrecht, Holland: Kluwer.

Margolis, Joseph. 1990. Reconciling realism and relativism. In *The rhetorical turn: Invention and persuasion in the conduct of inquiry.* Herbert W. Simons. ed., 308–19. Chicago: University of Chicago Press.

Massey, Gerald. 1981. The fallacy behind fallacies. *Midwest Studies in Philosophy.* 6:489–500. (Excerpted in Hansen and Pinto, *Fallacies:* 159–71.)

McCabe, Mary Margaret. 1994. Arguments in context: Aristotle's defense of rhetoric. In *Aristotle's rhetoric: Philosophical essays.* David J. Furley and Alexander Nehamas. eds., 129–65. Princeton, N.J.: Princeton University Press.

Menssen, Sandra. 1993. Do women and men use different logics? A reply to Carol Gilligan and Deborah Orr. *Informal Logic.* 15:123–38.

Meyer, Michel. 1989. *From metaphysics to rhetoric.* Dordrecht, Holland: Kluwer.

———. 1986. Problematology and rhetoric. In *Practical reasoning in human affairs: Studies in honor of Chaim Perelman.* James L. Golden and Joseph J. Pilotta. eds., 119–52. Dordrecht, Holland: D. Reidel Publishing.

Meyerson, George. 1994. *Rhetoric, reason and society: Rationality as dialogue.* London: Sage Publications.

Missimer, Connie A. 1986. *Good arguments:An introduction to critical thinking.* Englewood Cliffs, N.J.: Prentice-Hall.

Murphy, John M. 1995. Critical rhetoric as political discourse. *Argumentation and Advocacy.* 32:1–15.

Murphy, Julien S. 1995. *The constructed body:AIDS, reproductive technology, and ethics.* Albany: State University of New York Press.

Natanson, Maurice and Henry W. Johnstone Jr. 1965. eds. *Philosophy, rhetoric, and argumentation.* University Park: Pennsylvania State University Press.

Nehamas, Alexander. 1994. Pity and fear in the *Rhetoric* and the *Poetics.* In *Aristotle's rhetoric:Philosophical essays.* David J. Furley and Alexander Nehamas. eds., 257–82. Princeton, N.J.: Princeton University Press.

Norris, Christopher. 1982. *Deconstruction: Theory & practice*. London: Methuen & Co.

Nussbaum, Martha C. 1994. *The therapy of desire: Theory and practice in Hellenistic ethics*. Princeton, N.J.: Princeton University Press.

Nye, Andrea. 1990. *Words of power*. New York: Routledge.

Oddie, Judge. 1991. *Science and the administration of justice*. London: Justice.

Orr, Deborah. 1989. Just the facts Ma'am: Informal logic, gender and pedagogy. *Informal Logic*. 11:1–10.

Perelman, Chaim. 1989a. The new rhetoric and the rhetoricians: Remembrances and comments. In *The new rhetoric of Chaim Perelman: Statement & response*. Ray D. Dearin. ed., 239–51. New York: University Press of America.

———. 1989b. Formal logic and informal logic. In *From metaphysics to rhetoric*. Michel Meyer. ed., 9–14. Dordrecht, Holland: Kluwer.

———. 1982. *The realm of rhetoric*. William Kluback. trans. Notre Dame: University of Notre Dame Press.

———. 1979a. *The new rhetoric and the humanities: Essays on rhetoric and its applications*. Dordrecht, Holland: D. Reidel Publishing.

———. 1979b. The rational and the reasonable. In *The new rhetoric and the humanities: Essays on rhetoric and its applications*. Dordrecht, Holland: D. Reidel Publishing.

———. 1967. *Justice*. New York: Random.

———. 1963. *The idea of justice and the problem of argument*. John Petrie. trans. London: Routledge.

———and L. Olbrechts-Tyteca. 1989. Act and person in argument. In *The new rhetoric of Chaim Perelman: Statement & response*. Ray D. Dearin. ed., 43–68. New York: University Press of America.

———. 1969, *The new rhetoric: A treatise on argumentation*. John Wilkinson and Purcell Weaver. trans. Notre Dame: University of Notre Dame Press.

Pinto, Robert C. 1995. The relation of argument to inference. In *Perspectives and Approaches: Proceedings of the Third ISSA Conference on Argumentation,* vol. 1. Frans van Eemeren et al. eds., 271–86. Amsterdam: Sic Sat.

———. 1994. Logic, epistemology and argument appraisal. In *New essays in informal logic*. Ralph H. Johnson and J. Anthony Blair. eds., 118–24. Windsor, Ontario: Informal Logic.

Plato. 1921. *Theaetetus.* H. N. Fowler. trans. Cambridge: Harvard University Press.

Potter, Jonathan. 1996. *Representing reality: Discourse, rhetoric and social construction.* London: Sage Publications.

Putnam, Hilary. 1981. *Reason, truth and history.* Cambridge: Cambridge University Press.

Quine, W. V. 1972. *Methods of logic.* 3rd edition. New York: Holt.

Rassinier, Paul. 1977. *Debunking the genocide myth.* Los Angeles, CA: Noontide Press.

Ray, John W. 1978. Perelman's universal audience. *Quarterly Journal of Speech.* 64:361–75.

Read, Stephen. 1995. *Thinking about logic: An introduction to the philosophy of logic.* Oxford: Oxford University Press.

———. 1988. *Relevant logic: A philosophical examination of inference.* Oxford: Blackwell.

Regina v. Zundel. 1987. *Ontario Reports.* 58:129–203.

Rescher, Nicholas. 1977. *Dialectics: A controversy oriented approach to the theory of knowledge.* Albany: State University of New York Press.

Reuters News Agency. 1990. Iraqi atrocities cited by amnesty. *The Globe and Mail,* 19 December Toronto:A1–2.

Ricoeur, Paul. 1977. *The rule of metaphor: Multidisciplinary studies of the creation of meaning in language.* Robert Czerny, with Kathleen McLaughlin and John Costello, SJ. trans. Toronto: University of Toronto Press.

Roberts, R. H. and J. M. M. Good. 1993. *The recovery of rhetoric: Persuasive discourse and disciplinarity in the human sciences.* Charlottesville: University Press of Virginia.

Rorty, Amelie Oksenberg. 1996. ed. *Essays on Aristotle's rhetoric.* Los Angeles: University of California Press.

———. 1996. Structuring rhetoric. *Essays on Aristotle's rhetoric.* Amelie Oksenberg Rorty. ed., 1–33. Los Angeles: University of California Press.

Rose, Hilary. 1993. Rhetoric, feminism and scientific knowledge or from either/or to both/and. In *The recovery of rhetoric: Persuasive discourse and disciplinarity in the human sciences.* R. H. Roberts and J. M. M. Good. eds., 203–23. Charlottesville: University Press of Virginia.

Rowland, Robert C. 1995. In defense of rational argument: A pragmatic justifications of argumentation theory and response to postmodern critique. *Philosophy and Rhetoric.* 28:350–64.

Rowse, Arthur E. 1991. Flacking for the emir. *The Progressive.* 55:20–22.

Rushdie, Salman. 1988. *The satanic verses.* New York: Viking.

Russman, Thomas A. 1995. Postmodernism and the parody of argument. *Argumentation.* 9:123–35.

Sacks, Oliver. 1995. *An anthroplogist on Mars: Seven paradoxical tales.* Toronto: Vintage.

Scriven, Michael. 1976. *Reasoning.* New York: McGraw-Hill Inc.

Scult, Allen. 1989. Perelman's universal audience: One perspective. In *The new rhetoric of Chaim Perelman: Statement & response.* Ray D. Dearin. ed., 153–62. New York: University Press of America.

Searle, John. 1969. *Speech acts: An essay in the philosophy of language.* Cambridge: Cambridge University Press.

Siegel, Harvey. 1988. *Educating reason: Rationality, critical thinking and education.* New York: Routledge.

Simons, Herbert W. 1990. ed. *The rhetorical turn: Invention and persuasion in the conduct of inquiry.* Chicago: University of Chicago Press.

Solmsen, F. 1929. Die entwicklung der aristotelischen Logik und Rhetorik, Berlin.

Sperber, Dan and Deidre Wilson. 1986. *Relevance: Communication and cognition.* Cambridge: Harvard University Press.

———. 1982. Mutual knowledge and relevance in theories of comprehension. In *Mutual knowledge.* N. V. Smith. ed., 61–85. London: Academic Press.

Tindale, Christopher W. 1996. Fallacies in transition: An assessment of the pragma-dialectical perspective. *Informal Logic.* 18:17–33.

———. 1995. Walton and the standard treatment. In *Analysis and evaluation: Proceedings of the third ISSA conference on argumentation,* vol 2. Frans H. van Eemeren, et al. eds., 274–85. Amsterdam: Sic Sat.

———. 1994 Contextual Relevance in Argumentation." In *New essays in informal logic.* Ralph H. Johnson and J. Anthony Blair. eds., 67–81. Windsor, Ontario: Informal Logic.

———. 1993. Reasonableness and the limits to persuasion. *The Canadian Journal of Rhetorical Studies.* 3:133–48.

———. 1992. Audiences, relevance, and cognitive environments. *Argumentation.* 6:177–88.

———. 1986. The speaking subject: Speech acts, grammatology, and the phenomenology of speech. Ph.D. diss., University of Waterloo. Ottawa: National Library of Canada.

Toulmin, Stephen. 1990. *Cosmopolis: The hidden agenda of modernity.* Chicago: University of Chicago Press.

———. 1958. *The uses of argument.* Cambridge: Cambridge University Press.

———, Richard Rieke, and Allan Janik. 1984. *An introduction to reasoning.* 2d edition. New York: Macmillan.

Verbiest, Agnes. 1995. Woman and the gift of reason. *Argumentation.* 9:821–36.

Vidal-Naquet, Pierre. 1992. *Assassins of memory: Essays on the denial of the Holocaust.* Jeffrey Mehlman. trans. New York: Columbia University Press.

Vorobej, Mark. 1992. Defining Deduction. *Informal Logic.* 14:105–18.

Walton, N. Douglas. 1996. *Arguments from ignorance.* University Park: Pennsylvania State Press.

———. 1995a. *A pragmatic theory of fallacy.* Tuscaloosa: University of Alabama Press.

———. 1995b. Appeal to pity: A case study of the *argumentum ad misericordiam. Argumentation.* 9:769–84.

———. 1995c. Types of argument. In *The Oxford companion to philosophy.* Ted Honderich. ed., 48–49. Oxford: Oxford University Press.

———. 1992a. *Plausible argument in everyday conversation.* Albany: State University of New York Press.

———. 1992b. Types of dialogue, dialectical shifts and fallacies. In *Argumentation illuminated.* Frans H. van Eemeren, et al. eds., 133–47. Amsterdam: Sic Sat.

———. 1992c. *The place of emotion in argument.* University Park: Pennsylvania State University Press.

———. 1991a. *Begging the question: Circular reasoning as a tactic of argumentation.* New York: Greenwood.

———. 1991b. Hamblin and the standard treatment of fallacies. *Philosophy and Rhetoric.* 24:353–61.

———. 1990. What is reasoning? What is an argument? *Journal of Philosophy.* 87:399–419.

———. 1989. *Informal logic: A handbook for critical argumentation.* Cambridge: Cambridge University Press.

———. 1987a. *Informal fallacies: Towards a theory of argument criticisms.* Amsterdam: John Benjamins.

———. 1987b. What is a fallacy?" In *Argumentation: Across the lines of discipline*. Frans H. van Eemeren, et al. eds., 323–30. Dordrecht/Holland: Foris Publications.

———. 1982. *Topical relevance in argumentation*. Amsterdam: John Benjamin Publishing Co.

———. 1979. Philosophical basis of relatedness logic. *Philosophical Studies*. 36:115–36.

———and Erik C. W. Krabbe. 1995. *Commitment in dialogue: Basic concepts of interpersonal reasoning*. Albany: State University of New York Press.

Warren, Karen. 1988. Critical thinking and feminism. *Informal Logic*. 10:31–44.

Weinstein, Mark. 1994. Informal logic and applied epistemology. In *New essays in informal logic*. Ralph H. Johnson and J. Anthony Blair. eds., 140–61. Windsor, Ontario: Informal Logic.

———. 1990. Towards a research agenda for informal logic and critical thinking. *Informal Logic*. 12:121–43.

Wenzel, Joseph W. 1989. Relevance—and other norms of argument: A rhetorical exploration. In *Norms in argumentation*. Robert Maier. ed., 85–95. Dordrecht, Holland: Foris Publications.

———. 1987a. The rhetorical view of argumentation: Exploring a paradigm. *Argumentation*. 1:73–88.

———. 1987b. The rhetorical perspective on argument. In *Argumentation: Across the lines of discipline*. Frans H. van Eemeren, et al. eds., 101–9. Dordrecht, Holland: Foris Publications.

———. 1985. Toward a normative theory of argumentation: Van Eemeren and Grootendorst's code of conduct for rational discussions. In *Argumentation and social practice: Proceedings of the fourth SCA/AFA conference on argumentation*. J. Robert Cox, et al. eds., 139–53. Annandale, Va.: Speech Communication Association.

———. 1980. Perspectives on argument. In *Proceedings of the summer conference on argumentation*. J. Rhodes and S. Newell. eds. Speech Communication Association.

———. 1979. Jurgen Habermas and the dialectical perspective on argumentation. *Journal of the American Forensic Association*. 16:83–94.

Whately, Richard. 1963. Historic doubts relative to Napoleon Buonoparte. In *Elements of Rhetoric* [1846]. Carbondale: Southern Illinois University Press.

238 References

Willard, Charles Arthur. 1995. Failures of relevance: A rhetorical view. In *Fallacies: Classical and contemporary readings.* Hans V. Hansen and Robert C. Pinto. eds., 145–58. University Park: Pennsylvania State University Press.

———. 1992. A Perelman festschrift. *Argumentation and Advocacy.* 29:32–7. (Review of Meyer, *From metaphysics to rhetoric.*)

———. 1990. Authority. *Informal Logic.* 12:11–22.

———. 1989. *A Theory of argumentation.* Tuscaloosa: University of Alabama Press.

Woods, John. 1995. Fearful Symmetry. In *Fallacies: Classical and contemporary readings.* Hans V. Hansen and Robert C. Pinto. eds., 181–93. University Park: Pennsylvania State University Press.

———. 1994. Is the theoretical unity of the fallacies possible? *Informal Logic.* 16:77–85.

———. 1988a. Pragma-Dialectics: A radical departure in fallacy theory. *ISSA Newsletter.* 4:5–15.

———. 1988b. Buttercups, GNP's and quarks: Are fallacies theoretical entities? *Informal Logic.* 10:67–76.

———. 1980. What is informal logic? *Informal logic: The first international symposium.* J. Anthony Blair and Ralph Johnson. eds. 57–68. Pt. Reyes, Calif.: Edgepress.

———and Brent Hudak. 1989. By parity of reasoning. *Informal Logic.* 11:125–39.

Woods, John and Douglas N. Walton. 1989. *Fallacies: Selected papers 1972–1982.* Dordrecht/Holland: Foris Publications.

———. 1982. *Argument: The logic of the fallacies.* Toronto: McGraw-Hill Ryerson.

Wreen, Michael. 1994a. What is a Fallacy? In *New essays in informal logic.* Ralph H. Johnson and J. Anthony Blair. eds., 93–102. Windsor, Ontario: Informal Logic.

———. 1994b. Look, Ma! No Frans! *Pragmatics and Cognition.* 2:285–306.

———. 1988. Admit no force but argument. *Informal Logic.* 10:89–95.

Index